D1083389

Risk Topography

A National Bureau of
Economic Research
Conference Report

Risk Topography
Systemic Risk and
Macro Modeling

Edited by **Markus Brunnermeier and
Arvind Krishnamurthy**

The University of Chicago Press

Chicago and London

MARKUS BRUNNERMEIER is the Edwards S. Sanford Professor of
Economics at Princeton University and a research associate of the
National Bureau of Economic Research. ARVIND KRISHNAMURTHY is
the Harold L. Stuart Professor of Finance in the Kellogg School of
Management at Northwestern University and a research associate
of the National Bureau of Economic Research.

The University of Chicago Press, Chicago 60637
The University of Chicago Press, Ltd., London
© 2014 by the National Bureau of Economic Research
All rights reserved. Published 2014.
Printed in the United States of America

23 22 21 20 19 18 17 16 15 14   1 2 3 4 5

ISBN-13: 978-0-226-07773-4 (cloth)
ISBN-13: 978-0-226-09264-5 (e-book)
DOI: 10.7208/chicago/9780226092645.001.0001

Library of Congress Cataloging-in-Publication Data

Risk topography : systemic risk and macro modeling / edited by
    Markus Brunnermeier and Arvind Krishnamurthy.
        pages cm. — (National Bureau of Economic Research
    conference report)
    Contains selection of the papers of two National Bureau
of Economic Research (NBER) conferences on systemic risk
measurement held in October 2010 in New York and in April 2011
in Chicago.
    Includes bibliographical references and index.
    ISBN 978-0-226-07773-4 (cloth : alk. paper) — ISBN
    978-0-226-09264-5 (e-book) 1. Risk—Congresses. 2. Financial risk
    management—Congresses. 3. Macroeconomics—Econometric
    models—Congresses. I. Brunnermeier, Markus Konrad, editor of
    compilation. II. Krishnamurthy, Arvind, editor of compilation.
    III. Series: National Bureau of Economic Research conference
    report.
    HB615.R5575 2014
    338.5—dc23

                                                    2013040582

♾ This paper meets the requirements of ANSI/NISO Z39.48-1992
(Permanence of Paper).

Relation of the Directors to the
Work and Publications of the
National Bureau of Economic Research

1. The object of the NBER is to ascertain and present to the economics profession, and to the public more generally, important economic facts and their interpretation in a scientific manner without policy recommendations. The Board of Directors is charged with the responsibility of ensuring that the work of the NBER is carried on in strict conformity with this object.

2. The President shall establish an internal review process to ensure that book manuscripts proposed for publication DO NOT contain policy recommendations. This shall apply both to the proceedings of conferences and to manuscripts by a single author or by one or more co-authors but shall not apply to authors of comments at NBER conferences who are not NBER affiliates.

3. No book manuscript reporting research shall be published by the NBER until the President has sent to each member of the Board a notice that a manuscript is recommended for publication and that in the President's opinion it is suitable for publication in accordance with the above principles of the NBER. Such notification will include a table of contents and an abstract or summary of the manuscript's content, a list of contributors if applicable, and a response form for use by Directors who desire a copy of the manuscript for review. Each manuscript shall contain a summary drawing attention to the nature and treatment of the problem studied and the main conclusions reached.

4. No volume shall be published until forty-five days have elapsed from the above notification of intention to publish it. During this period a copy shall be sent to any Director requesting it, and if any Director objects to publication on the grounds that the manuscript contains policy recommendations, the objection will be presented to the author(s) or editor(s). In case of dispute, all members of the Board shall be notified, and the President shall appoint an ad hoc committee of the Board to decide the matter; thirty days additional shall be granted for this purpose.

5. The President shall present annually to the Board a report describing the internal manuscript review process, any objections made by Directors before publication or by anyone after publication, any disputes about such matters, and how they were handled.

6. Publications of the NBER issued for informational purposes concerning the work of the Bureau, or issued to inform the public of the activities at the Bureau, including but not limited to the NBER Digest and Reporter, shall be consistent with the object stated in paragraph 1. They shall contain a specific disclaimer noting that they have not passed through the review procedures required in this resolution. The Executive Committee of the Board is charged with the review of all such publications from time to time.

7. NBER working papers and manuscripts distributed on the Bureau's web site are not deemed to be publications for the purpose of this resolution, but they shall be consistent with the object stated in paragraph 1. Working papers shall contain a specific disclaimer noting that they have not passed through the review procedures required in this resolution. The NBER's web site shall contain a similar disclaimer. The President shall establish an internal review process to ensure that the working papers and the web site do not contain policy recommendations, and shall report annually to the Board on this process and any concerns raised in connection with it.

8. Unless otherwise determined by the Board or exempted by the terms of paragraphs 6 and 7, a copy of this resolution shall be printed in each NBER publication as described in paragraph 2 above.

Contents

VII. INTERNATIONAL SECTOR

Acknowledgments

This volume grew out of two National Bureau of Economic Research (NBER) conferences on systemic risk measurement held in October 2010 in New York and in April 2011 in Chicago. The project was funded through the generous support of the Sloan Foundation, the Zell Center for Risk Research at the Kellogg School of Management, and the Julis-Rabinowitz Center at Princeton University.

We are grateful for the participation and comments of many people at these conferences, only some of whom are represented in the chapters in this book. For their formal but unpublished presentations at the conferences we thank Lewis Alexander, Richard Berner, Claudio Borio, Antonella Foglia, Michael Gibson, Francis Gross, Philipp Hartmann, Ing Haw Cheng, Anil Kashyap, Andrei Kirilenko, Don Kohn, Joe Langsam, John Liechty, Adam Lavier, Michael Palumbo, Mattias Persson, Hélène Rey, Jesus Saurina Salas, Til Schuermann, and Wei Xiong.

We also thank Carl Beck, Lita Kimble, and the NBER staff for helping with the logistical arrangements for the conference, and Helena Fitz-Patrick for her help with the publication process.

Introduction

Markus Brunnermeier and Arvind Krishnamurthy

The financial crisis of 2007 to 2008 was an urgent call for rethinking the measurement of economic activity and for developing macroeconomic models where finance plays an important role. Existing measurement systems did not reveal the fragility of the financial sector, and particularly the magnitude of its exposure to real estate risk. Mainstream macroeconomic models could not assess the impact of a meltdown of the financial sector ("systemic risk") because the financial sector typically did not play a central role in these models.

Brunnermeier, Gorton, and Krishnamurthy (2012) draw an analogy between the situation during and after the crisis and similar developments during the 1930s in the midst of the Great Depression. It was at this time that Richard Stone, Simon Kuznets, Arthur Burns, Wesley Mitchell, and their colleagues developed the first official measures of economic activity for the overall economy, that is, the National Income and Product Accounts, and the chronology of business cycles. Richard Froyen (2009, 13) put it this way:

> One reads with dismay of Presidents Hoover and then Roosevelt designing policies to combat the Great Depression of the 1930s on the basis of such sketchy data as stock prices indices, freight car loadings, and incomplete indices of industrial production. The fact was that comprehensive measures of national income and output did not exist at the time. The

Markus Brunnermeier is the Edwards S. Sanford Professor of Economics at Princeton University and a research associate of the National Bureau of Economic Research. Arvind Krishnamurthy is the Harold L. Stuart Professor of Finance at the Kellogg School of Management at Northwestern University and a research associate of the National Bureau of Economic Research.

For acknowledgments, sources of research support, and disclosure of the authors' material financial relationships, if any, please see http://www.nber.org/chapters/c12506.ack.

Depression, and with it the growing role of government in the economy, emphasized the need for such measures and led to the development of a comprehensive set of national income accounts.[1]

In the fall of 2010 and the spring of 2011, the National Bureau of Economic Research (NBER) held two conferences that brought together leading academic researchers, central bankers, and other financial market experts to discuss ideas on advancing measurement and macroeconomic modeling to face these challenges. This book contains a selection of the papers that were presented at the conferences.

Existing measurement systems, such as the national income accounts and the Federal Reserve's Flow of Funds focus on measuring flows and stock variables. Recent events have highlighted the importance of measuring risks. Simply focusing on flow or stock variables is insufficient, especially in a world of derivatives that may divorce initial risk exposures and cash flows. For example, entering a futures position does not involve large cash flows initially even though both parties expose themselves to potentially large risks. Thus a theme that runs through the measurement proposals that are analyzed in this book is the importance of measuring risks to form a comprehensive "risk topography" of the economy.

A large part of macro risk is endogenously generated by the system. Systemic crises are the result of a negative shock, or trigger, affecting a fragile or vulnerable economy. While these triggers may vary from crisis to crisis, the underlying vulnerabilities have much greater commonality across episodes. The chapters in this book inform us about vulnerabilities as opposed to triggers. For example, in the context of the recent crisis, the trigger was ostensibly the bursting of a real estate bubble, while amplification occurred through a number of vulnerabilities in the financial and household sector. We have focused on the vulnerabilities in part because they are recurring phenomena across crises and thus most amenable to systematic study.

There are a variety of vulnerabilities that observers point to during financial crises. Network models capture so called "domino effects." Market participants that are linked through contractual arrangements suffer if one of their contracting partners defaults. This can trigger a whole chain reaction throughout the system. Spillovers can also occur when participants are not directly linked. For example, if many financial institutions are exposed to a given asset class, and some institutions are distressed and have to reduce their asset holdings, then asset prices may fall, triggering losses across all institutions. These types of spillovers are not limited to contractually linked institutions and are arguably more powerful in that they affect a large set of institutions. Indirect spillover effects depend crucially on the response of market participants. If most participants decide to hold on to their assets or even step in and buy more, then they act as shock absorbers. On the other

---

1. This quotation is also cited by Landefeld, Seskin, and Fraumeni (2008).

hand, if after an adverse shock they also sell assets and withdraw funds, they become shock amplifiers. Their response depends primarily on their liquidity mismatch, leverage, capital, and overall risk exposure. Thus, aggregated measures of these variables are likely to be important in assessing underlying vulnerabilities. The chapters in this book discuss these types of vulnerabilities as well as others involving the corporate and household sectors.

While many of the vulnerabilities discussed in the book have been pointed to in prior theoretical work, they have not been systematically measured and the question remains of how quantitatively important they are in driving macroeconomic patterns during systemic crises. Which types of vulnerabilities are more important? How do they interact? We expect that the types of measurements advanced in this book will help observers better identify significant vulnerabilities and thus serve as an early warning system for crises. We also expect that the data, as it is accumulated over time, will shape the development of macroeconomic models of systemic risk by providing the essential data on which to calibrate and discriminate across competing models. This latter point concerning the interplay between data collection and macro theory is the second theme that runs through this book. The emphasis on macro stresses that amplification, vulnerabilities, and fragility are general equilibrium phenomena.[2]

Ultimately, better measurement can also improve the regulatory framework for financial institutions. For example, without clear measures of banks' macro risk exposures and a corresponding macroeconomic model that can quantify financial stability, it is impossible to determine whether the capital requirement for banks should be, say, 7 percent or 20 percent.

The book will be of most value to those in regulatory positions who, since the crisis, have been involved in efforts to improve current measurement systems. The book is also of interest to academics that plan to conceptualize effective measurement and make future use of the collected data to discriminate across various macroeconomic models with financial frictions. The book outlines the issues that need to be addressed by a new measurement system that captures the linkage between finance and the macroeconomy. Many of the chapters explain how a given measurement can be used to further understand systemic risk and thus illustrate the potential of using measurement to inform models. The book also addresses conceptual questions: How should a policymaker think about measurement of a financial world of increasing complexity and uncertainty? What are the tradeoffs in making measured data public? In addition to conceptual measurement issues, the book offers explicit measurement strategies that can be implemented either

---

2. These points regarding focusing on a risk topography that can be used in a general equilibrium macro model are drawn from and expanded on in our collaboration with Gary Gorton (see Brunnermeier, Gorton, and Krishnamurthy 2012).

immediately (some of which have already been implemented following the conferences) or within a couple of years.

Following the introduction, the first chapter in this book, by Lars Peter Hansen, discusses some of the challenges that arise when measurement outpaces theory. Hansen's chapter recalls discussions from seventy years ago on national income accounting and Arthur Burns and Wesley Mitchell's (1946) well-known book on the measurement of business cycles. Tjalling Koopman's review of the Burns and Mitchell book is famous in its own right ("Measurement without Theory") and criticizes the authors for being "unbendingly empiricist," charging that their approach limits the usefulness of their measurement. The approaches taken in this book may be criticized on similar grounds. However, history has validated Burns and Mitchell's empirical approach and as Hansen notes, "an unabashedly empirical approach can most definitely be of considerable value, especially in the initial stages of a research agenda." The national income accounting measurement agenda that earned Nobel Prizes for Simon Kuznets and Richard Stone was initially guided by incomplete theories of the economy, but the measures have proven central to economists' understanding of the economy. Likewise, we see this book as offering approaches to measurement that will better our understanding of macrofinancial links.

Hansen's chapter also notes that since the measurement agenda is in its initial stages, it is important to diversify across possible approaches and also to ensure that measurements by government agencies continue to be responsive to research needs. Theories will change with new data and this will suggest the collection of other data. The Job Openings and Labor Turnover Survey (JOLTS) produced by the Bureau of Labor Statistics (BLS) provides a clear example of the interplay between theory and data collection efforts. Economists including Peter Diamond, Dale Mortensen, and Chris Pissarides have written theoretical articles on job search. These models were evaluated using data sets pieced together from data collected for other purposes by the Census Bureau and the BLS's Labor Turnover Survey. The JOLTS data was informed by the new search theory and has greatly advanced our understanding of labor markets. The resulting empirical insights then subsequently allowed researchers to better discriminate across various models.

The second chapter of the book by Augustin Landier and David Thesmar addresses the trade-offs in making data public. A common view from the private sector is that making information public can negatively affect the incentives of agents and reduce welfare. An example that is often given is that revealing data on banks' trading positions may reduce market making activity and liquidity. Banks may even be exposed to predatory trading activity. In academic debates, an argument given for suppressing information is that the release of precise public information can coordinate agent actions in a manner that is welfare reducing. For example, it can induce a bank run. On the other hand, as we have discussed, publicizing information is valuable in identifying vulnerabilities early on. In addition, it might stimulate further research on macrofinancial modeling, which can better guide regulatory policy. Landier and Thesmar discuss these and other issues in their chapter. They argue that there are three dimensions to consider when releasing information: granularity of data, frequency of data reporting, and lags in data disclosure. They consider the costs and benefits of disclosure along these dimensions. The analysis bears on questions such as: At what frequency should data be collected and made available? How long should the regulator wait before releasing the data? At what level of detail (granularity) should information be released, and if the public information is detailed, should it be made anonymous?

The remainder of the book, chapters 3 through 16, analyzes specific measurement approaches covering different sectors of the economy. We have organized these chapters into five parts. The first part includes Hansen's and Landier and Thesmar's chapters covering conceptual measurement issues. The second part concerns the measurement of risk exposures within the financial sector. The third part discusses measuring leading response indicators, such as liquidity and leverage, and other factors that may indicate vulnerability of a particular sector. The fourth part is concerned with financial intermediation and credit markets, covering both the funding and lending side of intermediaries. The fifth part tackles the household sector, whose leverage dynamics have played an important role in the real estate boom/bust. The sixth part covers the nonfinancial corporate sector and discusses data to diagnose how financial frictions may affect corporate investment. The last part discusses international issues.

The book need not be read in this order. We highlight a number of specific chapters analyzing concrete strategies for measurement that could be quickly and easily implemented. These chapters include Duffie's "10-by-10-by-10" proposal (chapter 3), McDonald's margin chapter (chapter 5), Geanakoplos and Pedersen's leverage chapter (chapter 8), Bassett et al.'s chapter on bank lending (chapter 10), and Parker's household finance "LEADS" proposal (chapter 13). Other chapters outline measurement concepts that can be implemented only over longer horizons, or step back and argue for the importance of measuring a particular sector or motivating a particular measurement concept.

Chapter 3 by Darrell Duffie offers a system for monitoring risks of systemically important financial firms that is simple, immediately implementable, and yet has enormous potential to identify vulnerabilities in the financial system. His 10-by-10-by-10 approach focuses on a core group of ten financial firms, measuring risk exposures for a specified set of ten scenarios, and measuring the ten largest counterparty exposures of each firm in this scenario. This approach is immediately implementable because many financial firms collect this sort of information regularly for enterprise risk management purposes. Thus, Duffie's approach builds on current practice and takes the second essential step of standardizing the risk management information across firms and eliciting information that can be compared and aggregated. Additionally, even though the focus is on a small group of financial firms, the fact that financial activity is concentrated among a few firms in most countries means that this monitoring system can shed light on the most important vulnerabilities in the financial system. Given the concentration of activity and the fact that core firms are often counterparties to noncore firms, the monitoring system may also shed light on activities of smaller financial firms. Furthermore, the proposal can easily be extended to a larger number of firms, scenarios, and counterparties.

Duffie outlines examples of the type of information that can be gleaned from the 10-by-10-by-10 system. If Treasury yields were to rise dramatically, how much would systemically important financial institutions gain or lose in total, from each other, and from others? From a macroprudential standpoint, the existence of a common large exposure to some risk factor suggests a potential vulnerability. The data can also reveal channels of contagion via a network. For example, if all firms have large counterparty exposure stemming from a given risk factor to a single firm, then that firm becomes a central node for contagion. In the recent crises, the 10-by-10-by-10 data may have pointed to the importance of AIG, even if AIG was not one of the ten financial firms on which data was collected.

Chapter 4 is by Juliane Beganau, Monika Piazzesi, and Martin Schneider and presents a way to remap the Federal Reserve's Flow of Funds to represent asset positions in terms of risk exposures along key risk factors. Modern finance views an asset as a random stream of payments. The market value of the asset today is the present value of the payment stream at the appropriate state prices. Clearly, only measuring and reporting the market value of an asset, as is the norm for trading assets in accounting statements, represents a small portion of the information about the asset. As an example, the market value of an interest rate swap derivative that is entered into today by a bank at a midmarket price is equal to zero. But of course the swap reflects significant nonzero exposure to changes in interest rates for the bank. Worse, reporting the book value of an asset, as is the norm for held-to-maturity assets in bank accounting, represents even less information about the asset. The focus on stocks of market value or book value assets may have been appropriate fifty years ago, but is not informative in a world of derivative securities, off-balance sheet vehicles, and other financial innovations.

The chapter offers a way to summarize payment stream information that is superior to asset market or book values. Assets are payment streams with exposures to a few underlying risk factors. For example, for fixed-income instruments including bonds and swaps, the literature on the term structure of interest rates shows that one can reduce the payment information of these assets into a few (e.g., three) underlying factors (e.g., level, slope, and curvature). This powerful observation implies that much of the fixed-income universe can be summarized as risk exposures to three factors. Moreover, the factor exposures of different assets can be linearly aggregated to summarize the overall exposure of a bank, a group of banks, a sector, or even an economy, to these risk factors. In essence, the chapter envisions remapping the Flow of Funds in terms of these exposures to risk factors. The authors argue that there is substantial information in currently reported data to take steps in this direction. Indeed, in a related paper (Beganau, Piazzesi, and Schneider 2012), the authors show how to use Bank Call Report data to infer interest rate factor exposures for a number of the largest banks in the United States.

Chapter 5 is by Robert L. McDonald and describes how information from margins that are provided by traders to derivatives (e.g., futures or swaps) clearinghouses can be used to estimate risk and liquidity risk exposures. The central idea in the chapter is that margin/collateral protects counterparties against credit losses and is thus an economic measure of exposure that differs by asset and by the topology of risk. Thus, for example, information on the aggregate amount of margin, say, on interest rate futures reflects the size of interest rate exposures transacted in the economy. McDonald makes a strong case that margin information that is currently collected can be valuably used to measure exposures, and also discusses how regulations under Dodd-Frank may be implemented to most effectively use margin information. The current version of Dodd-Frank fails to use this information, despite the fact that McDonald's ideas are among the most implementable of the measurement schemes outlined in this book.

Chapter 6, by Viral V. Acharya, is complementary to chapter 5. While McDonald focuses on derivatives that are cleared in exchanges, Acharya focuses on the derivatives that remain entirely over the counter. Currently most derivatives transactions fall into the latter category, and even with regulatory incentives to migrate derivatives clearing onto exchanges, it is likely that a significant share of derivatives trades will remain over the counter. Acharya offers an excellent overview of the ways in which financials currently disclose information on their derivative positions in public filings, noting the lack of a standard across firms and the shortcomings in currently reported information. He then discusses how to standardize reporting and what to report. In principle, there is a great deal of salient information ranging from derivative exposures by maturity, to exposures by counterparty, to contingent exposures (i.e., on a given stress). Like McDonald, he emphasizes the importance of margin call exposure, notably what he labels the "margin coverage ratio" (MCR) that compares a firm's cash position to its margin call exposure under stress scenarios.

Chapters 7 and 8 focus on response indicators. Systemic risk has an endogenous component that is driven by the response of economic actors. For example, if the financial sector is highly levered, then even a small decline in asset values can trigger fire-sales of assets, which further lower asset values. Likewise, if banks have little liquidity and a preponderance of short-term debt, then they risk bank runs.

Chapter 7 by Markus Brunnermeier, Arvind Krishnamurthy, and Gary Gorton discusses ways to measure liquidity. While the measurement of a quantity like bank capital is fairly clear, measuring the "liquidity" of a bank's balance sheet is far less straightforward. The chapter begins by discussing the theoretical literature on liquidity and explaining how to measure liquidity from the standpoint of these models. It then turns to practical challenges in liquidity measurement through a series of illustrative examples. Brunnermeier, Krishnamurthy, and Gorton then describe a liquidity mismatch index (LMI), motivated by theory, and reflecting the practical challenges in liquidity measurement. An important feature of the LMI is that it can be aggregated across firms. Thus the measure naturally describes liquidity mismatch at the firm, industry, and economy-wide levels. The chapter discusses the ways in which the LMI can be used to assess systemic risk. As a "response indicator" about market participants' reaction to an adverse shock, it is an important building block in the risk topography framework outlined in Brunnermeier, Gorton, and Krishnamurthy (2012).

Chapter 8, by John Geanakoplos and Lasse Heje Pedersen, discusses the measurement of leverage. The chapter begins by discussing the importance of leverage measurement as a response indicator, and as a factor in financial crises. An important observation made by Geanakoplos and Pedersen is that leverage on new loans and leverage on old (preexisting) loans are two conceptually different measures that are each informative. The authors point out that the leverage on new loans is a measure of current credit conditions. The average or old leverage instead signals the economy's past vulnerability to negative shocks. The authors point out that new leverage can be well captured by measuring margin requirements—haircuts on repo loans, or loan-to-value requirements on durable goods purchases. Indeed, coming from different points of view, Acharya, McDonald, as well as Geanakoplos and Pedersen describe the value of measuring margins at the asset level, underlining the value of such a measurement.

Chapters 9, 10, and 11 tackle financial intermediation and credit markets. While the textbook financial intermediary borrows short and lends long, in practice there is a great deal of texture in both the short and long of this intermediation. These chapters delve into this texture.

Chapter 9 focuses on the repo market and the security lending markets, which are key short-term funding markets for banks and have witnessed run-like behavior in the crisis (see Gorton and Metrick 2010; Krishnamurthy, Nagel, and Orlov 2012). Despite the importance of these markets, there is little data on the prices and quantities of trade in these markets. Tobias Adrian, Brian Begalle, Adam Copeland, and Antoine Martin provide a comprehensive overview of the structure of the repo markets, their function, the available data sources on repo and what is known about it, as well as what is not known. One of their observations is that repo is transacted primarily in two ways, via a triparty system and via a bilateral system. The available data from the crisis suggests that these systems behaved very differently, with far more stability of the haircuts in the triparty market compared to the bilateral market. Without data on these markets, it is hard to pinpoint what drove these differences. Yet, without such an understanding it is also hard to spot vulnerabilities in the short-term funding markets. This chapter describes the type of data that is needed in order to better understand these important short-term funding markets.

Chapters 10 and 11 consider the lending side of intermediaries. A key amplification mechanism identified by the theoretical literature is the possibility of a credit crunch whereby a disruption in the supply of new bank loans, through losses on existing loans, for example, reduces spending and production, exacerbating a downturn, and further increasing losses on existing bank loans. These chapters offer suggestions on how to measure a credit crunch that may be developing.

In chapter 10 William F. Bassett, Simon Gilchrist, Gretchen C. Weinbach, and Egon Zakrajšek point out the difficulties in analyzing new bank loans based on existing data. Most existing sources mix existing loans and new loans, measuring the total amount of loans at a given point in time, or failing to distinguish between loans made under existing commitments and new commitments. Their chapter offers an explicit and easily implementable suggestion to alter the data collected in Call Reports in a manner that can get at the key flows of new lending.

Chapter 11 by Atif Mian discusses the benefits of implementing a credit registry, which contains microlevel data detailing lending between every commercial borrower and bank. Such credit registry data are increasingly available in many countries, and have been used in studies by Mian in the case of Pakistan and Spain. As is well understood, a key difficulty in identifying a credit crunch is in disentangling whether a contraction in the volume of bank loans is due to loan supply factors or loan demand factors. Mian discusses in the context of his past work how a credit registry can help in identifying supply separate from demand. Although a credit registry is demanding in terms of data requirements, Mian points out the many ways in which such data can help identify credit supply shocks and further researchers' understanding of the link between financial intermediation and the macroeconomy.

Chapters 12, 13, and 14 address the household sector. Chapter 12 by Robert E. Hall lays out the case for the importance of measuring the household sector. As Hall argues, households have played a central role in recent events: they increased borrowing and leverage dramatically in the period from 2002 to 2006, and since then have suffered from house price collapses and "levered losses." As a consequence, households have cut back on expenditures, with detrimental effects on output and employment. Given that the majority of households are dependent on financial institutions for credit, measuring the household sector is essential to understanding connections between financing and macroeconomic activity.

What are the main aspects of the household sector that need to be measured? Chapter 13 by Jonathan A. Parker lays out a comprehensive approach to measuring the household sector, which he titles LEADS (liabilities, earnings, assets, demographics, and financial sophistication). Parker argues that detailed information is needed to measure liquid wealth (assets minus liabilities) as well as lifetime wealth (wealth plus future income and benefits) in order to understand the covariance of a given household's wealth with macroeconomic factors. With such information, one can characterize the exposure of groups of households to a macroeconomic factor such as real estate prices. This would allow regulators to better understand how a fall in real estate may affect household expenditure behavior. To get at the wealth variable, we need information on liabilities, earnings, assets, and demographics. Parker describes the current data available to construct wealth as well as other data that may be required. This discussion will be valuable to anyone involved in measurement of the household sector. Parker also makes a strong case to measure the financial sophistication of households. There are likely many unsophisticated households who may be subject to systematic errors in their financial planning. Such errors may compound the impact of a macroeconomic shock. Parker concludes, with the eye of a researcher, by describing how data should be made public to maximize its use in research.

Chapter 14 by Amir Sufi drills in on one particular risk stemming from the household sector. Sufi seeks data to determine when an increase in household leverage may pose a risk to the macroeconomy. He suggests that such a risk arises when the increase is driven by an expansion of credit supply. Drawing on his own work with Mian, he outlines data and a methodology that can be used to measure credit supply expansions. The data is in some regard similar to the credit registry data that Mian outlines in chapter 11 for firms, but applied to households. In particular, Sufi suggests microlevel panel data on household consumption and wealth. Much of this data exists currently but is not accessible to researchers. Thus, Sufi's chapter is a call for organizing existing data and making this data available.

Chapter 15 by V. V. Chari turns to nonfinancial firms. Many theoretical models highlight the impact of financial frictions on firms' investment decisions. That is, if many firms have high leverage and limited liquidity, then a downturn may force firms to cut back on investment, which can have macroeconomic consequences. Chari presents the available aggregate data on flows between nonfinancial firms and the rest of the economy and shows that such data does reveal evidence of financial frictions. Financial frictions are only present in subsets of the firms, and to understand these frictions one needs microlevel data. Chari discusses the available data sets and notes that the biggest need is for financial statements of privately held firms. Compustat data covers large public firms, but these are the firms least affected by financial frictions. While data on privately held firms exist within the IRS, they are not public. Chari suggests a manner by which the data can be publicized and made available to researchers.

Chapter 16 by Eugenio Cerutti, Stijn Claessens, and Patrick McGuire discusses cross-border issues. Prominent narratives of the recent financial crisis emphasize the global nature of banking. Imbalances in one region of the world can quickly propagate to others and exacerbate macroeconomic risks. Cerutti, Claessens, and McGuire argue that to understand global banking, we need data at the bank level covering operations across countries. As an example from the recent crisis, cross-currency funding played an important role and led to the establishment of central bank foreign-exchange swap lines. To study this type of issue, one needs data at the bank level on foreign-exchange swap use and foreign sources of funding. But such data does not exist currently. Bank-level data that are collected by supervisors are not widely shared, generally not even across supervisory jurisdictions, and only broad aggregates are publicly disclosed. While there has been some progress on filling these data gaps by the International Monetary Fund (IMF) and the Bank for International Settlements (BIS), there remain significant deficiencies. This chapter draws attention to these important issues and calls for further progress to close these international data gaps.

To conclude this introduction, we return to the analogy of national income accounting. The development of national income accounts has been critical for much of our knowledge of the way economies function. The financial crisis has shown that our understanding of the function of finance in the macroeconomy is still very incomplete. In addition to measuring only stock and flow variables, the recent financial crisis has shown the importance of risk measurement.

In this book we aim to assemble many important building blocks—or at least the conceptual cornerstones—for a modern risk measurement system. Of course, one may ask whether we have missed important components and failed to identify knowledge gaps. One gap that we are aware of concerns expectations. It is important to get some indication that market participants are driven by collective misjudgments and distorted expectations. We tried but failed to commission a chapter that proposes new survey methods to elicit market participants' expectations and tail risk perceptions. The chapters in this book are particularly focused on vulnerabilities that can lead to an amplified response to negative shocks. As a large part of the risk is endogenous and self-generated by the system, the measurement can only be understood in connection with general equilibrium models. Additional data will allow researchers and regulators to discriminate across models and is thus essential to improve our understanding of macrofinancial links. We hope that the chapters in this book will aid in academic and regulatory efforts to address these issues.

References

Begenau, Juliane, Monika Piazzesi, and Martin Schneider. 2012. "Banks' Risk Exposures." Working Paper, Stanford University.

Burns, Arthur F., and Wesley C. Mitchell. 1946. *Measuring Business Cycles*. New York: National Bureau of Economic Research.

Brunnermeier, Markus, Gary Gorton, and Arvind Krishnamurthy. 2012. "Risk Topography." In *NBER Macroeconomics Annual 2011*, edited by Daron Acemoglu and Michael Woodford. Chicago: University of Chicago Press.

Froyen, Richard. 2009. *Macroeconomics: Theories and Policies*. Upper Saddle River, NJ: Prentice Hall.

Gorton, Gary, and Andrew Metrick. 2010. "Securitized Banking and the Run on Repo." *Journal of Financial Economics* 104 (3): 425–51.

Krishnamurthy, Arvind, Stefan Nagel, and Dmitry Orlov. 2012. "Sizing up Repo." NBER Working Paper no. 17768, Cambridge, MA.

Landefeld, J. Steven, Eugene P. Seskin, and Barbara M. Fraumeni. 2008. "Taking the Pulse of the Economy: Measuring GDP." *Journal of Economic Perspectives* 22 (2): 193–216.

I

Measurement and Disclosure

1

Challenges in Identifying and Measuring Systemic Risk

Lars Peter Hansen

1.1 Introduction

Discussions of public oversight of financial markets often make reference to "systemic risk" as a rationale for prudent policy making. For example, mitigating systemic risk is a common defense underlying the need for macroprudential policy initiatives. The term has become a grab bag, and its lack of specificity could undermine the assessment of alternative policies. At the outset of this essay I ask, should systemic risk be an explicit target of measurement, or should it be relegated to being a buzz word, a slogan or a code word used to rationalize regulatory discretion?

I remind readers of the dictum attributed to Sir William Thomson (Lord Kelvin):

> I often say that when you can measure something that you are speaking about, express it in numbers, you know something about it; but when you cannot measure it, when you cannot express it in numbers, your knowledge is of the meagre and unsatisfactory kind: it may be the beginning of knowledge, but you have scarcely, in your thoughts advanced to the stage of *science*, whatever the matter might be.[1]

Lars Peter Hansen is the David Rockefeller Distinguished Service Professor in Economics, Statistics, and the College at the University of Chicago and a research associate of the National Bureau of Economic Research.

In writing this chapter, I benefited from helpful suggestions by Amy Boonstra, Gary Becker, Mark Brickell, John Heaton, Jim Heckman, Arvind Krishnamurthy, Monika Piazzesi, Toni Shears, and Stephen Stigler, and especially by Markus Brunnermeier, Andy Lo, Tom Sargent, and Grace Tsiang. For acknowledgments, sources of research support, and disclosure of the author's material financial relationships, if any, please see http://www.nber.org/chapters /c12507.ack.

1. From lecture to the Institution of Civil Engineers, London (3 May 1883), "Electrical Units of Measurement," *Popular Lectures and Addresses* (1889), Vol. 1, 80–81.

While Lord Kelvin's scientific background was in mathematical physics, discussion of his dictum has pervaded the social sciences. An abbreviated version appears on the Social Science Research building at the University of Chicago and was the topic of a published piece of detective work by Merton, Sills, and Stigler (1984). I will revisit this topic at the end of this essay. Right now I use this quote as a launching pad for discussing systemic risk by asking if we should use measurement or quantification as a barometer of our understanding of this concept.

One possibility is simply to concede that *systemic risk* is not something that is amenable to quantification. Instead it is something that becomes self-evident under casual observation. This is quite different from Kelvin's assertion about the importance of measurement as a precursor to some form of scientific understanding and discourse. Kelvin's view was that for measurement to have any meaning requires that (a) we formalize the concept that is to be measured, and (b) we acquire data to support the measurement.

The need to implement new laws with expanded regulation and oversight puts pressure on public sector research groups to develop quick ways to provide useful measurements of systemic risk. This requires shortcuts, and it also can proliferate superficial answers. These short-term research responses will be revealing along some dimensions by providing useful summaries from new data sources or at least data sources that have been largely ignored in the past. Stopping with short-term or quick answers can lead to bad policy advice and should be avoided. It is important for researchers to take a broader and more ambitious attack on the problem of building quantitatively meaningful models with macroeconomic linkages to financial markets. Appropriately constructed, these models could provide a framework for the quantification of systemic risk.

In the short run, we may be limited in our ability to provide meaningful quantification. Perhaps we should defer and trust our governmental officials engaged in regulation and oversight to "know it when they see it." I have two concerns about leaving things vague, however. First, it opens the door to a substantial amount of regulatory discretion. In extreme circumstances that are not well guided by prior experience or supported by economic models that we have confidence in, some form of discretion may be necessary for prudent policy making. However, discretion can also lead to bad government policy, including the temptation to respond to political pressures. Second, it makes criticism of measurement and policy all the more challenging. When formal models are well constructed, they facilitate discussion and criticism. Delineating assumptions required to justify conclusions disciplines the communication and commentary necessary to nurture improvements in models, methods, and measurements. This leads me to be sympathetic to a longer-term objective of exploring the policy-relevant notions of the quantification of systemic risk. To embark on this ambitious agenda, we should do so with open eyes and a realistic perspective on the measurement challenges. In what follows, I explore these challenges, in part, by drawing on the experience from other such research agendas within economics and elsewhere.

In the remainder of this essay: (a) I explore some conceptual modeling and measurement challenges, and (b) I examine these challenges as they relate to existing approaches to measuring systemic risk.

1.2   Measurement with and without Theory

Sparked in part by the ambition set out in the Dodd-Frank Act and similar measures in Europe, the Board of Governors of the Federal Reserve System and some of the constituent regional banks have assembled research groups charged with producing measurements of systemic risk. Such measurements are also part of the job of the newly created Office of Financial Research housed in the Treasury Department. Similar research groups have been assembled in Europe. While the need for legislative responses puts pressure on research departments to produce quick "answers," I believe it is also critical to take a longer-term perspective so that we can do more than just respond to the last crisis. By now, a multitude of proposed measures exist and many of these are summarized in Bisias et al. (2012), where *thirty-one* ways to measure systemic risk are identified. While the authors describe this catalog as an "embarrassment of riches," I find this plethora to be a bit disconcerting. In describing why, in the next section, I will discuss briefly some of these measures without providing a full-blown critique. Moreover, I will not embark on a commentary of all thirty-one listed in their valuable and extensive summary. Prior to taking up that task, I consider some basic conceptual issues.

I am reminded of Koopmans's discussion of the Burns and Mitchell (1946) book on measuring business cycles. The Koopmans (1947) review has the famous title "Measurement without Theory." It provides an extensive discussion and sums things up saying:

> The book is unbendingly empiricist in outlook. . . . But the decision not to use theories of man's economic behavior, even hypothetically, limits the value to economic science and to the maker of policies, of the results obtained or obtainable by the methods developed. (172)

The measurements by Burns and Mitchell generated a lot of attention and renewed interest in quantifying business cycles. They served to motivate development of both formal economic and statistical models. An unabashedly empirical approach can most definitely be of considerable value, especially in the initial stages of a research agenda. What is less clear is how to use such an approach as a direct input into policy making without an economic model to provide guidance as to how this should be done. An important role for economic modeling is to provide an interpretable structure for using available data to explore the consequences of alternative policies in a meaningful way.

In the remainder of this section, I feature two measurement challenges that should be central to any systemic research measurement agenda. How do we distinguish *systemic* from *systematic* risk? How do we conceptualize and quantify the *uncertainty* associated with systemic *risk* measurement?

1.2.1   Systematic or Systemic

The terms *systematic* and *systemic* risk are sometimes confused, but their distinction is critical for both measurement and interpretation. In sharp contrast with the former concept, the latter one is well studied and supported by extensive modeling and measurement. "Systematic risks" are macroeconomic or aggregate risks that cannot be avoided through diversification. According to standard models of financial markets, investors who are exposed to these risks require compensation because there is no simple insurance scheme whereby exposure to these risks can be averaged out.[2] This compensation is typically expressed as a risk adjustment to expected returns.

Empirical macroeconomics aims to identify aggregate "shocks" in time series data and to measure their consequences. Exposure to these shocks is the source of systematic risk priced in security markets. These may include shocks induced by macroeconomic policy, and some policy analyses explore how to reduce the impact of these shocks to the macroeconomy through changes in monetary or fiscal policy. Often, but not always, as a separate research enterprise, empirical finance explores econometric challenges associated with measuring both the exposure to the components of systematic risk that require compensation and the associated compensations to investors.

"Systemic risk" is meant to be a different construct. It pertains to risks of breakdown or major dysfunction in financial markets. The potential for such risks provides a rationale for financial market monitoring, intervention, or regulation. The systemic risk research agenda aims to provide guidance about the consequences of alternative policies and to help anticipate possible breakdowns in financial markets. The formal definition of *systemic risk* is much less clear than its counterpart *systematic risk*.

Here are three possible notions of systemic risk that have been suggested. Some consider systemic risk to be a modern day counterpart to a bank run triggered by liquidity concerns. Measurement of that risk could be an essential input to the role of central banks as "lenders of last resort" to prevent failure of large financial institutions or groups of financial institu-

---

2. A more precise statement would be that these are the risks that could require compensation. In equilibrium models there typically exist aggregate risks with exposures that do not require compensation. Diversification arguments narrow the pricing focus to the systematic or aggregate risks.

tions. Others use systemic risk to describe the vulnerability of a financial network in which adverse consequences of internal shocks can spread and even magnify within the network. Here the measurement challenge is to identify when a financial network is potentially vulnerable and the nature of the disruptions that can trigger a problem. Still others use the term to include the potential insolvency of a major player in or component of the financial system. Thus systemic risk is basically a grab bag of scenarios that are supposed to rationalize intervention in financial markets. These interventions come under the heading of "macroprudential policies." Since the Great Recession was triggered by a financial crisis, it is not surprising that there were legislative calls for external monitoring, intervention, or regulation to reduce systemic risk. The outcome is legislation such as the rather cumbersome and still incomplete 2,319 page Dodd-Frank Wall Street Reform and Consumer Protection Act. The sets of constructs for measurement to support prudent policy making remain a challenge for future research.

Embracing Koopmans's call for models is appealing as a longer-term research agenda. Important aspects of his critique are just as relevant as a commentary on current systemic risk measurement as they were for Burns and Mitchell's business cycle measurement.[3]

1.2.2   Systemic Risk or Uncertainty

There are important conceptual challenges that go along with the use of explicit dynamic economic models in formal ways. Paramount among these is how we confront risk and uncertainty. Economic models with explicit stochastic structures imply formal probability statements for a variety of questions related to implications and policy. In addition, uncertainty can come from limited data, unknown models, and misspecification of those models. Policy discussions too often have a bias toward ignoring the full impact of uncertainty quantification. But abstracting from uncertainty measurement can result in flawed policy advice and implementation.

There are various approaches to uncertainty quantification. While there is well-known and extensive literature on using probability models to support statistical measurement, I expect special challenges to emerge when we impose dynamic economic structure onto the measurement challenge. The discussion that follows is motivated by this latter challenge. It reflects my own perspective, not necessarily one that is widely embraced. My perspective is consonant, however, with some of the views expressed by Haldane (2011, 2012) in his discussions of policy simplicity and robustness when applied to regulating financial institutions.

---

3. One way in which the systemic risk measurement agenda is more advanced than that of Burns and Mitchell is that there is a statistical theory that can be applied to many of the suggested measurements of systemic risk. The ability to use "modern methods of statistical inference" was one of the reasons featured by Koopmans for why formal probability models are valuable, but another part of the challenge is the formal integration with economic analysis.

I find it useful to draw a distinction between risk and alternative concepts better designed to capture our struggles with constructing fully specified probability models. Motivated by the insights of Knight (1921), decision theorists use the terms *uncertainty* and *ambiguity* as distinguished from risk. See Gilboa and Schmeidler (1989) for an initial entrant to this literature and Gilboa, Postlewaite, and Schmeidler (2008) for a recent survey. Alternatively, we can think of statistical models as approximations and we use such models in sophisticated ways with conservative adjustments that reflect the potential for misspecification. This latter ambition is sometimes formulated as a *concern for robustness*. For instance, Petersen, James, and Dupuis (2000) and Hansen and Sargent (2001) confront a decision problem with a family of possible probability specifications and seek conservative responses.

To appreciate the consequences of Knight's distinction, consider the following. Suppose we happen to have full confidence in a model specification of the macroeconomy appropriately enriched with financial linkages needed to capture system-wide exposure to risk. Since the model specifies the underlying probabilities, we could use it both to quantify systemic risk and to compute so-called counterfactuals. While this would be an attractive situation, it seems not to fit many circumstances. As systemic risk remains a poorly understood concept, there is no "off-the-shelf " model that we can use to measure it. Any stab at building such models, at least in the near future, is likely to yield, at best, a coarse approximation. This leads directly to the question: how do we best express skepticism in our probabilistic measurement of systemic risk?

Continuing with a rather idealized approach, we could formally articulate an array of models and weight these models using historical inputs and subjective priors. This articulation appears to be overly ambitious in practice, but it is certainly a good aim. Subjective inputs may not be commonly agreed upon and historical evidence distinguishing models may be weak. To make this approach operational leads naturally to a sensitivity analysis for priors including priors over parameters and alternative models.

A model by its very nature is wrong because it simplifies and abstracts. Including a formal probabilistic structure enriches predictions from a model, but we should not expect such an addition to magically fix or repair the model. It is often useful to throw other models "into the mix," so to speak. The same limitations are likely to carry over to each model we envision. Perhaps we could be lucky enough to delineate a big enough list of possible models to fill gaps left by any specific model. In practice, I suspect we cannot achieve complete success and certainly not in the short term. In some special circumstances, the gaps may be negligible. Probabilistic reasoning in conjunction with the use of models is a very valuable tool. But too often we suspect the remaining gaps are not trivial, and the challenge in using the models is capturing how to express the remaining skepticism. Simple models can contain powerful insights even if they are incomplete along some dimensions. As statisticians with incomplete knowledge, how do we embrace such models or collections of them while acknowledging skepticism that should justifiably go along with them? This is an enduring problem in the use of dynamic stochastic equilibrium models and it seems unavoidable as we confront the important task of building models designed to measure systemic risk. Even as we add modeling clarity, in my view we need to abandon the presumption that we can measure fully *systemic risk* and go after the conceptually more difficult notion of quantifying *systemic uncertainty*. See Haldane (2012) for a further discussion of this point.

What is at stake here is more than just a task for statisticians. Even though policy challenges may appear to be complicated, it does not follow that policy design should be complicated. Acknowledging or confronting gaps in modeling has long been conjectured to have important implications for economic policy. As an analogy, I recall Friedman's (1960) argument for a simplified approach to the design of monetary policy. His policy prescription was premised on the notion of "long and variable lags" in a monetary transmission mechanism that was too poorly understood to exploit formally in the design of policy. His perspective was that the gaps in our knowledge of this mechanism were sufficient that premising activist monetary policy on incomplete models could be harmful. Relatedly, Cogley et al. (2008) show how alternative misspecification in modeling can be expressed in terms of the design of policy rules. Hansen and Sargent (2012) explore challenges for monetary policy based on alternative specifications of incomplete knowledge on the part of a so-called "Ramsey planner." The task of this planner is to design formal rules for implementation. It is evident from their analyses that the potential source of misspecification can matter in the design of a *robust rule*. These contributions do not explore the policy ramifications for system-wide problems with the functioning of financial markets, but such challenges should be on the radar screen of financial regulation. In fact, implementation concerns and the need for simple rules underlie some of the arguments for imposing equity requirements on banks. See, for instance, Admati et al. (2010). Part of policy implementation requires attaching numerical values to parameters in such rules. Thus concerns about systemic uncertainty would still seem to be a potential contributor to the implementation of even seemingly simple rules for financial regulation.

Even after we acknowledge that policymakers face challenges in forming systemic risk measures that could be direct and explicit tools for policy, there is another layer of uncertainty. Sophisticated decision makers *inside* the models we build may face similar struggles with how to view their economic environments. Why might this be important? Let me draw on contributions from two distinct strands of literature to speculate about this.

Caballero and Simsek (2010) consider models of financial networks. In such models financial institutions care not only about the people that they interact with, say, their neighbors, but also the neighbors of neighbors, and so forth. One possibility is that financial entities know well what is going on at all nodes in the financial network. Another is that while making probabilistic assessments about nearby neighbors in a network is straightforward, this task becomes considerably more difficult as we consider more indirect linkages, say, neighbors of neighbors of neighbors and so forth. This view is made operational in the model of financial networks of Caballero and Simsek (2010).

In a rather different application Hansen (2007) and Hansen and Sargent (2010) consider models in which investors struggle with alternative models of long-term economic growth. While investors treat each of the models as misspecified, they presume that the models serve as useful benchmarks in much the same way as in stochastic specifications of robust control theory. Historical evidence is informative, but finite data histories do not accurately reveal the best model. Important differences in models may entail subtle components of economic growth that can have long-term macroeconomic consequences. Concerns about model misspecification become expressed more strongly in financial markets in some time periods than others. This has consequences for the valuation of capital in an uncertain environment and on the market trade-offs confronted by investors who participate in financial markets. In the example economies considered by Hansen (2007) and Hansen and Sargent (2010), what they call uncertainty premia become larger after the occurrence of a sequence of bad macroeconomic outcomes.

In summary, the implications of systemic uncertainty whether in contrast or in conjunction with systemic risk are both important for providing policy advice and understanding market outcomes. External analysts, say, statisticians, econometricians, and policy advisors, confront specification uncertainty when they build dynamic stochastic models with explicit linkages to the financial markets. Within dynamic models with micro foundations are decision makers or agents that also confront uncertainty. Their resulting actions can have a big impact on the system-wide outcomes. Assessing both the analysts' and agents' uncertainties are critical components to a productive research agenda.

1.3   Current Approaches

Let me turn now to some of the recent research related to systemic risk. Just the wide scope of the Bisias et al. (2012) survey reminds us that there is not yet an agreed upon approach to this measurement. To me, it suggests that identifying what measurements will be the most fruitful to support our understanding of linkages between financial markets and the macroeconomy is an open issue. In a superficial way, the sheer number of approaches would seem to address the Kelvin dictum. The problem is complex and it has many dimensions to it and thus requires multiple measurements. But I am doubtful that this is a correct assessment of the situation. Alternative measures are supported implicitly by alternative modeling assumptions and it is hard to see how the full array of measurements provides a coherent set of tools for policy makers. Many of the measurements to date seem closer in spirit to the Burns and Mitchell approach and fall way short of the Koopmans standard. From a policy perspective, I fear that we remain too close to the Potter-Stewart "we know it when we see it" view of systemic risk.

What follows is a discussion of a few specific approaches for assessing systemic risk along with some modeling and data challenges going forward.

1.3.1   Tail Measures

One approach measures codependence in the tails of equity returns to financial institutions. Some form of codependence is needed to distinguish the impact of the disturbances to the entire financial sector from firm-specific disturbances. Prominent examples of this include the work of Adrian and Brunnermeier (2008) and Brownlees and Engle (2011). Measuring tail dependence is particularly challenging because of limited historical data. To obtain estimates requires implicit extrapolations from the historical time series of returns because of the very limited number of extreme values of the magnitude of a financial crisis. While codependence helps to identify large aggregate shocks, all such shocks are in effect treated as a conglomerate when extracting information from historical evidence. The resulting measurements are interesting, but they put aside some critical questions that are needed to understand better policy advice. For example, while equity returns are used to identify an amalgam of aggregate shocks that could induce crises, how does the *mechanism* by which the disturbance is transmitted to the macroeconomy differ depending on the *source* of the disturbance? Not all financial market crises are macroeconomic crises. The big drops in equity markets on October 19, 1987, and April 14, 2000, did not trigger major macroeconomic declines. Was this because of the source of the shock or because of the macroeconomic policy responses? Understanding both the source and the mechanism of the disturbance would seem to be critical to the analysis of policy implications. Further empirical investigation of financial linkages with macroeconomic repercussions should be an important next step in this line of research.

It is wrong to say that this tail-based research is devoid of theory, and in fact Acharya et al. (2010) suggest how to use tail-risk measures as inputs into calculations about the solvency of the financial system. Their paper includes an explicit welfare calculation, and their use of measurements of tail dependence is driven in part by a particular policy perspective. Their theoretical supporting analysis is essentially static in nature, however. The macroeconomic consequences of crises events and how they unfold over time is largely put to the side. Instead, the focus is on providing a measure of the public cost of providing capital in order to exceed a specific threshold. This research does result in model-based measurements of what is called *marginal expected shortfall* and *systemic risk*. These measurements are updated regularly on the V-Lab web page at New York University. The use by Acharya et al. (2010) is an interesting illustration of how to model systemic risk and may well serve as a valuable platform for a more ambitious approach.

The focus on equity calculations limits the financial institutions that can be analyzed. The so-called shadow banking sector contains potentially important sectors or groups of firms that are not publicly traded. One could argue that if the monitoring targets are only SIFI's (so-called systemically important financial institutions), then the focus on publicly traded financial firms is appropriate. But system-wide policy concerns might be directed at the potential failure of collections of nonbank financial institutions including ones that are not publicly traded and hence omitted by calculations that rely on equity valuation measures.

1.3.2   Contingent Claims Analysis

In related research, Gray and Jobst (2011) apply what is known as contingent claims analysis. This approach features risk adjustments to sectoral balance sheets while featuring the distinct roles of debt and equity. It builds on the use of option pricing theory for firm financing where there is an underlying stochastic process for the value of the firm assets. Equity is a call option on these assets and debt is the corresponding put option. Gray and Jobst (2011) discuss examples of this approach extended to sectors of the economy including the government. In their applications, they measure sectoral balance sheets with a particular interest in financial crises. This approach neatly sidesteps statistical challenges by using "market expectations" and risk-adjusted probabilities in conjunction with equity-based measures of uncertainty and simplified models of debt obligations. Extending contingent claims analysis from the valuation of firms to systems of firms and governments is fruitful. Note, however, if our aim is to make welfare assessments and direct linkages to the macroeconomy, then the statistical modeling and measurement challenges that are skirted will quickly resurface. Market expectations and risk-neutral probability assessments offer the advantage of not needing to distinguish actual probabilities from the marginal utilities of investors in financial markets, but this advantage can only be pushed so far. A more fundamental understanding of the market-based "appetite for risk" and a characterization of the macroeconomic implications of the shocks that command large risk prices require further modeling and a more prominent examination of historical evidence. Such an understanding is central when our ambition is to engage in the analysis of counterfactuals and hypothetical changes in policies.[4]

---

4. The potential omission of firms not publicly traded limits this approach for the reasons described previously.

1.3.3   Network Models

Network models of the financial system offer intriguing ways to summarize data because of its focus on interconnectedness. These models open the door to some potentially important policy questions, but there are some critical shortcomings in making these models fully useful for policy. A financial firm in a network may be highly connected, interacting with many firms. Perhaps these links are such that the firm is "too interconnected to fail." A critical input into a policy response is how quickly the networks structure will evolve when such a firm fails. As is well recognized, in a dynamic setting these communications links will be endogenous, but this endogeneity makes modeling in a tractable way much more difficult and refocuses some of the measurements needed to address policy concerns.

1.3.4   Dynamic, Stochastic Macroeconomic Models

Linking financial market disruption to the macroeconomy requires more than just using "off-the-shelf" dynamic stochastic equilibrium models, say, of the type suggested by Christiano, Eichenbaum, and Evans (2005) and Smets and Wouters (2007). By design, models of this type are well suited for econometric estimation and they measure the consequences of multiple shocks and model explicitly the transition mechanisms for those shocks. Identification in these multishock models is tenuous. More importantly they are "small-shock" models. In order to handle a substantial number of state variables, they appeal to small noise approximations for analytical tractability. Since the financial crisis, there has been a rush to integrate financial market restrictions into these models. Crises are modeled as times when ad hoc financial constraints bind.[5] To use local methods of analysis, separate approximations are made around crisis periods. See Gertler and Kiyotaki (2010) for a recent development and discussion of this literature. There is some promising recent research developing and applying computational methods that allow for a more global approach to analyzing nonlinear dynamic economic models. More application and experience with such methods should open the door to a better understanding of stochastic models with linkages between financial markets and the macroeconomy.

Enriching dynamic stochastic equilibrium is a promising research agenda, but this literature has only scratched the surface on how to extend these models to improve our understanding of the macroeconomic consequence to upheaval in financial markets. It remains an open research question as to how best (a) to model financial constraints, both in terms of theoretical grounding and empirical importance; (b) to characterize the macroeconomic

---

5. I use the term *ad hoc* in a less derogatory manner than many other economists. I remind readers of a dictionary definition: concerned or dealing with a specific subject, purpose, or end.

consequences of crisis level shocks that are very large but infrequent; and (c) to model the origins of these shocks.[6]

1.3.5   Pitfalls in Data Dissemination and Collection

Measurement requires data. Going forward, there is great opportunity for the Office of Financial Research in the United States and its counterparts elsewhere to provide new data for researchers. Some of the data in its most primitive form will be confidential. Concern for confidentiality will create challenges for sharing this information with external researchers. One approach is to restrict the use of such data to be "in house." This will limit the value of the data collection. If the objective is to ensure the high quality of research within government agencies, it is valuable to make important components of the data available to external researchers. This external access permits replication of results, and nurtures innovative modeling and measurement.[7] Moreover, external analysis can provide a check against research with preordained conclusions or inadvertent support for policies such as "too big (or too something) to fail." While providing external access requires that data be distributed in manners that respect individual confidentiality, the possibility of making such data available is a reality. The Census Bureau has already confronted such challenges successfully.

There are additional data issues that require scrutiny. Distortions in the collection of publicly available data can hinder the measurement of aggregate risk exposures because of the temptation to disguise the problematic nature of policies in place. Moreover, even when intentions are good, preexisting policies can make the assessment of risk using historical data more challenging by partially mitigating risks in ways that are not sustainable in the future. Brickell (2011) identifies this latter challenge and argues that it may have contributed to errors in assessing housing market risk in the years before the Great Recession. These types of concerns place an extra burden on empirical researchers to model the biases in data collection induced by both public and private incentives for distortion.

Given this state of econometric modeling and measurement, I see a big gap to fill between statistical analyses measuring comovements in the tails of financial market equity returns and empirical analyses measuring the impact of shocks to the macroeconomy. This gap limits, at least temporarily, the scope of the analysis of systemic risk. Closing this gap provides an important opportunity for the future. The compendium of systemic risk measures identified in Bisias et al. (2012) should be viewed merely as an inter-

---

6. For instance, the Macroeconomic Financial Modeling group funded by the Alfred P. Sloan Foundation explores the challenges to building quantitatively ambitious models that address these and other related challenges.

7. Andy Lo has made the related point that potentially relevant sectors, such as the insurance sector, are not under the formal scrutiny of the federal government and hence there may be an important shortfall in the data available to the Office of Financial Research.

esting start. We should not lose sight of the longer-term challenge to provide systemic risk quantification grounded in economic analysis and supported by evidence. The need for sound theoretical underpinnings for producing policy-relevant research identified by Koopmans many decades ago still applies to the quantification of systemic risk. Policy analysis stemming from econometric models aims to push beyond the realm of historical evidence through the use of well-grounded economic models. It is meant to provide a framework for the conduct of hypothetical policies that did not occur during the historical observation period. To engage in this activity with the ambition to understand better how to monitor or regulate the financial sector to prevent major upheaval in the macroeconomy requires creative adjustments in both our modeling and our measurement.

1.4   Conclusion

We should not underestimate the difficulty of measuring systemic risk in a meaningful way. But success offers the potential for valuable inputs into policy making. Wearing my econometrician's hat has led me to emphasize measurement challenges and the associated uncertainty caused by limited data or unknown statistical models used to generate the data. Of course clever econometricians can always invent challenges, and in many respects part of the econometrician's job is to provide credible ways to quantify measurement uncertainties. After all, quantitative research in economics grounded by empirical evidence should be more than just reporting a single number but instead ranges or distributions that include sensitivity to model specification. Good econometrics is supported simultaneously by good economics and good statistics. Exploring the consequences of potential model misspecification necessarily requires inputs from both economics and statistics. Economic models help us understand what statistical inputs are most consequential to economic outcomes and good statistics reveal where the measurements are least reliable. Moreover, such econometric explorations will benefit discussions of policy by providing repeated reminders of why gaps in our knowledge can have important implications.

Allow me to close by returning to the Kelvin dictum and drawing on some intellectual history of it as it relates to social science research. The decision to place this dictum on the Social Science Research building at the University of Chicago caught the attention of some distinguished scholars. This building housed the economics department for many years and the Cowles Commission for Research in Economics during the years 1939 to 1955 when many young scholars came there to explore linkages between economics, mathematics, and statistics.[8] Two of the original pillars of the "Chicago

---

8. After moving to Yale in 1955, the Cowles Commission was renamed the Cowles Foundation.

school," Knight and Viner, had notable reactions to the use of the Kelvin quote and proposed amendments:[9]

Knight: If you cannot measure a thing, go ahead and measure it anyway.

Viner: and even when we can measure a thing, our knowledge will be meager and unsatisfactory.

Perhaps just as intriguing as Knight's and Viner's scepticism are the major challenges that were levied to Lord Kelvin's own calculations about the age of the sun. These challenges provide an object lesson in support of model uncertainty. Kelvin argued that the upper bound of the sun's age was twenty to forty million years, although his earlier estimates included the possibility of a much larger number, up to 100 million years. Kelvin's evidence and that provided by others were used to question the plausibility of the Darwinian theory of evolution. Darwin's own calculations suggested that much more time was needed to justify the evolutionary processes. In hindsight, Lord Kelvin's estimates were over one hundred times lower than the current estimate of 4.5 billion years. Kelvin's understatements were revised upward by substantive advances in our understanding of radioactivity as an energy source. This historical episode illustrates rather dramatically an impact of model uncertainty on the quality of measurement. While Knight's and Viner's words of caution were motivated by their perception of social science research several decades ago, their concerns extend to other research settings as well. It is difficult to fault Lord Kelvin for not anticipating the discovery of a new energy source. Nevertheless, I do not wish to conclude that the potential for model misspecification should induce us to abandon earnest attempts at quantification. Instead quantification should be a valued exercise, and part of this exercise should include a characterization of sensitivity to alternative model specifications. Unfortunately, there are no guarantees that we have captured the actual form of the misspecification among the possibilities that we consider, but at least we can avoid some of the pitfalls of using models in naive ways.

Quantitative ambitions have the virtue of providing clarity for what is to be measured. Models provide measurement frameworks and facilitate communication and criticism. While simple quantifications of systemic risk may be a naive hope, producing better models to support policy discussion and analysis is a worthy ambition. Building a single consensus model is unrealistic in the near term, but even exploring formally the consequences of alternative models adds discipline to policy advice. Without such modeling pursuits, we are left with a heavy reliance on discretion in governmental course of action. Perhaps discretion is the best we can do in some extreme circumstances, but formal analysis should provide coherency and transparency to economic policy.

9. See Merton, Stills, and Stigler (1984).

While systemic-risk modeling and measurement is a promising research agenda, caution should prevail about the impact of model misspecification on the measurements and the consequences of those measurements. A critical component to this venture should be to assess and guard against adverse impacts of the use of measurements from necessarily stylized models. Complete success along this dimension is asking too much, otherwise we would just "fix" our models. Nevertheless, confronting the various components of uncertainty with some formality will help us to use models in sensible and meaningful ways. As our knowledge and understanding advance over time, so will our comprehension and characterization of uncertainty in our model-based, quantitative assessments.

References

Acharya, Viral V., Christian Brownlees, Robert Engle, Farhang Farazmand, and Matthew Richardson. 2010. "Measuring Systemic Risk." In *Regulating Wall Street*, edited by Viral V. Acharya, Thomas F. Cooley, Matthew Richardson, and Ingo Walter, 85–119. Hoboken, NJ: John Wiley and Sons, Inc.

Admati, Anat R., Peter M. DeMarzo, Martin F. Hellwig, and Paul Pfleiderer. 2010. "Fallacies, Irrelevant Facts, and Myths in the Discussion of Capital Regulation: Why Bank Equity Is Not Expensive." Research Papers 2065. Stanford University, Graduate School of Business.

Adrian, Tobias, and Markus K. Brunnermeier. 2008. "CoVaR." Technical report, Federal Reserve Bank of New York, Staff Reports.

Bisias, Dimitrios, Mark Flood, Andrew W. Lo, and Stavros Valavanis. 2012. "A Survey of Systemic Risk Analytics." Working Paper 0001, Office of Financial Research, US Department of Treasury.

Brickell, Mark. 2011. "Lessons Gleaned from Flawed Mortgage Risk Assessments." *Financial Times*, April 13.

Brownlees, Christian, and Robert Engle. 2011. "Volatility, Correlation and Tails for Systemic Risk Measurement." Technical report. Available at: http://ssrn.com/abstract=1611229 .

Burns, Arthur F., and Wesley C. Mitchell. 1946. *Measuring Business Cycles*. New York: National Bureau of Economic Research.

Caballero, Ricardo, and Alp Simsek. 2010. "Fire Sales in a Model of Complexity." Working Paper no. 09-28, Department of Economics, MIT.

Christiano, Lawrence J., Martin Eichenbaum, and Charles L. Evans. 2005. "Nominal Rigidities and the Dynamic Effects of a Shock to Monetary Policy." *Journal of Political Economy* 113 (1): 1–45.

Cogley, Timothy, Riccardo Colacito, Lars Peter Hansen, and Thomas J. Sargent. 2008. "Robustness and U.S. Monetary Policy Experimentation." *Journal of Money, Credit and Banking* 40 (8): 1599–623.

Friedman, Milton. 1960. *A Program for Monetary Stability*. New York: Fordham University Press.

Gertler, Mark, and Nobuhiro Kiyotaki. 2010. "Financial Intermediation and Credit Policy in Business Cycle Analysis." In *Handbook of Monetary Economics*, vol. 3, edited by Benjamin M. Friedman and Michael Woodford, 547–99. Amsterdam: Elsevier.

Gilboa, Itzhak, and David Schmeidler. 1989. "Maxmin Expected Utility with Non-Unique Prior." *Journal of Mathematical Economics* 18 (2): 141–53.

Gilboa, Itzhak, Andrew W. Postlewaite, and David Schmeidler. 2008. "Probability and Uncertainty in Economic Modeling." *Journal of Economic Perspectives* 22 (3): 173–88.

Gray, Dale F., and Andreas A. Jobst. 2011. "Modelling Systemic Financial Sector and Sovereign Risk." *Sveriges Riksbank Economic Review* 2:68–106.

Haldane, Andrew G. 2011. "Capital Discipline." Technical report, Bank of England. Based on a speech given to the AEA meeting in Denver, Colorado. January.

———. 2012. "The Dog and the Frisbee." Paper presented at the Federal Reserve Bank of Kansas City's 36th Economic Policy Symposium, Jackson Hole, Wyoming. August.

Hansen, Lars Peter. 2007. "Beliefs, Doubts and Learning, Valuing Macroeconomic Risk." *American Economic Review* 97 (2): 1–30.

Hansen, Lars Peter, and Thomas J. Sargent. 2001. "Robust Control and Model Uncertainty." *American Economic Review* 91 (2): 60–6.

———. 2010. "Fragile Beliefs and the Price of Uncertainty." *Quantitative Economics* 1 (1): 129–62.

———. 2012. "Three Types of Ambiguity." *Journal of Monetary Economics* 59 (5): 422–445.

Knight, Frank H. 1921. *Risk, Uncertainty, and Profit*. Boston: Hart, Schaffner and Marx; Houghton Mifflin Co.

Koopmans, Tjalling C. 1947. "Measurement without Theory." *Review of Economics and Statistics* 29 (3): 161–72.

Merton, Robert K., David L. Sills, and Stephen M. Stigler. 1984. "The Kelvin Dictum and Social Science: An Excursion into the History of an Idea." *Journal of the History of Behavioral Sciences* 20:319–31.

Petersen, Ian R., Matthew R. James, and Paul Dupuis. 2000. "Minimax Optimal Control of Stochastic Uncertain Systems with Relative Entropy Constraints." *IEEE Transactions on Automatic Control* 45:398–412.

Smets, Frank, and Rafael Wouters. 2007. "Shocks and Frictions in US Business Cycles: A Bayesian DSGE Approach." *American Economic Review* 97 (3): 586–606.

2

Regulating Systemic Risk through Transparency
Trade-Offs in Making Data Public

Augustin Landier and David Thesmar

According to many observers, the financial crisis is a product of the lack of transparency of the financial system. In a recent speech, Fed chairman Ben Bernanke acknowledged that opaqueness was a "structural weakness in the shadow banking system" and an important element in the narrative of the crisis.[1] Examples of such opaqueness are over-the-counter (OTC) markets such as the credit default swap (CDS) market, for which there is little detailed data about holdings, prices, and collateral posted. This made it difficult for the regulator to understand the web of counterparty exposures and have an independent assessment of the overall resilience of the system.

Besides what was available to the regulator, public disclosure of financial information was probably insufficient. For instance, the lack of microdata on the content of securitized products made it difficult for investors to price risk correctly. Market participants trading securitized products such as collateralized debt obligations (CDOs) and collateralized mortgage obligations (CMOs) were relying on imprecise, and sometimes flawed, ratings (Benmelech and Dlugosz 2009). Beyond pricing, public availability of data is argued to enhance the role that researchers outside the government (from universities, think tanks, or other private institutions) can play in assisting, and to some extent monitor, regulators.[2]

Augustin Landier is a professor at the Toulouse School of Economics (TSE). David Thesmar is professor of finance at the HEC Paris.

We thank Markus Brunnermeier, Arvind Krishnamurthy, Luigi Zingales, and other participants at the NBER systemic risk meeting in Chicago in May 2011. For acknowledgments, sources of research support, and disclosure of the authors' material financial relationships, if any, please see http://www.nber.org/chapters/c12508.ack.

1. Speech given at the 2010 Squam Lake conference. http://www.federalreserve.gov/news events/speech/bernanke20100616a.htm.

2. Mary Graham (2002).

This chapter is about the costs and benefits of public disclosure of financial data. Theoretically, however, increasing transparency may reduce welfare as well as increase it. For instance, Dang, Gorton, and Holmström (2010) argue that common ignorance of market participants about the precise nature of some assets might be a desired feature rather than a bug of the financial system. Such assets might deliberately be constructed as opaque to remain information insensitive. Releasing more information in the public domain might thus be welfare decreasing. Other voices, notably from the private sector, warn that extreme transparency might be detrimental to incentives of financial agents to produce information and to innovate.

In this chapter, we develop a framework to understand the costs and benefits of public disclosure of financial data. We believe such a framework can help regulators to determine the format under which data should be publicly accessible, as a function of the type of information under consideration. In our framework, the welfare impact of public access to data depends on three dimensions: (a) the frequency of data collection, (b) the time lag of their public release, and (c) their level of granularity/anonymity. Granularity and anonymity are linked as less granular (more aggregated) data make it easier to protect anonymity.

In doing so, our framework addresses the following questions:

- At what frequency should data be collected and made available?
- How long should the regulator wait before releasing the data?
- At what level of detail (granularity) should information be released? If the public information is detailed, should it be made anonymous?

Frequency, lag, and granularity are important choice variables for regulators who wish to publicly disclose data; yet, there is no systematic doctrine about their optimal level. To give examples, some data are currently publicly available at very fine levels of granularity (13Fs filings provide at the institution level an exhaustive position-by-position view of individual long-equity holdings at a quarterly frequency). By contrast some other data are available only at an aggregated level (e.g., new lending by banks or bank cross-country exposures). But these choices owe more to history and political compromises than to a systematic cost and benefit analysis.

In the first section of the chapter, we review the various economic costs associated to public data release and review the corresponding academic literature. In the second section, we present several dimensions of data that can be optimized to mitigate each of these costs. Last, we review the positive impact that might be expected from public access to financial data and develop a framework to manage on a case-by-case basis the cost-benefit trade-off, notably through the choice of disclosure lags and granularity.

2.1   The Potential Costs of Transparency:
A Review of Economic Forces at Stake

There is a basic intuitive economic reason why more information is a priori better than less: individual decisions are closer to being privately optimal when agents have more accurate information. Because in a frictionless economy private and social efficiency do not differ, it follows that full public disclosure of information is always desirable from a welfare perspective if we abstract from frictions. However, this prediction does not hold anymore in the presence of economic frictions. In this section, we review the various kinds of frictions that can create a welfare cost to the public release of financial information.

2.1.1   The (Shrinking) Material and Clerical Costs

A direct cost of transparency is simply that of producing, storing, certifying, and disseminating information. For a long time, such costs have been an important margin in deciding the optimal level of public disclosure. Today, while these costs might not be trivial, they have been enormously diminished (the cost of saving one bit of information on hard disk storage space has decreased by almost 1.5 million times since 1980).

Moreover, much financial information that one might be inclined to disclose consists of information that financial firms already produce for internal use. For instance, disaggregated data on holdings and liabilities is a necessary ingredient of sound risk management by financial institutions. Thus, the need to transmit them to regulators and/or to the public might not be a high additional cost to companies. In what follows, we will focus on other costs than these simple material costs of producing and managing information.

2.1.2   Secrecy Might Be Vital to Some Activities in Finance

A second line of arguments against imposing higher transparency is that it might discourage the production of information by financial intermediaries and consequently decrease market efficiency. To have incentives to produce information, economic agents need to be able to use it to make profits, which might require a temporary monopoly power on that information. For instance, after paying the cost to identify an arbitrage opportunity, a hedge fund manager might need time to exploit the opportunity before it gets revealed to the public. If positions are disclosed quickly, the fund might not have had time to enter positions at a sufficient scale to recoup the initial cost.

Thus, by decreasing rents of arbitrageurs, transparency might, according to that view, reduce market efficiency (this is related to the Grossman-Stiglitz paradox). Opacity in finance might be useful in protecting rents from information production, akin to trade secrets or patents in other high-tech industries. One empirical example where this property-right argument has some empirical bite, however, seems to be that of the analyst's coverage. Gomes, Gorton, and Madureira (2007) study the consequences of the adoption of the Regulation Fair Disclosure ("Reg FD") by the US Securities and Exchange Commission in October 2000, a regulation that prevents firms from selectively disclosing information to some market participants (typically a few selected analysts), but not others. They find that this regulation led to a loss of analyst coverage for small firms and to a higher cost of capital. Their interpretation is that by eliminating the temporary monopoly power of some analysts on information, the regulation discouraged them to work on small firms.

In finance, the property-right argument is hard to reconcile with recent trends in the cost of information accumulation and evolution of rents in the sector.[3] There is evidence that wages and profits in the financial sector have risen to abnormally high levels (see, e.g., Philippon and Reshef 2008). At the same time, the cost of gathering, storing, and processing information has decreased massively. Hence, for the current level of financial rents to be optimal, we need information acquisition to have become extremely (socially) valuable in today's economies.

2.1.3   Transparency May Generate Instability

Various academic theories provide models where the disclosure of more public information can generate financial instability, increased volatility, and/or reduced liquidity. We provide in this subsection a categorization of these theories.

When It Creates Asymmetric Information

Several papers argue that when complex information is released to the public, only the most sophisticated agents are able to process it. Thus, increased transparency can generate asymmetric information among agents, which in turn can make markets less liquid or even collapse à la Akerlof (1970). The more complex the information to be released is, the stronger this effect. For instance, Pagano and Volpin (2012) have a model along this line of research where they emphasize the view that transparency enhances liquidity only if market participants are equally skilled at information processing. In their model, some investors have limited ability to process information. Thus, releasing more public information can increase adverse selection in the market and reduce liquidity. Similarly, Dang, Gorton, and Holmström, (2010) also develop a model where common ignorance facilitates trading.

---

3. Moreover, the empirical evidence from nonfinancial industries also indicates that strong intellectual property protection often decreases innovation speed (see, e.g., Williams [2010] or Boldrin and Levine [2007]).

More transparency can lead to the inefficient emergence of adverse selection. Their paper suggests that certain types of market securities, such as securitized products, are designed to be information insensitive and thus deliberately constructed to be opaque. Markets for such securities can function better if all agents are kept uninformed about details so that no one suspects other agents of trading with superior information. Holmström (2008) notes that when De Beers sells wholesale diamonds, the stones are placed in opaque packets that buyers are forbidden to explore, to avoid the occurrence of a lemon's problem.

Empirical evidence looking at the introduction of a fundamental change of the US bond market tends, however, to find positive liquidity effects of transparency: after July 2002, the Transaction Reporting and Compliance Engine (TRACE) requires bond dealers to report all trades in publicly issued corporate bonds. The National Association of Security Dealers makes the transaction data freely accessible to the public. Several studies find that the cost of trading corporate bonds has decreased following the increase in transparency (see Goldstein, Hotchkiss, and Sirri (2007); Edwards, Harris, and Piwowar (2007); Bessembinder and Maxwell 2008).

When It Creates Coordination Failures

The "global games" literature has examined the impact of public information in coordination games where agents have both private and public information. Morris and Shin (2002) show that the provision of more precise public information can be detrimental to welfare. The reason is that agents (rationally) overreact to public information compared to the social optimum, and hence noise in public signals can cause social inefficiencies. An increase in the precision of public information may have the perverse effect of increasing aggregate volatility, as economic activity becomes more sensitive to common noise. The reason is that private signals are not used in a socially optimal manner in the presence of strong public signals.

In the same vein, Amador and Weill (2010) show that the availability of more public information can limit the incorporation of private signals into prices and thus be welfare decreasing (see also Duffie, Malamud, and Manso 2009). In the presence of multiple equilibria, public information can also lead to the selection of a bad equilibrium.

Morris and Shin (2007) have a model where coarser information has a greater chance of being understood by all market participants than granular information, and thus leads to better coordination among agents. They emphasize a trade-off between the quantity of information and its shared nature. If coordination requires a common understanding of information, it is possible for increased transparency to be welfare decreasing. This is because some market observers (possibly a small minority) fail to understand the information.

When It Facilitates Predatory Trading

Investors in financial distress can be forced to quickly unwind their positions. When the holdings of such investors are known by other traders, such liquidations can give rise to predatory trading: informed traders anticipate the fire sale and initially trade in the same direction as the distressed institution, which amplifies the shock to asset prices. Brunnermeier and Pedersen (2005) provide a continuous time model that solves for the price trajectory in the presence of fire sales and quantify the amplifying impact of predatory trading on price swings. They emphasize the risk of systemic destabilization induced by such predatory trading and use as a motivating example the alleged trading against positions of Long-Term Capital Management (LTCM) in the fall of 1998, which led to the concern that LTCM's financial difficulties might destabilize the financial system as a whole. This kind of destabilizing speculation is facilitated when both the individual shocks leading to fire sales (such as performance or outflows) and the individual holdings of investors are public information.

Empirically, Coval and Stafford (2007) study the price impact of mutual funds outflows. They emphasize the fact that public disclosure of funds holdings makes future flow-driven transactions predictable. This creates an incentive to front run the anticipated fire sales of distressed mutual funds that are experiencing large capital outflows. Such front-running strategies are shown to be profitable. They decrease the price at which these distressed funds are able to liquidate positions. Looking at hedge fund holding data, Greenwood and Thesmar (2011) find little evidence of such front running by hedge funds. On average, hedge fund trading is not correlated with mutual fund fire sales. For some stocks, this correlation is positive (front running), but for others, this correlation is negative (liquidity provision).

When It Generates Perverse Incentives to Offset Regulation

Higher transparency imposed to institutions can generate large offsetting effects. Faced with higher disclosure requirements, financial institutions might strategically attempt to find ways to manipulate disclosures in a self-serving manner. The economic forces behind such offsetting effects are well known: agents try to strategically manipulate to their advantage the signals that are used by regulators or principals to evaluate them (Holmström 1999; Holmström and Milgrom 1991). Such inefficient "signal jamming" can lead to substantial distortions.

Directly related to the offsetting effects of disclosure requirements, a large literature studies how publically traded companies engage in earnings smoothing and various accounting manipulations to optimize market reactions to their corporate financial reporting. Bergstresser and Philippon (2006) show that discretionary accruals are used strategically by CEOs to manipulate reported earnings. Graham, Harvey, and Rajgopalc (2005) find that 78 percent of a representative sample of top executives admits to "sacrificing long-term value to smooth earnings." In the same vein, Chevalier and Ellison (1997) show that mutual fund managers who are performing well relative to the market gamble to make year-end lists of "top performers"; this is again an example of "jamming" publically observed signals.

Such offsetting effects due to regulatory constraints have actually been at play in the current crisis: the shadow banking system was partly developed as a way to bypass regulatory constraints, notably capital requirements. Asset-backed commercial paper conduits became an increasingly large source of funding for commercial banks, reaching US $1.4 trillion in June 2007 (see Acharya, Schnabl, and Suarez 2011 and Brunnermeier 2009).

2.2   The Three Determinants of the Costs and Benefits to Publicly Disclose Financial Data

The costs of public disclosure listed earlier are potentially affected by three parameters. These parameters are all choice variables of the regulator who is in charge of disseminating the information. In this section, we describe these parameters and their effect on the costs of transparency. We defer the discussion on their impact on benefits of disclosure to the next section.

The three determinants of the costs and benefit of transparency are the following:

- Granularity: There are two levels of granularity—that of the reporting entity, and that of the reported positions. Regarding positions, data can be at the individual position level (e.g., quantity of common stocks of company i held) or at a more aggregate level (e.g., quantity of stocks in industry i held). Similarly, reports can give holdings at the individual legal entity level or at a more aggregate level. For instance 13F reports provide fully granular data on long-equity holdings: each reporting entity has to file its positions in each individual company. By contrast, Bank for International Settlements (BIS) reports are more aggregated, as they give the consolidated exposure of all the banks of country i to any given foreign country j. Note that granularity and anonymity are to be determined jointly: to make data anonymous (i.e., such that the reporting entity cannot be identified by the user), it is usually needed to pick an appropriate level of aggregation; otherwise, users might infer from the data what institution/individual is reporting. For example, the ranking of banks by asset size is known, and thus data that would provide total balance sheet-size information would be de facto non-anonymous.
- Frequency: Data can be reported at various frequencies. When frequencies are too low (e.g., annual or quarterly), a risk exists that institu-

tions engage in window dressing by changing holdings right before they have to report. To avoid such gaming of the system without incurring the inconvenience of high frequency reporting, institutions could be asked to provide average numbers over a given period as advised in the Geneva Report.

- Lag of disclosure: Data regarding holdings at date t can be reported at time t' and made available at a later date $t'' > t'$ to the public. The public disclosure lag is $t'' - t$ and the reporting lag is $t' - t$. For instance, form 13F is required to be filed to the SEC by large institutional owners within forty-five days of the end of a calendar quarter and is made available immediately on the SEC's website; that is, $t' - t = t'' - t = 45$ days.

Let us now turn to the impact of these three determinants on the costs of transparency. Lag of disclosure and granularity are key margins to reduce these costs. The revelation of "cold" information won't induce lemons problems, coordination failures, nor a substantial loss in trading profitability. A delay of six months to one year seems reasonable in most cases. Zingales (2009, 421) suggests delays of one to two years before full disclosure of individual data in private equity and hedge funds. His argument is the following: "This delay will eliminate any competitive concern, since the half-life of a portfolio strategy is very short on Wall Street (Grinold and Kahn [2000] estimate it as 1.2 years), while still providing the benefit of a serious statistical analysis of this market, which will improve allocation." Still, some agents might argue that key proprietary processes might be reverse engineered by observing data and could be detrimental to profitability. Facing such arguments, the regulator has to estimate whether this is a credible threat to the business; if so, the solution is to reveal data at more aggregate levels, thus limiting the possibility of reverse engineering. However, less granular information on holdings might be easier to manipulate than lists of individual holdings (granular information).

2.3   The Potential Gains from Public Disclosure

We now turn to the potential welfare gains from public access to financial data. In each case, we will review the extent to which the benefits depend on frequency, lags, and granularity. A frequent question in financial economics is why firms do not set the right level of disclosure by themselves (Leuz and Wysocki 2008). After all, if information is useful to buyers of securities, they should be willing to pay a higher price to be informed. In the case of systemic risk, the reason for the underprovision of public information by private actors is simple: firms do not internalize the impact that their level of disclosure can have on the stability of the financial system via the knowledge of other participants (including the regulator). There is thus a motive for compulsory disclosure of information.

2.3.1   "Crowdsourcing" and the Value of "Free-Range" Research

One option available to regulators is to behave as gatekeepers regarding the data and provide access to them only to selected teams of researchers who present a project that is considered valuable for regulatory purposes. However, there are several reasons that might make such restrictive access suboptimal.

First, many research projects are not well defined at an early stage and it is often only after thorough data exploration that researchers are able to spot new relevant questions or anomalies worth being investigated. If data are not publically accessible, such exploration is less likely to take place. Second, any gatekeeping institution is likely to become excessively protective about the use of data and favor internal or more connected researchers. It is difficult to conceive a governance mechanism that would surely defeat the emergence of such monopolistic behavior.

Data availability directly feeds research intensity: Kevin Murphy shows that the average number of CEO pay papers produced per year has doubled after the executive compensation data for large US companies (EXECUCOMP) became available in 1992. In several instances, such research has had direct regulatory impact. An instance of influential forensic analysis by academics in finance is the work of Heron and Lie (2007, 2009). Using public executive compensation data, they uncovered a widespread practice of backdating option grant dates among US executives. They estimate that 18.9 percent of option grants of top US executives during the period 1996 to 2005 were backdated. Their study led to a large Securites and Exchange Commission (SEC) inquiry into this illegal practice. The impact of researchers using their free access to the data to identify new topics or anomalies worth being investigated by regulators is historically validated by several other examples. Notably, numerous academic studies have investigated the behavior of mutual funds taking advantage of public holdings and performance data provided by the SEC. For instance, Carhart et al. (2002) document that the prices of stocks owned by mutual funds exhibit positive abnormal returns at the end of the quarter. Duong and Menschke (2008) find no evidence for such manipulation by mutual funds post 2000 suggesting that the increased scrutiny following the publication of the results has led to a decrease in manipulation of that sort. 13F filings have widely been used in research to study the potentially destabilizing role of institutional investors in financial markets. Brunnermeier and Nagel (2004) explore the behavior of hedge funds during the Internet bubble and show that they were long technology stocks during most of the bubble, thus playing a destabilizing role. Insider trading data are also largely exploited by researchers. It is easy to imagine how much more could be done if wider data were available. For instance, the fact that short positions are not available in 13Fs has limited the scope of research on the market impact of hedge funds.

The internal politics of bureaucratic organizations might create a climate favorable to status quo bias and reluctance to ask disturbing questions. An open-source approach to the use of data might mitigate these biases, by letting researchers from various horizons free to ask questions that might seem a priori unwarranted. The "wisdom of crowds" effect stemming from a large pool of external researchers that are not filtered by (or affiliated to) the regulator can hardly be replicated in-house. Small groups of experts tend to be prone to consensus and are less likely to ask the disturbing questions. Researchers internal to regulatory agencies might become too confident in the system and miss the buildup of excessive risk taking. New forms of risks might emerge from unpredictable parts of asset classes that specialized researchers might dismiss as innocuous out of habit. Such cognitive and organizational "groupthink" effects and their causes are explored in Benabou ([2010]; see also Janis [1982]).[4]

For the wisdom of crowd effect to take place, granular data might be important because categories used by regulators to aggregate data can slowly become obsolete. In some cases, regulators might even deliberately provide hard-to-use aggregates to preserve their monopoly in the use of the data. New sources of risks are likely to come from unexpected parts of the system, or innovations such as "game-changing" products that do not fit existing categories. To address such changing environments, access to granular data is key. Cheng and Xiong (2013) show how, using granular (but not public) data from the Commodity Futures Trading Commission (CFTC), the impact of indexed traders on commodity prices can be inferred. Their analysis cannot be undertaken using the public aggregate data reported by the CFTC.

Disclosure lags (as long as they are not too extreme) will not diminish the interest of researchers for data, nor the relevance of their contributions: based on 2003 to 2004 data, researchers may have produced highly relevant research for taking regulatory decisions in 2007 to 2008.

2.3.2 Avoiding Regulatory Capture

Regulatory capture occurs when the regulated industry manages to bias the regulator's decisions in its favor (Stigler 1971).[5] Incentives of regulators might be improved if internal data are made available to the large public ex post, so that researchers and other outside experts can externally monitor regulatory decisions. Moreover, even absent incentive problems from regu-

---

4. The wisdom of crowds effect we are referring to is by no means akin to a form of "self-regulation." Quite the contrary, contributions from unaffiliated researchers can enrich and complement the work of regulators and help them reach efficient decisions.
5. Several commentators (e.g., Johnson 2009) have argued that regulatory capture of public agencies might have been a driving force behind the financial crisis, resulting in a lax regulatory environment placing faith in "self-regulation" via risk models internal to banks.

lators (i.e., even if they turned out to automatically make socially optimal choices), the possibility to judge ex post that their decisions were ex ante justified based on their information set is important: it reinforces the legitimacy of their choices and the confidence of market participants.

Here again, a relatively long disclosure lag (e.g., a couple of years) is not very detrimental to the benefits of transparency, but it is important to get access to data with the same granularity as the regulator to replicate his or her information set.

2.3.3   Complementarity with the Internal Reporting System of Financial Institutions

The standardization of back-office booking of positions among banks and other financial institutions creates a mutually beneficial situation for both regulators and financial institutions. On the one hand, it makes regulation more efficient: reports to regulators can be directly fed by internal risk-management systems. Also, highly granular (position level) reports might be important to accelerate the standardization of new products between banks and making regulators quickly aware of the emergence of such new products. The advantage of forcing the adoption of a common asset classification is to force banks to improve back office and risk management and help coordination among them.

On the other hand, standardization of back-office booking also makes internal risk-management systems more efficient, which in turn elicits cooperation from the financial industry. A good example is the case of transaction identifiers. In its willingness to create a reporting standard, the Office of Financial Research seeks to impose a "Legal Entity Identifier," a detailed identifying number for each financial transaction, including derivatives. The gains of doing so for the financial industry are important. First, having common identifiers makes settlement easier, which lowers back-office costs. Second, it lowers the cost of mergers as it becomes easier to integrate different risk-management systems into a single one. This made the industry coopoerative; in particular, big entities who had grown through successive acquisitions.

For this positive coordination effect of data disclosure to take place, public disclosure is, in theory, not needed (it is enough that regulators get the information). However, public data can help private actors identify crowded trades and stay away from them. This argument might be reversed in the presence of bailout expectations, as financial institutions might then have collective incentives to load on similar risks (see, e.g., Fahri and Tirole 2012). For disaggregate data to be informative about counterparty risk, it is important for them to be specific about the exact reporting entity; for example, separate out assets for which the bank is liable and assets for which banks are not, which suggests aiming for relatively fine granularity. Note that such feedback into risk management needs to take place in real time. It follows that in order to induce such private risk-management effects, short lags are more important than when the purpose of public data release is used by the academic community.

2.4 Conclusion

While this chapter focuses on the finance industry, there are general lessons that can be drawn from our analysis for other areas of regulation (such as environmental and medical data). After reviewing the potential costs of public disclosure of financial data, we have shown how they can be mitigated by the choice of long disclosure lags and coarser levels of granularity (i.e., more aggregate data). In reviewing the gains from access to public data, based on observing the use of already available public data, we emphasize the fact that long lags of disclosure (such as a couple of years) might not be a major impediment to the production of relevant contributions by academic researchers, but might negatively impact the feedback into private risk management. However, the relevance of academic contributions is more likely to be impacted by the choice of granularity of the data. In particular, aggregate data seem more vulnerable to obfuscation by private actors and possibly by regulators themselves.

References

Acharya, Viral V., Philipp Schnabl, and Gustavo Suarez. 2013. "Securitization without Risk Transfer." *Journal of Financial Economics* 107 (3): 515–36.

Akerlof, George A. 1970. "The Market for 'Lemons': Quality Uncertainty and the Market Mechanism." *Quarterly Journal of Economics* 3 (August): 488–500.

Amador, Manuel, and Pierre-Olivier Weill. 2010. "Learning from Prices: Public Communication and Welfare." *Journal of Political Economy* 118 (5): 866–907.

Benabou, Roland. 2010. "Groupthink." Working Paper, Princeton University.

Benmelech, Efraïm, and Jennifer Dlugosz. 2009. "The Alchemy of CDO Credit Ratings." *Journal of Monetary Economics* 56 (5): 617–34.

Bergstresser, Daniel, and Thomas Philippon. 2006. "CEO Incentives and Earnings Management." *Journal of Financial Economics* 80:511–29.

Bessembinder, Hendrik, and William Maxwell. 2008. "Transparency and the Corporate Bond Market." *Journal of Economic Perspectives* 22 (2): 217–34.

Boldrin, Michele, and David Levine. 2007. "Against Intellectual Monopoly." Unpublished Manuscript. University of California, Los Angeles. http://www.dklevine.com/general/intellectual/against.htm.

Brunnermeier, Markus. 2009. "Deciphering the Liquidity and Credit Crunch of 2007–08." *Journal of Economic Perspectives* 23 (1): 77–100.

Brunnermeir, Markus, and Stefan Nagel. 2004. "Hedge Funds and the Technology Bubble." *Journal of Finance* 59 (5): 2013–40.

Brunnermeier, Markus, and Lasse Pedersen. 2005. "Predatory Trading." *Journal of Finance* 60:1825–63.

Carhart, Mark, Ron Kaniel, David Musto, and Adam Reed. 2002. "Leaning for the Tape: Evidence of Gaming Behavior in Equity Mutual Funds." *Journal of Finance* 57 (2): 661–93.

Cheng, Ing-Haw and Wei Xiong. 2013. "The Financialization of Commodity Markets." NBER Working Paper no. 19642, Cambridge, MA.

Chevalier, Judith, and Glenn Ellison. 1997. "Risk Taking by Mutual Funds as a Response to Incentives." *Journal of Political Economy* 105 (6): 1167–1200.

Coval, Joshua, and Erik Stafford. 2007. "Asset Fire Sales (and Purchases) in Equity Markets." *Journal of Financial Economics* 86 (2): 479–512.

Dang, Tri vi, Gary Gorton, and Bengt Holmström. 2010. "Opacity and the Optimality of Debt for Liquidity Provision." Working Paper.

Duong, Truong, and Felix Menschke. 2008. "Risk Taking and Incentives of Money Market Mutual Fund Managers." Unpublished Manuscript.

Duffie, D., Malamud, S., and Manso, G. 2009. "Information Percolation with Equilibrium Search Dynamics." *Econometrica* 77 (5): 1513–74.

Edwards, Amy, Lawrence Harris, and Michael Piwowar. 2007. "Corporate Bond Market Transaction Costs and Transparency." *Journal of Finance* 62 (3): 1421–51.

Farhi, Emmanuel, and Jean Tirole 2012. "Collective Moral Hazard, Maturity Mismatch, and Systemic Bailouts." *American Economic Review* 102 (1): 60–93.

Goldstein, Michael, Edith Hotchkiss, and Erik Sirri. 2007. "Transparency and Liquidity: A Controlled Experiment on Corporate Bonds." *Review of Financial Studies* 20 (2): 235–73.

Gomes, Armando, Gary Gorton, and Leonardo Madureira. 2007. "SEC Regulation Fair Disclosure, Information, and the Cost of Capital." *Journal of Corporate Finance* 13 (2–3): 300–34.

Graham, John, Campbell Harvey, and Shiva Rajgopalc. 2005. "The Economic Implications of Corporate Financial Reporting." *Journal of Accounting and Economics* 40:3–73.

Graham, Mary. 2002. *Democracy by Disclosure*. Washington, DC: Brookings Institution Press.

Greenwood, Robin and David Thesmar. 2011. "Stock Price Fragility." *Journal of Financial Economics* 102 (3): 471–90.

Heron, Randall A., and Erik Lie. 2007. "Does Backdating Explain the Stock Price Pattern around Executive Stock Option Grants?" *Journal of Financial Economics* 83:271–95.

———. 2009. "What Fraction of Stock Option Grants to Top Executives Have Been Backdated or Manipulated?" *Management Science* 55 (4): 513–25.

Holmström, Bengt. 1999. "Managerial Incentive Problems: A Dynamic Perspective." *Review of Economic Studies* 66 (1): 169–82.

———. 2008. "Discussion of 'The Panic of 2007,' by Gary Gorton." In Maintaining Stability in a Changing Financial System, Proceedings of the Jackson Hole Conference, Federal Reserve Bank of Kansas City.

Holström, Bengt, and Paul Milgrom. 1991. "Multitask Principal-Agent Analyses: Incentive Contracts, Asset Ownership, and Job Design." *Journal of Law, Economics and Organization* 7 (0): 24–52.

Janis, Irving. 1982. *Groupthink*. Boston: Houghton Mifflin Company.

Johnson, Simon. 2009. "The Quiet Coup." *The Atlantic*, May 1, 2009, http://www.theatlantic.com/magazine/archive/2009/05/the-quiet-coup/307364/.

Leuz, Christian, and Peter Wysocki. 2008. "Economic Consequences of Financial

Reporting and Disclosure Regulation: A Review and Suggestions for Future Research." Unpublished Manuscript.

Morris, Stephen, and Hyun Song Shin. 2002. "Social Value of Public Information." *American Economic Review* 92 (5): 1521–34.

———. 2007. "Optimal Communication." *Journal of the European Economic Association* 5 (2–3): 594–602.

Pagano, Marco, and Paolo Volpin. 2012. "Securitization, Transparency, and Liquidity." *Review of Financial Studies* 25:2417–53.

Philippon, Thomas, and Ariel Reshef. 2008. "Wages and Human Capital in the US Financial Industry: 1909–2006." Working Paper, New York University.

Stigler, George J. 1971. "The Theory of Economic Regulation." *Bell Journal of Economics* 2 (1): 3–21.

Williams, Heidi. 2010. "Intellectual Property Rights and Innovation: Evidence from the Human Genome." NBER Working Paper no. 16213, Cambridge, MA.

Zingales, Luigi. 2009. "The Future of Securities Regulation." *Journal of Accounting Research* 47 (2): 391–426.

II

Risk Exposures

3

Systemic Risk Exposures
A 10-by-10-by-10 Approach

Darrell Duffie

Here, I present and discuss a "10-by-10-by-10" network-based approach to monitoring systemic financial risk. Under this approach, a regulator would analyze the exposures of a core group of systemically important financial firms to a list of stressful scenarios, say ten in number. For each scenario, about ten such designated firms would report their gains or losses. Each reporting firm would also provide the identities of the ten, say, counterparties with whom the gain or loss for that scenario is the greatest in magnitude relative to all counterparties. The gains or losses with each of those ten counterparties would also be reported, scenario by scenario.

Gains and losses would be measured in terms of market value and also in terms of cash flow, allowing regulators to assess risk magnitudes in terms of stresses to both economic values and also liquidity. Exposures would be

Darrell Duffie is the Dean Witter Distinguished Professor of Finance at the Graduate School of Business at Stanford University and a research associate of the National Bureau of Economic Research.

I am grateful for comments from Viral Acharya, Lewis Alexander, Niki Anderson, Peter Axilrod, Dick Berner, Markus Brunnermeier, Stacey Coleman, Rob Engle, Mike Fishman, Mark Flood, John Gidman, Tobi Guldimann, Anil Kashyap, John Khambu, Arvind Krishnamurthy, Joe Langsam, Clinton Lively, Stephen O'Connor, Mike Piwowar, Hélène Rey, and Chester Spatt, none of whom necessarily agree with any of the views expressed here. In June 2007, I suggested a preliminary version of this approach to the Financial Advisory Roundtable of the Federal Reserve Bank of New York. This chapter was prepared for a meeting on October 17, 2010, of the Systemic Risk Measurement Initiative of the National Bureau of Economic Research, of which I am a research associate. This approach has been presented to a number of regulators in Europe and the United States, whose comments have been extremely helpful. I am especially grateful to the editors of this volume, Markus Brunnermeier and Arvind Krishnamurthy. For nonacademic relationships that may present a potential conflict of interest, please see my web page at www.stanford.edu/~duffie/. For acknowledgments, sources of research support, and disclosure of the author's material financial relationships, if any, please see http://www.nber.org/chapters/c12512.ack.

measured before and after collateralization. One of the scenarios would be the failure of a counterparty. The "top ten" counterparties for this scenario would therefore be those whose defaults cause the greatest losses to the reporting firm.

In eventual practice, the number of reporting firms, the number of stress scenarios, and the number of major counterparties could all exceed ten, but it is reasonable to start with a small reporting system until the approach is better understood and agreed upon internationally.

This systemic risk-monitoring system would be more effective if adopted by regulators in several major jurisdictions. Pooled reports that are based on coordinated choices of stress scenarios would reveal systemic risk more comprehensively.

With such a monitoring system in place, a regulator charged with supervision of the stability of the financial system would be in a position to quickly answer a range of questions concerning concentrations of stress on the central nodes and links of the system. Examples of the questions that could arise include the following:

1. Is it true that some large hedge funds have taken significant foreign-exchange positions with systemically important banks? Who are these hedge funds? Do any of them also pose potentially large counterparty default exposures to any of these banks? How large are the associated market-value and cash-flow impacts?

2. If treasury yields were to rise dramatically, how much would systemically important financial institutions gain or lose in total, from each other and from others?

3. How prominent are central clearing counterparties (CCPs) among the top counterparties to systemically important firms?

4. What sorts of major financial firms have short positions with respect to real estate markets, and with whom do they hold their largest positions in this asset class?

5. Do the exposure results obtained from the reporting firms allow us to identify any previously undetected systemically important firms?

Although 10-by-10-by-10 reports would be collected from a small number of designated firms, the results would likely shed light on risk flows between these firms and potentially many other firms. Because of this, a regulator may be able to identify nonreporting firms that are candidates to be designated as systemically important, and perhaps also be added to the list of reporting firms. This process of augmenting the reported network can be iterated. An analysis of 10-by-10-by-10 data could also trigger follow-up supervisory conversations between regulators and individual firms, or groups of firms. For example, a regulator might wish to alert a group of banks that they have significant exposures in the same asset class and in the same direction with a concentrated common set of counterparties.

It is to be emphasized that this approach to systemic risk monitoring is much broader than a counterparty default exposure measurement system, although counterparty default exposures are included in it. For a given scenario, large gains shed as much light on risk flows through the financial system as do large losses. Moreover, even if reported gains and losses do not threaten the viability of reporting firms or their immediate counterparties, they may be important clues to the magnitudes of risk flows in given asset classes, and may allow regulators to consider the potential for contagion through fire sales.

Under this monitoring scheme, once revised and implemented, the reporting entities would provide the stipulated measures periodically, say quarterly, to designated regulators. Regulators from various jurisdictions would pool and then analyze the data. The overall objective would be to monitor the exposure of the financial system to systemically important stresses. The joint exposure of the system to the performance of particular asset classes, macroeconomic events, and entities (or chains of entities) could, as a result, be clarified. Summary information could be publicly disclosed, for example, in the form of histograms or population statistics, making a reasonable trade-off of the costs and benefits of releasing firm-specific or detailed data. For example, the Financial Services Authority of the United Kingdom has provided semiannual reports of the default exposures of UK banks to hedge fund counterparties. Public knowledge of summary information regarding stresses across the financial system of various types may contribute to an endogenous lowering of critical stresses through repricing and portfolio adjustments.

Regulators may choose to be cautious, however, about creating additional uncertainty, or potentially even triggering runs, through public reporting of detailed firm-specific contemporaneous stress information.[1] Rather, their objective may be to alert themselves and the public to potential sources of financial instability before they reach dangerous levels.

Full and immediate public disclosure of firm-specific stress reports could also dampen the incentives of reporting firms to act as liquidity providers, temporarily warehousing risk, as modeled by Grossman and Miller (1988) and Brunnermeier and Pedersen (2009). Intermediaries would expect more severe price impacts when unloading large positions if the sizes of their positions are known publicly. Bid-offer spreads would widen, and market liquidity could suffer as a result. For similar reasons, in the face of instant public disclosure of their positions, the incentives to gather fundamental information would be reduced, worsening the price-discovery function of financial markets.

---

1. The security of the data is clearly a concern, and this should figure carefully into the design of the reporting system. It should be possible, if desired, to use encryption methods to ensure that even some regulators are unable to fully disaggregate the data.

Separate analysis would likely suggest criteria for the selection of important stress scenarios, as well as precise instructions for stress measurement.
It is natural to specify extreme-but-plausible scenarios for changes in market
prices, or performance of nonpriced instruments, that could occur within,
say, one quarter. The relevant shocks are those likely to have occurred conditional on a major financial crisis. Illustrative examples of these scenarios
could include the following:

1. The default of a major entity
2. A 4 percent simultaneous change in all credit yield spreads
3. A 4 percent shift of the US-dollar yield curve
4. A 25 percent change in the value of the dollar relative to a basket of
major currencies
5. A 25 percent change in the value of the euro relative to a basket of
major currencies
6. A 25 percent change in a major real estate index
7. A 50 percent simultaneous change in the prices of all energy-related
commodities
8. A 50 percent change in a global equities index

The asset classes covered by these scenarios are broad, keeping the reporting system relatively simple and robust. While individual financial firms
may be heavily exposed to long-short strategies within an asset class, major
financial crises are more likely to be connected with severe price movements
across a large asset class.

Much of the required reporting methodology is within the scope of current state-of-the-art risk-management systems used by major financial institutions.[2] For example, it is somewhat routine for major banks to monitor
their largest credit exposures, incorporating for each major counterparty
all significant contractual positions, covering loans, bonds, equities, over-

---

2. For example, J.P. Morgan's 10Q disclosure for June 2010 states: "The Firm conducts
economic-value stress tests using multiple scenarios that assume credit spreads widen significantly, equity prices decline and significant changes in interest rates across the major currencies.
Other scenarios focus on the risks predominant in individual business segments and include
scenarios that focus on the potential for adverse movements in complex portfolios. Scenarios
were updated more frequently in 2009 and, in some cases, redefined to reflect the significant
market volatility which began in late 2008. Along with VaR, stress testing is important in measuring and controlling risk. Stress testing enhances the understanding of the Firm's risk profile
and loss potential, and stress losses are monitored against limits. Stress testing is also utilized in
one-off approvals and cross-business risk measurement, as well as an input to economic capital
allocation. Stress-test results, trends and explanations based on current market risk positions
are reported to the Firm's senior management and to the lines of business to help them better
measure and manage risks and to understand event risk-sensitive positions." SEC Financial
Reporting Release 48 and International Financial Reporting Standard 7 mandate disclosure
of value at risk or sensitivities to various market stresses. The IFRS7 requires sensitivities to
interest rates, currencies, and "other price risk" (for example, that from equities and commodities), including the impact on profits and on firm equity for "reasonably possible" changes in
the relevant variable (Section 40). The New York Fed, through its supervisory monitoring
program, collects information from reporting banks on the sensitivities to key risk factors of
the market values of their trading and held-to-maturity assets that are marked to market. The

the-counter derivatives, and loan guarantees. Likewise, the gain or loss in market value associated with a return scenario of the sort shown in the abovementioned list is often captured within existing risk-management systems by replacing the current market prices used for monitoring the values of positions with the stipulated artificial prices, and then recalculating position values.[3] The total change in value is the reported gain or loss. All positions that are contractually linked to the indicated price scenario must be identified, scenario by scenario. At least in terms of methodology, this is a conventional approach for large sophisticated banks and large hedge funds. Notably, this approach is "model-free." That is, from the viewpoint of reporting firms, the stress scenarios are precisely defined deterministic scenarios provided by the regulator. The reporting firms would not use model-based probabilistic methods, such as those applied for value-at-risk measurement.

In order to calculate the cash-flow impacts of a scenario, substantial contractual detail would need to be captured by a risk-management system. Cash-flow impacts include those associated with collateral exchanges, option exercises, termination settlement of OTC derivatives, debt payments (or lack thereof), and so on. Some of the likely reporting firms may not have the information technology needed to collect and aggregate the cash-flow impacts of shocks to major asset classes, particularly with respect to specific counterparties. This capability, going beyond that required for measuring Basel III liquidity coverage ratios, would need to be added to their risk-reporting systems.

Brunnermeier, Gorton, and Krishnamurthy (2012) have proposed a new measure of balance-sheet liquidity that would be complimentary to the cash-flow stress measures proposed here. Notably, their liquidity measure addresses the ability of a reporting firm to withstand a liquidity shock.

For asset classes that are not marked to market, such as the nontraded loan books of major banks, scenarios can be converted by regulators into stipulated default losses or other performance losses, as has been done in some cases for the recent system-wide bank-capital stress tests of the United States and the Eurozone.

A macroeconomic scenario, such as a reduction in the growth rate of gross domestic product, can be converted by regulators into stipulated return shocks for positions that are marked to market, or into stipulated rates of loss for nontraded loan books. One is interested in the expected gain or loss in value (or cash-flow impact) of each asset class, conditional on the

---

Federal Reserve System currently collects additional information on the sensitivities of the portfolios of banks to specified risk factors. The comments of Fed governor Daniel Tarullo, of February 2010, suggest ongoing efforts in this direction, and the need to further study systemic linkages.

3. An alternative is a "delta-based" approach, by which the sensitivity of a position value to a unit shift in the underlying price is multiplied by the stipulated price change. With extreme scenarios, the delta-based approach would be inaccurate for nonlinear positions, such as options.

scenario. These return or performance shocks would be estimated by the regulator and provided to all reporting firms as inputs to their reporting methodology. In this way, standardization is promoted. Standardization is particularly valuable in a network setting in which one hopes to follow the transmission of financial shocks from node to node through the network. Standardization also reduces noise and moral hazard that would otherwise arise in the interpretation by reporting firms of broadly defined macro-economic stresses.

Likewise, in designing a stress scenario, a regulator interested in the all-in impact of a shock to a particular asset class could stipulate the given return shock to that asset class, as well as the expected returns to all other major asset classes conditional on the return shock to the target asset class.[4] As such, each scenario is specified by regulators and passed to reporting firms as a list of deterministic returns or performance shocks to all asset classes.

Some care would be needed to ensure that all, or at least the vast majority, of a reporting firm's positions are mapped to associated exposures by asset classes. This is already standard practice for the risk-management systems in use by many large financial firms, but the list of asset classes and the methodologies that are currently used for these instrument-to-asset-class mappings differ across firms.

One of the stipulated scenarios, the default of a single entity, entails a calculation of the total loss associated with the failure of an issuer, bor-rower, or OTC counterparty, combining all contractual exposures, including debt, equity, securities lending, and derivatives. The regulator could specify a fractional loss of value given default, or require reports based on zero recoveries. The associated ten counterparties for this stress would be those whose defaults would lead to the greatest losses to the reporting firm. These entities could often include sovereigns, quasi sovereigns, and financial utili-ties such as central clearing parties.

The UK Financial Services Authority (FSA) already conducts a regular survey of the exposures to hedge funds (only) of UK banks. For example, in July 2010, the FSA reported that the maximum potential credit exposure (which includes the effect of ten-day, 99 percent value at risk) of any one bank to any one hedge fund was approximately $600 million.

A significant amount of work may be needed in order to refine the defini-tions of the exposure measures, including distinctions between gross and net losses. For example, a given scenario loss could be measured as follows:

1. On a mark-to-market basis, assuming no collateral and allowing for netting only within legally enforceable master netting agreements. In this case, the measured gain or loss would effectively assume that any potentially netting offsets of gains or losses with a single counterparty cannot be real-

---

4. I am grateful to Rob Engle for this suggestion.

ized except where clearly required by master netting agreements, and would be measured before offsetting reductions allowed by collateralization.

2. On a net mark-to-market basis, after the use of collateral and legally enforceable netting.

3. On a cash-flow basis, within a prescribed time period such as thirty days, the duration standard for the Basel III liquidity coverage ratio requirement.

Notwithstanding the ability of a reporting entity to offset losses by applying collateral, gross-of-collateral exposure measures may assist regulators in understanding the magnitudes of risks for a given asset class flowing across specific links in the financial system, and also permit them to consider the potential impact of asset fire sales, including sales of collateral. The objective is to capture systemic linkages, whether or not by virtue of collateral, that expose the reporting financial institution to significant losses. Likewise, the largest counterparties for a given scenario are selected on the basis of the absolute magnitude of the gain or loss, and not on the basis of the loss to the reporting institution.

3.1 Some Shortcomings

A shortcoming of the 10-by-10-by-10 approach is that the total sensitivity of a financial entity to some relatively broadly defined risk factor may be moderate, while at the same time the entity has dangerously large long and short exposures within the broadly specified risk class. For example, the 2006 failure of the hedge fund Amaranth Advisors LLC was caused by approximately $6.5 billion in losses on roughly equally sized long and short positions in natural gas futures contracts for two different delivery months, March and April 2007, respectively. Similarly, the significant losses of certain "quant equity" hedge funds in August 2007 stemmed from long and short equity positions that left these funds relatively unexposed to a shift in the overall level of major stock indices. The general concern that the defined risk factors may be too broad to capture some important narrowly concentrated exposures is mitigated by the likelihood that firm-threatening exposures to relative movements within a well chosen broad risk factor are likely to be held by a relatively small set of firms. In any case, nothing rules out the selection of long-short or cross-market stresses if these are believed to be among the most important potential shocks to the financial system.

Another shortcoming of the 10-by-10-by-10 approach is that it would miss widely dispersed potential sources of systemic risk that do not flow through major financial institutions. For example, the US savings and loan crisis of the 1980s did not present large, directly measurable stresses to systemically important financial institutions. The 10-by-10-by-10 approach captures only those sources of stress that pass through the center of the financial system. Regulators could perhaps augment with additional network-based stress analysis that reaches more broadly into the financial system.

The magnitudes of losses caused by a specific stress do not on their own determine whether a firm has the necessary capital and liquidity to withstand the stress without failure. The data provided through 10-by-10-by-10 reports may be useful in judging the ability of firms to withstand important shocks, but for that purpose would need to be accompanied by additional firm-specific capital and liquidity measures. In that sense, 10-by-10-by-10 reports could provide useful data for the supervisory analysis of systematically important firms.

Essentially any stress measurement system is subject to a financial risk-management analogue of the Heisenberg uncertainty principle, by which increasing the precision of one's measurement of one aspect of a system merely increases uncertainty regarding other dimensions of the system. This endogeneity is similar to that of the well-known "Lucas critique." The shareholders and some of the employees of a financial institution often have an incentive to take more risk than is socially optimal because they do not internalize the costs of systemic risk. When a regulator focuses on a particular risk measure, a reporting financial institution may adjust its risk-taking behavior so as to lower this risk measure while raising its risk elsewhere.

For example, regulators commonly focus on "value at risk," the loss on a given portfolio that is exceeded with a small defined probability, say 5 percent. A reporting financial institution may, as a result, choose to increase its exposure to losses that occur with a smaller probability than 5 percent. Similarly, if a regulator measures the exposure of a bank to a 25 percent change in the value of an asset, the bank could buy and sell options on the asset so as to lower this particular exposure, while raising its exposure to a 30 percent change in the value of the asset. In the face of concerns about this form of window dressing, a regulator could request the impacts to a graduated range of shock magnitudes, from moderate to large. In general, by limiting the stress measures to a small number of extremely broad asset classes, the Heisenberg uncertainty principle is significantly mitigated, but is not eliminated.

Eventually, regulators may have sufficient instrument-level data to directly conduct risk analyses without reliance on reporting by the firms they are monitoring. This would dramatically increase the range of tests and studies that could be conducted, and lower concerns over standardization of the implementation across reporting firms, as well as window-dressing behavior. On the other hand, the cost and time delays associated with comprehensive and accessible instrument-level regulatory databases currently seem large, to say the least. In any case, the ability of each reporting firm to administer stress reports within its own risk-management system is of some independent risk-management value.

The greater the standardization of risk measures, the greater is the danger of "groupthink"; that is, an unhelpful common focus or agreement on what matters, in the presence of unconsidered relevant alternatives. Groupthink that is caused by a common industry-wide risk-measurement approach could lower the chance that important alternative sources of systemic risk would be identified by creative individual analysis, or would be brought forward for treatment once identified.

Further, standardization of risk measures may encourage common approaches to hedging or speculation that could destabilize markets if a significant number of important financial institutions rush toward a common exit from dangerous positions that are identified by a dramatic increase in a specific standardized risk measure.

3.2   Could This Have Made a Difference in the Last Financial Crisis?

The financial crisis of 2007 to 2009 was triggered by significant losses in assets linked to subprime residential mortgages. As the crisis developed, the systemic risks became increasingly related to broader real estate-related asset classes, to broader debt-market pricing, and to counterparty exposures; for example, through derivatives and repo markets. Is it plausible that, without a hindsight advantage, a *"n-by-n-by-n"* monitoring scheme could have made a significant difference in the ability of regulators to visualize the buildup of systemic risk that occurred prior to the onset of the crisis?

Residential mortgages form one of the largest underlying asset classes to which systemic investors are exposed, and a common epicenter for financial crises. It is more than plausible that one or more of the stress scenarios specified by regulators would have picked up a substantial buildup of network exposure to mortgage-related assets well in advance of the crisis. After all, we now know that several major likely reporting financial institutions, including UBS, Citibank, Bank of America, and Merrill Lynch, each had tens of billions of dollars of losses related to the subprime mortgages alone. The underlying position sizes took many quarters to build.

With the benefit of *"n-cubed"* reports, regulators would have observed the growing exposures of the reporting institutions themselves. Perhaps these exposures were already available to regulators through other forms of bank supervisory reporting. The *n*-cubed reports would also have revealed increasing and changing network flows of risk related to mortgages. In particular, even if it had not been an *n*-cubed reporting firm, AIG would likely have been identified as a significant source of counterparty exposure to several systemically important reporting financial institutions. We now know this because, in the breech, regulators were forced to rescue AIG because of the life-threatening exposures to AIG of a number of major global banks, through the losses they would have otherwise incurred through their contractual positions with AIG on mortgage-related contracts with AIG. Again, these exposures would have taken a number of quarters to build toward the extremely large sizes they ultimately reached, and so the buildup would likely have been identified in advance. If, as a result, AIG had been asked "join the grid" and begin reporting to an "$(n + 1)$-cubed" monitoring system, the resulting network risk map would have presumably identified AIG's own aggregate exposure to the underlying residential mortgage asset class. (A side benefit is that AIG's directors would have had a better chance to have become informed of their firm's growing exposure to the asset class.) Further, additional nonreporting firms that were exposed to AIG would likely have been identified, including perhaps some foreign banks, had they not already been reporting to a global version of the n-cubed system.

One should also consider whether, even with the benefit of an n-cubed monitoring system, regulators would have taken appropriate note of the changing network risk flows related to mortgage-related assets. Because the mortgage-related asset class is always enormous, would the increasingly dangerous exposures to AIG have set off concerns and been elevated for further action by macro- or microprudential supervisors? Perhaps.

If the monitoring system had been too complex or had it provided an overwhelming amount of undigested data, the growing dangers could have remained "in plain sight" but undetected. If the system had been too sparse, some important points of fragility could have been be missed.

A lesson of the crisis is the importance of access to carefully designed network-based risk monitoring systems, and of investigating the causes of changes in the character of risk flows as they occur.

References

Basel Committee on Banking Supervision. 2004. "Principles for the Management and Supervision of Interest Rate Risk." Basel: Bank for International Settlements. July. http://www.bis.org/publ/bcbs108.pdf?noframes=1.

Brunnermeier, Markus, Gary Gorton, and Arvind Krishnamurthy. 2012. "Risk Topography." In *NBER Macroeconomics Annual 2011*, edited by Daron Acemoglu and Michael Woodford, 149–83. Chicago: University of Chicago Press.

Brunnermeier, Markus, and Lasse Pedersen. 2009. "Market Liquidity and Funding Liquidity." *Review of Financial Studies* 22:2201–38.

Financial Services Authority. 2010. "Assessing Possible Sources of Systemic Risk from Hedge Funds: A Report on the Findings of the Hedge Fund as Counterparty Survey and Hedge Fund Survey." London: United Kingdom Financial Services Authority. July. www.fsa.gov.uk/pubs/other/hedge_funds.pdf.

Grossman, S. J., and M. H. Miller. 1988. "Liquidity and Market Structure." *Journal of Finance* 43:617–33.

Tarullo, Daniel. 2010. "Equipping Financial Regulators with the Tools Necessary to Monitor Systemic Risk." Testimony before the Senate Subcommittee on Security and International Trade and Finance, Committee on Banking, Housing, and Urban Affairs, Washington, DC, February 12. http://www.federalreserve.gov/newsevents/testimony/tarullo20100212a.htm.

4

Remapping the Flow of Funds

Juliane Begenau, Monika Piazzesi,
and Martin Schneider

The Flow of Funds Accounts are a crucial data source on credit market positions in the US economy. In particular, they combine regulatory data from various sources to produce a consistent set of flow and stock tables in major credit market instruments by sector. There is also a detailed breakdown of the financial sector by type of institution. This is exactly the kind of data needed to understand how financial innovation changes the amount of borrowing and lending in the economy and reshapes the financial industry. The events of the last five years have underscored the importance of positions data to guide economic analysis.

As do most available data sets on credit market positions, the Flow of Funds Accounts report accounting measures such as book value or fair value. In contrast, most economic analysis views asset positions as random payment streams that are valued by state prices. The latter view is particularly useful to assess the sensitivity of a position to changes in market conditions. For example, one may ask what happens to the value of a position when monetary policy lowers the short end of the yield curve. The answer follows from discounting the payment stream with (hypothetical) state prices that reflect the steeper yield curve. More generally, once positions are viewed as payment streams, the risk in a position can often be parsimoniously rep-

Juliane Begenau is a PhD candidate in economics at Stanford University. Monika Piazzesi is the Joan Kenney Professor of Economics at Stanford University and a research associate and director of the Asset Pricing Program at the National Bureau of Economic Research. Martin Schneider is professor of economics at Stanford University and a research associate of the National Bureau of Economic Research.

We thank Markus Brunnermeier, Darrell Duffie, John Geanakoplos, Arvind Krishnamurthy, and conference participants at the NBER systemic risk conference. For acknowledgments, sources of research support, and disclosure of the authors' material financial relationships, if any, please see http://www.nber.org/chapters/c12556.ack.

resented by exposures to a small number of risk factors. Exposures are then comparable across positions and can readily be aggregated to create measures of risk for the entire portfolio held by an economic agent, such as a financial institution or a household.

Viewing positions as payment streams typically requires more information than book value or fair value. In particular, to construct the payment stream associated with a given instrument such as a coupon bond or installment loan, one would like to know:

- the maturity or next repricing date of the instrument;
- the promised interest rate, that is, the coupon rate for a bond or the loan rate;
- call or prepayment provisions, if applicable; and
- the credit rating of the issuer.

Importantly, much of this information is already contained in the data sets from which the Flow of Funds Accounts are constructed. This suggests that substantial improvements may be possible at low cost.

This article argues that quantitative analysis of credit market positions would benefit tremendously if the additional information about the structure of payment streams were more readily available. Section 4.1 states why credit market positions are important for policy analysis and economic research in general. Section 4.1.1 describes the currently available data sets. Section 4.1.2 explains how economists think about credit market positions in terms of payment streams. Section 4.1.3 states why information beyond basic accounting numbers is therefore useful. Section 4.1.4 describes how payment streams are represented using factor models, and section 4.1.5 shows how this leads naturally to measures of risk exposure. Finally, section 4.2 derives some concrete suggestions for data collection.

4.1   Why Economists Need Credit Market Position Data

Recent boom bust episodes brought about large credit market positions of individual economic agents, as well as entire sectors of the economy such as households. In the last few years, economics has already been paying more attention to credit market positions, and one would now expect this trend to accelerate.

Data on credit market positions are useful to economists because they help assess the balance sheet effects of shocks that alter the net worth of borrowers and lenders. For example, if inflation picks up or monetary policy raises the short-term interest rate, how much does this help home owners with fixed rate mortgages? How much does it hurt bank shareholders or mortgage bond holders? Can inflation stimulate the economy by redistributing toward financially constrained borrowers who have a larger propensity to spend?

Beyond the study of particular shocks, data on credit market positions can help derive a comprehensive description of risk exposure. Economic agents' credit market positions are portfolios of risky assets that are affected by a variety of shocks, including inflation and interest rate changes. As a result, macroprudential regulation should be based on the entire conditional distribution of economic agents' net worth.

The above-mentioned examples point to two issues that come up when working with data on credit market positions. The first is the need to ensure *comparability* across positions. To develop measures of risk, it must be possible to aggregate different positions into a single portfolio. There must, therefore, be sufficient information so that the—potentially offsetting—risk exposures of individual positions can be taken into account. Indeed, the risk of an institution is different if it uses derivatives to hedge balance sheet exposure than when it does not. Increasing transaction costs in a market has a different effect when that market is typically used to hedge exposure than when it is used to speculate. We argue later that thinking in terms of payment streams and state prices naturally addresses this issue.

The second issue is how to choose the right amount of *detail*. For many questions, it is helpful to go beyond simple aggregate measures of credit and net worth, and consider how positions differ by, for example, maturity or default risk. Indeed, the effect of monetary policy on a sector's net worth will be quite different if this sector borrows mostly long term than when it borrows mostly overnight. We argue that the factor structure of risks provides guidance on the detail required.

4.1.1   Data Sources on Credit Market Positions

There are at least three types of data sets that contain credit market positions. First, there are collections of accounting statements or regulatory filings by individual corporations—for example, annual company reports, SEC filings, or bank "call reports." The Flow of Funds Accounts of the United States compiles accounting data but aggregates positions to the national level. Second, there are household surveys that ask questions about wealth, such as the Survey of Consumer Finances and the Panel Study of Income Dynamics. A third, and more recent, source of data consists of databases that record particular credit market transactions undertaken by households or firms. On the household side, an example is county deeds records on house purchases, which in many counties also contain information on mortgages. On the firm side, there are commercial data sets on corporate bond and syndicated loan issuance. Transaction data are special because the unit of observation is a transaction, rather than an economic agent.

Most available data sets present credit market positions in terms of *book value* or *fair value* only. Traditional accounting rules call for recording the book value of an instrument. For example, in case of a mortgage, the book value is the face value of the loan, while for a coupon bond it is the principal, paid at the maturity date. More recently, some credit market positions—especially those in marketable fixed-income securities—have been marked to market on firm balance sheets. In this case, there is also information about the fair value of a position, an estimate of its resale value.

What exactly is reported depends on the particular data set. Company and regulatory institutions typically provide a mix of fair and book value, as do household surveys; the Flow of Funds Accounts report book values. As a rule, data sets in which the unit of observation is an economic agent provide little information on the nature of contracts beyond book value or fair value. In contrast, transaction data tend to come with more detailed information about contracts related to individual transactions.

4.1.2 Economic Analysis of Asset Positions: Payment Streams and State Prices

Economic analysis treats all assets, including credit market instruments, as *payment streams*. A payment stream is a sequence of random variables that says, for every date and every state of the world, what the asset pays off. If there was no uncertainty, then the payment stream would simply be the stream of promises made by the issuer of the instrument. More generally, the random payment stream reflects modifications to initial promises, such as lower payments in default.

The value of an asset in an economic model is typically determined by applying a set of *state prices* to its payment stream. Almost all economic models imply a set of state prices that can be used to compute values. Importantly, this includes models where heterogeneous economic agents face frictions such as transaction costs and borrowing constraints. Such models are likely to be particularly useful to study the real effects of borrowing and lending.

Thinking in terms of payment streams and state prices is well suited to answer questions about the balance sheet effects of shocks and the risk exposure of agents. Viewing positions as payment streams on a common set of states of the world makes them directly comparable. To assess the effect of a shock, such as a policy intervention, one typically first works out the direct effect of the shock on each payment stream (a larger probability of default or a change in duration due to earlier prepayment of debt, for example). One then works out the effect of the shock on state prices, which jointly affect the value of all payment streams.

4.1.3 Information beyond Accounting Numbers

Thinking about credit market positions as payment streams requires information beyond book value or fair value. One important ingredient is information about how contracts specify the structure of the payment stream. As a simple example, consider a Treasury bond. Its book value represents only one of the payments promised by the bond. The fair value says what the bond trades for, but it does not say why—that is, how the price depends on the structure of the payment stream and state prices. Actually constructing the payment stream requires knowing the coupon rate and the maturity date.

Information about contracts is typically not enough to construct payment streams. An exception is a world where payment streams are certain—if promises have a fixed schedule and are always kept, then the payment stream follows immediately from the promises written into the contract. More generally, promises may not have a fixed schedule (for example, when a bond is callable or a mortgage is prepaid) and promises may not be kept.

With uncertain payment streams, constructing a payment stream will involve some economic modeling. For example, a modeler must make assumptions on when mortgages are prepaid (depending on movements in interest rates and house prices), and when borrowers default. Dealing with these contingencies benefits from information about contracts that speaks to the randomness in payments (such as prepayment rules.) It can also benefit from additional information outside the contract, such as credit ratings that may provide guidance on modeling default probabilities.

4.1.4   Representing Payment Streams with Factor Models

Describing random payment streams—specifying payoffs for all dates and state of the world—may appear excessively complicated. In particular, what is the relevant set of "states of the world"? Fortunately, simple representations are available using a factor model approach. Factors are random variables that represent the major sources of market risk affecting payment streams. One then defines the relevant states of the world for a position next period as the innovations to the factors, as well as possibly idiosyncratic shocks to the position (such as borrower default). The modeling task is to describe the joint conditional distribution of the factors and idiosyncratic events. Factors are assumed to follow Markov dynamics: their distribution depends on the past only through their last realizations.

The criterion for selecting factors is how well the entire cross section of market prices (by maturity and credit quality, for example) can be approximated by the factor model. For credit market instruments, a small number of factors (often less than five, depending on the frequency of the data) has been found sufficient to describe the evolution of market prices. One factor is typically a short-term interest rate (such as the three-month T-bill rate) that captures movements in the level of the yield curve. Other common factors are the slope of the yield curve (e.g., the difference between the ten-year Treasury yield and the three-month T-bill rate), a "fear gauge" (such as the Merrill Lynch Option Volatility Estimate [MOVE] Index, a measure of bond-market volatility that serves as a bond-market analogue of the Volatility Index [VIX]), or a liquidity factor (such as the difference between on-the-run and off-the-run Treasury yields).

Capturing credit risk requires specification of the default event as well as the payments in default, and it may require additional factors to describe the probability of default. The default event can be a missed interest payment, or a missed interest and principal payment. Its arrival is assumed to depend on firm-specific as well as macroeconomic conditions (see Duffie [2011] for details.) In particular, to capture the fact that default is more likely in bad times and risk premia on corporate bonds are countercyclical, the probability of default may depend on factors like GDP growth or credit spreads such as the difference between swap and Treasury rates. The expected loss in default is often assumed to be proportional to the market value of the bond.

4.1.5   Factor Models and Risk Exposure

The factor model approach offers a convenient way to measure risk exposures. In particular, we can represent a payment stream as a portfolio containing only a small number of "spanning securities." The security payoffs reflect the risk in the factors. For a simple example, suppose that there is only one factor, the short-interest rate. Two securities are then sufficient to represent any position: cash and a long bond, the price of which responds to the short rate. More generally, if N is the number of factors, any payment stream can be represented by a portfolio consisting of cash and N long bonds.

The replicating portfolio has to be recalculated every period. Ideally, the portfolio should be updated every instant—replication with Markovian factor dynamics is exact only in continuous time. However, replication works approximately in discrete time (see e.g., Piazzesi and Schneider 2010). Replication is particularly attractive when the number of assets, and thus the number of payment streams under consideration, is much larger than the number of factors. In this case, the spanning portfolio is a far simpler representation of risk exposures than the original collection of payment streams.

Once the positions of individual economic agents or sectors of the economy are represented as portfolios of spanning securities, the portfolio weights become natural measures of risk exposure. With two factors, we might find that the retirement savings of the household sector can be represented as a portfolio that is about one-third in a two-year bond and two-thirds in a ten-year bond, with some small residual weight on cash. The example weights here reflect a duration somewhere between two and ten years. Since the factor model tells us how bond prices respond to shocks, we can calculate how the households' retirement wealth moves with changes in the level or the slope of the yield curve.

Portfolios of spanning securities are also easy to compare. For example, consider a bank that has a balance sheet subject to maturity mismatch, but also trades interest risk in the swap market. Both the bank's swap position and its nonderivative fixed-income position can be viewed as portfolios of spanning securities. It is then easy to check whether the swap portfolio hedges exposures in the other portfolio or not (see Begenau, Piazzesi, and Schneider [2012] for details on the replication of swap portfolios).

4.2   Concrete Suggestions for Data Collection

The previous considerations lead to a few simple suggestions for how common data sets could be made more user friendly for economic analysis. Here we have data collection efforts in mind, with the unit of observation being an economic agent or sector. In such data sets, credit market positions are usually aggregated into a reasonably small number of instrument classes ("long-term bonds," "loans," etc.) for which book value or fair value (or both) is recorded. Our basic suggestion is to add, for each instrument class and each date, a few numbers that describe (a) the structure of promised payments specified by the average contract in the class, and (b) the average credit quality of the class.

Stock versus flows. The following suggestions apply differently whether the data collected are stocks or flows, and collection of information about flows is preferable if possible. If stocks are collected, information about maturities, credit ratings, and callability is typically available only about the currently outstanding positions in each instrument class. For example, one may know the average maturity, credit rating, and interest rate for a pool of mortgages held by an institution. In contrast, if flows are collected, then there is information about newly issued instruments. For example, one will know the maturity, credit rating, and interest on a new vintage of mortgage pools.

Information about flows is preferable because different vintages of long-term instruments may have very different payment streams, and therefore different exposure to risk. For example, if the loan rate and credit rating differ across vintages of mortgage pools with similar maturity. Given information on flows, researchers could track different vintages of credit market instruments issues at different dates. Information on flows would ideally also include redemptions and defaults by vintage (period of origination)— for example, the share of mortgage face values that were prepaid, and the share of face values of corporate bonds that went into default, together with recovery rates.

Promised payments. Every credit market position comes with a stream of promised payments. Abstracting from prepayment, the stream of promises can be described by a few numbers. For coupon bonds, what is needed is the maturity and the coupon rate. For installment loans, the installment, and the maturity are enough. Prepayment options can typically be described by the shortest time from which the debt can be repaid. Finally, some debt contracts make random promises since they pay floating rates. Ideally, those would be broken out from other debt, and the maturity and spread over a benchmark rate reported separately.

Default. Payments are made by issuers who may default. To assess the risk of default, it would be useful to have some sense of the average credit rating of the issuers in a particular class of instruments. This information would then be used by the modeler to specify how default affects the payment stream as previously discussed.

Derivatives. Firms often use derivatives, either to hedge (or double down) on their exposure to certain factors. Derivative contracts such as swaps or options can also be viewed as a payment stream. Since promised payments typically depend on a small number of factors, derivative positions can again be replicated as portfolios of spanning securities.

Data on derivative holdings come from various sources. Regulatory filings typically contain gross notional values and fair values, possibly some information on maturities. However, to determine the risk exposures of a bank's swap position, it is also important to know the direction of the trades (whether the bank pays a fixed or floating rate) as well as the average swap rate that was locked in on the contract.

In the case of options, it is important to know whether these are put or call options, the average strike price, and whether these options are bought or sold. We expect that this information is more difficult to obtain from banks than the other items on our wish list. Still, the information is crucial for the public to have, because the current data situation does not permit an outsider to determine the risk exposure of banks or the financial sector as a whole—not even after a long time lag.

Foreign currency. Our discussion so far has assumed that all credit is denominated in dollars, as it is true for the overwhelming majority of positions in the United States as well as a large share of positions elsewhere. More generally, the view of positions as payment streams and their representation using factor models extends naturally to the case of multiple currencies. One would then typically include exchange rates as additional factors. The currency in which a position is denominated would become an additional piece of information that should be recorded with the position.

References

Begenau, Juliane, Monika Piazzesi, and Martin Schneider. 2012. "Banks' Risk Exposures." Working Paper, Stanford University.

Duffie, Darrell. 2011. *Measuring Corporate Default Risk*. Oxford: Oxford University Press.

Piazzesi, Monika, and Martin Schneider. 2010. "Interest Rate Risk in Credit Markets." *American Economic Review* 100 (2): 579–84.

5
Measuring Margin

Robert L. McDonald

5.1 Introduction

In discussions related to derivatives and regulatory policy, three questions often arise:

- Across the economy, how exposed are firms to derivatives?
- How is this exposure split across different asset classes?
- How sensitive is the magnitude of exposure to economic shocks?

Margin—collateral that protects the counterparty against losses from failure to pay—is an economic measure of exposure that differs by asset and by the topography of risk. In this chapter I discuss the idea that reporting of margin, disaggregated by product class and by entity, would provide a standardized measure of the specific net risks being borne with derivatives, and provide information about entity vulnerabilities to specific market shocks, along with sector concentrations in particular derivative asset classes.[1] The future configuration of contracts, institutions, trading, and market practices is difficult to forecast. As markets evolve, routine margin reporting would provide information about risks that would be potentially helpful to policymakers, analysts, and market participants.

Robert L. McDonald is the Erwin P. Nemmers Professor of Finance at the Kellogg School of Management, Northwestern University.

Prepared for the NBER Initiative on Systemic Risk and Macro Modeling. I am grateful to Markus Brunnermeier, Arvind Krishnamurthy, Richard Heckinger, John McPartland, and Robert Steigerwald for helpful discussions and comments, but of course errors are my own. For acknowledgments, sources of research support, and disclosure of the author's material financial relationships, if any, please see http://www.nber.org/chapters/c12510.ack.

1. Acharya (chapter 6, this volume) suggests even more detailed reporting on derivatives. Whereas I emphasize reporting of existing margins, Acharya emphasizes reporting of what he calls "potential exposure," including additional margin calls due to credit downgrades.

The Bank of International Settlements (BIS) estimates that at year-end 2010, the outstanding notional amount of over-the-counter (OTC) derivatives was $601 trillion (BIS 2011). According to the BIS, the vast majority (77 percent) of these contracts are interest rate derivatives (with over 10 percent of this amount as options), with foreign exchange derivatives second at 9.6 percent, and credit default swaps (CDS) third at about 5 percent. Equity contracts represent about 1 percent and commodity contracts about 0.5 percent. The BIS obtained this estimate by surveying market participants and eliminating the double counting that results from both A and B reporting the same derivative contract between A and B.

The BIS estimate is difficult to interpret for several reasons.[2] First, by definition the count includes positions that are effectively offsets. For example, if two dealers in the ordinary course of business enter into a series of nonidentical but functionally similar swaps, there are likely to be significant economic offsets, so that the net exposure of one dealer in the event of bankruptcy by the other dealer is small. How overstated is the notional amount reported by BIS?

Second, the number includes derivatives based on interest rates, equity, credit, foreign exchange, and commodities. A swap of a given notional amount will embody different risks depending on the underlying asset, maturity, and structure of the product. A $1 million vanilla equity swap will typically be riskier than a $1 million vanilla interest-rate swap. However, swaps, including interest-rate swaps, can be designed to have additional layers of leverage and thus be substantially riskier than vanilla swaps per dollar of notional value. A famous example of this is the Procter and Gamble swap (McDonald 2013, 253).

In section 5.2 I discuss the economic interpretation of margin for individual contracts and for portfolios of contracts. I present examples showing how margin is assessed in practice for different kinds of underlying assets. In section 5.3, I discuss different margin practices in centrally cleared and OTC markets. Depending upon whether the margining system is gross or

---

2. ISDA (2011) makes two additional adjustments to the BIS number. First, it eliminates foreign exchange swaps. Second, it reduces the BIS estimate for double counting of interest rate swaps cleared at LCH Clearnet. Regarding the treatment of foreign exchange swaps, ISDA subtracts the value of FX swaps on the grounds that these are short term and, bizarrely, that they are "older products." Duffie (2011), in a comment on the Treasury proposal to exempt FX swaps from clearing requirements, expresses skepticism that foreign exchange swaps should be treated differently than other derivatives. Regarding the treatment of cleared swaps, the adjustment for double counting arises from the observation that a single swap presented to a clearinghouse becomes two swaps, one each between the original counterparties and the clearinghouse. Clearing, therefore, leads to an increase in the measured notional value of swaps. This is correct, but it is also true that the use of a clearinghouse does create new counterparty relationships for a given contract. Both the FX and clearing adjustments illustrate the limited usefulness of aggregate numbers. Disaggregated statistics permit the statistical consumer to make whatever adjustments seem appropriate for the analysis at hand.

net, margin may be held by different parties. Section 5.4 presents several examples illustrating different margin calculations for cleared and noncleared transactions. Using these examples, I contrast margin with notional amount and VaR (value at risk) as measures of risk. In section 5.5, I discuss a controversial feature of Dodd-Frank, the end-user exemption. I show that this feature can be seen as creating implicit off-balance sheet borrowing by the exempt end user. Section 5.6 concludes.

5.2   Understanding Margin

Derivatives contracts have future settlement based on a reference price, but it is common to settle the contracts on an ongoing mark-to-market basis as prices change prior to contract maturity. The term "margin" encompasses at least two different kinds of payments related to this settlement in advance: the maintenance margin, which is referred to in the OTC market as the "independent amount," and the variation margin.[3] The maintenance margin, which is the focus of this chapter, is an amount that provides collateral against possible future loss before the next marking to market of the contract. Depending upon the context, market participants under current rules may or may not post maintenance margin. The variation margin, by contrast, is a payment that covers realized loss, thereby resetting the value of the derivative to zero, and preventing losses from cumulating.

Margin is collateral for a contractual obligation, and as such reflects the riskiness of the contract. Although the notional amount of a position can be difficult to interpret, the margin on a position is an economically meaningful value, routinely computed and used by market participants as a protection against counterparty default. Margin thus provides a common denominator with which to compare the risk of different contracts and positions. In this section I provide some examples to illustrate margin practices in several different contexts.

Throughout this discussion we will be assuming that the derivative contract under discussion resembles a futures contract or swap, in that it has no initial premium (i.e., no payment from one party to the other, distinct from margin), there is futurity, that is, the contract will require future performance, and at the future settlement date there is a possibility of payments from either one of the two parties to the other. Credit risk is therefore two sided. Contracts for which the buyer fully pays (such as options) are different because the buyer has no further obligation, and thus credit risk is one sided.

---

3. The CME also distinguishes between *initial margin* and *maintenance margin*. Initial margin is the amount a trader must provide at the initiation of a position, while maintenance margin is the amount below which the trader must provide additional margin. We will focus on maintenance margin in this discussion.

5.2.1   Margin in Theory

Assume that there are two firms, A and B, that enter into a derivative contract such as a vanilla swap. A firm posts margin to protect the counterparty against the failure of the other to make a required payment on the derivative. In practice, margin is often computed as the expected loss on the position that occurs with some probability. The amount of margin will depend upon the frequency with which the position value is measured and settled.

Various methods can be used to compute the margin amount, but it is helpful to think of margin as a tail VaR, which is the conditional expectation of a position value if it falls below a certain level. Let V_t be the value of the derivative for A, so that $-V_t$ is the value for B. Assuming that A is long, so that $V_{t+1} < V_t$ represents a loss, margin for A is

$$(1) \qquad M_t^A = -E_t[V_{t+1} - V_t \mid V_{t+1} < V_{t+1}^p, V_t],$$

where V_t is the value of the derivative position at time t (it can be positive or negative), V_{t+1}^p is the value of the claim such that

$$\Pr(V_{t+1} < V_{t+1}^p \mid V_t) = p,$$

V_{t+1}^p is exceeded with probability p, and M_t is margin at time t. For example, margin might be computed based on a value that is exceeded with 1 percent probability. Note that there is a time period implicit in the calculation of M_t^A. For exchanges, the time period is typically a day. In OTC markets, the time period can be several days, in which case margin will be correspondingly greater, other things being equal.

Margin for B, who is short, is

$$(2) \qquad M_t^B = E_t[V_{t+1} - V_t \mid V_{t+1} > V_{t+1}^{1-p}, V_t].$$

We define V_{t+1}^{1-p} as

$$\Pr(V_{t+1} > V_{t+1}^{1-p} \mid V_t) = p.$$

In practice, for futures traded at exchanges, margin is set symmetrically so that $M_t^A = M_t^B$. Symmetry is not necessary, however. For options, margin applies only to levered or written positions. Equations (1) and (2) provide a rough conceptual description of the margin calculations of many derivatives clearinghouses.

Equations (1) and (2) are statistical definitions of margin. These measures are not based on an economic theory of optimal margin, which would require modeling default and systemic risk.[4] The margin calculations also make no adjustment for the risk of the specific counterparty. Nevertheless, M_t^A and M_t^B correspond conceptually to clearinghouse practice.

---

4. Bolton and Oehmke (2011) develop a model of optimal derivatives use and collateral in a context where hedging has value for firms but entails real costs, and there is credit risk.

In this discussion we have not specified the time horizon over which marking to market occurs. In practice, clearinghouses compute margin with respect to daily price moves. In the OTC market, revaluations may occur only weekly, in which case margins are larger due to less frequent marking to market. Margin is often approximated as a multiple of the asset standard deviation. A weekly return standard deviation will be approximately $\sqrt{5}$ times the daily standard deviation. If margin were being used to compare exposures across classes of derivatives, it would be necessary to know the mark-to-market horizon in order to compare the underlying positions.

5.2.2 Netting and Portfolio Margining

The preceding discussion defined margin for a single asset. For a portfolio of assets, margin can be computed in the same way. Suppose there are two derivatives with values V_t and Q_t held in quantities α_v and α_q. Let $W_t = \alpha_v V_t + \alpha_q Q_t$ denote the value of the portfolio. (Buyers and sellers can be distinguished by setting α_v and α_q appropriately.) The tail VaR for this portfolio is

$$(3) \qquad M_t^P = -E_t[W_{t+1} - W_t \mid W_{t+1} < W_{t+1}^P, W_t],$$

where $M_t(W)$ denotes the margin for asset W. By the Cauchy-Schwarz inequality,

$$(4) \qquad \alpha_v M_t(V) + \alpha_q M_t(Q) \geq M_t(W).$$

Setting margin for the position W using equation (3) is called *portfolio margining*, with the margin based on the aggregate risk of the portfolio components rather than the individual risks.[5]

The calculation in equation (4) depends upon the return correlations of V and Q. Correlations may vary over time and increase across asset classes in times of stress. As a result, portfolio margining is generally used only within specific asset classes, where correlations are likely to be high and relatively stable.

5.2.3 Margin Examples

The economic risk, and thus the margin, associated with a given notional amount differs by asset class and other characteristics, including maturity

---

5. Suppose that V and Q are marked to market over different horizons, which we will call 1 period and V periods. To understand portfolio margining in this case, let σ_v and σ_q represent the two 1-period standard deviations (corresponding to the more frequent mark-to-market interval) and ρ the return correlation. Suppose that Q is marked to market every $T > 1$ periods. The variance of the portfolio over T periods will be $\sigma^2 = \alpha_v^2 \sigma_v^2 + \alpha_q^2 \sigma_q^2 T + 2\rho \alpha_v \alpha_q \sigma_v \sigma_q \sqrt{T}$. The horizon T does not affect the variance of V in this calculation because the position is refreshed every period and there is never more than one period of exposure. As we vary T, we have

$$\frac{\partial \sigma}{\partial T} = \frac{1}{2\sigma}\left(\alpha_q^2 \sigma_q^2 + \rho \alpha_v \alpha_q \sigma_v \sigma_q \frac{1}{\sqrt{T}}\right).$$

As T increases, margin increases due to the risk of Q.

and the structure of the contract. In the following we use CME Group margin levels to illustrate possible differences in margin amount for a $100 million notional position in different assets.

Consider a contract to hedge a future $100 million ninety-day loan with a rate that will be linked to LIBOR on the lending date. One way to hedge this loan is by entering into a Eurodollar futures contract, which is an exchange-traded contract. The notional value of the contract is $1 million, so hedging the loan requires a position in 100 contracts.[6]

For each exchange-traded contract, the CME Group website reports the initial margin—the amount that must be posted to enter into an outright position (long or short) in one contract—and the maintenance margin, which is the minimum amount permitted in the margin account. Exchange-traded contracts are marked to market daily. In June 2011, the CME Group website reported that initial margin and maintenance margin for the Eurodollar contract was $608/$450 for contracts with an expiration date of less than one year, $743/$550 for contracts with an expiration date between one and three years, and $1,013/$750 for longer-dated contracts. In all three cases the maintenance margin is 74 percent of the initial margin, which in turn is less than 0.1 percent of the notional amount of $1 million. For our purposes, maintenance margin is the required minimum and thus corresponds most closely to equations (1) and (2).

Thus, hedging the $100 million loan would require that traders on each side of the contract maintain a margin balance of between $45,000 and $75,000, depending on the maturity of the contracts. In this example, we would observe open interest of 100 contracts and, because there is both a long and a short, total margin of roughly $90,000 to $150,000, depending upon maturity.

There are trading strategies such as spreads that would result in different margin amounts. For example, consider a trader who goes long fifty Eurodollar contracts expiring in one month and short fifty Eurodollar contracts expiring in a later month. The risk of a spread is lower than the risk of an outright position, so the spread—which also generates open interest of 100 contracts—would require initial margin of between $23,600 and $57,400, depending on maturity. This is about half the margin for a 100 contract outright position.

Some trading strategies require substantially smaller margin amounts per contract. For example, going long one December 2012 contract, long three June 2013 contracts, short three March 2013 contracts, and short one September 2013 contract—a so-called condor—would have initial margin of $68. If a trader entered into twelve such positions, there would be open

6. In this example it is irrelevant whether or not the party is hedging a lending or borrowing position. However, hedging a loan would entail going long Eurodollar futures, which are designed to behave like a bond, making money when the interest rate goes down. A short position would hedge borrowing.

Table 5.1 **Maintenance margin for different representative futures at CME Group exchanges, assuming a $100 million notional amount in the case of outright trades and a $100 million notional amount on each side in the case of spread trades (this is twice the number of contracts)**

| | | | Margins | |
| | | | Outright | Spread |
Asset	Ticker	Number of contracts	($)	($)
Eurodollar	ED	100	45,000	20,000
Treasury bond	US	1,000	2,000,000	300,000
S&P 500 index	SP	320	6,400,000	80,000
Crude oil (WTI)	CL	1,000	5,250,000	300,000
Natural gas (Henry Hub)	NG	2,174	4,347,826	869,565
Gold	GC	667	3,000,000	54,667
Copper	HG	1,000	4,250,000	225,000
Corn	C	3,077	5,384,615	2,307,692

Source: CMEGroup.com.

Note: The "Number of contracts" column reports the number of contracts with a $100 million notional amount.

interest of ninety-six contracts and total margin of $816. Depending on the spread strategy, required margin can vary by a factor of ten.

5.2.4   Margin for Different Assets

Table 5.1 shows representative margin levels for positions with a notional value of $100,000,000 for different contracts.[7] The main point of table 5.1 is that for a given notional amount, the risk of a position, as measured by margin, can vary significantly.[8] Even ignoring the Eurodollar contract, margin can vary by a factor of three (T-bonds vs. the S&P 500 index), and margin on spread positions can vary still more widely. For some assets, spreads are low risk (the S&P 500 index and gold, for example), while for others, spreads are relatively risky (corn and natural gas).

7. Table 5.1 is intended only to be illustrative, but it is worth noting that there can be a great deal of contract-to-contract variation in margin characteristics, even holding fixed the underlying asset or commodity. The table emphasizes differences across assets, but the differences in margin for a given asset, across different expirations, can also be considerable. For example, crude oil maintenance margins on outright positions start at $6,250 for the near months, and decline to $5,000 for contracts more distant than twenty months. Corn spread margins are $750/contract for spreads that cross harvests (e. g., summer against winter months), and $300/contract for spreads in the same season. The examples in table 5.1 are necessarily somewhat arbitrary.

8. The Eurodollar contract has a deceptively low margin. A common use of the contract is the hedging of swaps. The equivalent of a ten-year swap would be a set of Eurodollar contracts with forty different maturities. Multiplying the Eurodollar margin by forty yields a margin of $1.8 million, close to that of Treasury bonds.

5.3   Margin in Practice

In this section I discuss how margin is handled at a central clearinghouse and in the OTC market. It is important to keep in mind that all derivatives are in zero net supply. Also, for futures and swaps with zero value, both the buyer and seller post margin because either could experience a loss.

5.3.1   Clearinghouse Margin Practice

A typical clearinghouse becomes the counterparty for all traders: the seller to all buyers and the buyer to all sellers. This process by which the clearinghouse substitutes itself as counterparty is called *novation*. A clearinghouse does not novate all counterparty relationships, but typically deals directly only with clearing members, who in turn have obligations to the clearinghouse.[9] Other traders interact with the clearinghouse through clearing members.

A clearinghouse will have procedures and safeguards to protect clearing members against default by other clearing members. One common practice is for the clearinghouse to hold margin. For example, the CME Group in 2010 (CME Group, Inc. 2010) reported holding $82 billion of performance bonds. Depending upon the requirements of the clearinghouse and regulators, this reported margin number can have different interpretations. The following discussion is intended to outline the possible practices concerning margin, rather than the specific practices of any particular exchange.

Outright Positions

Consider the left-hand side of figure 5.1, in which there are two clearing members, and clearing member 1 has two customer accounts. Suppose that customer A is long two contracts, customer B is short one contract, and clearing member 2 is short one contract. Margin is M per contract, so total margin deposited by customers at clearing member 1 is $3M$, and clearing member 2 must deposit M. The disposition of the margin depends on clearinghouse rules, but the important point is that the total margin of $4M$ on deposit from customers measures their one-period economic exposure resulting from their derivatives positions.[10]

What happens to the $4M$ on deposit? The clearinghouse could mandate that clearing members post with the clearinghouse all margin received, in which case the clearinghouse would show performance bond holdings of

---

9. Clearing members will contribute to a clearinghouse guarantee fund, must be in financial good standing, and may have an obligation to contribute further to the clearinghouse in the event another clearing member defaults.

10. Note that there are credit relationships in the clearinghouse model that do not involve payment of margin. Generally, clearing member 1, not the clearinghouse, is the counterparty for customers A and B. If clearing member 1 were to fail, the clearinghouse would protect other clearing members against losses, but customers of clearing member 1 could potentially suffer losses, depending upon the precise legal obligation of the clearinghouse.

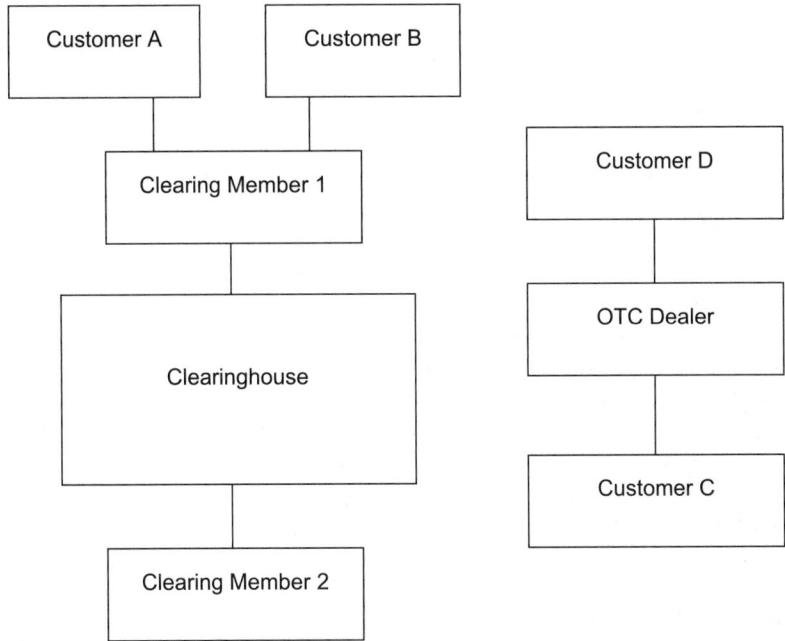

Fig. 5.1   Derivatives counterparties with and without a clearinghouse

$4M$. This treatment of margin by the clearinghouse is referred to as *gross margining*. Alternatively, rules could be such that the clearinghouse would, in the event of a failure, have a net obligation of one contract to clearing member 1, and the clearinghouse could then require a deposit only of M, the margin on one contract, from each clearing member. Clearing member 1 would continue to hold the remaining $2M$. This is a *net margining* system.

Thus, depending upon its rules, the clearinghouse could hold two units of margin, four units of margin, or something in between. In a net margin system, clearing member 1 would hold the two units of margin that are not held by the clearinghouse. The specific rights and obligations of customers, clearing members, and the clearinghouse under the two systems are potentially quite complicated and are beyond the scope of this discussion. The point is that the margin held by the clearinghouse provides different measures under the two systems.

Cross-Margined Positions

As discussed previously, margin can be based on a total portfolio position, taking into account diversification. Clearinghouses routinely use portfolio margining for calendar spreads (e.g., long September and short October in the same asset or commodity) and spread positions in different equity indexes (e.g., long Dow-Jones and short the S&P 500). Going long and short the same contract is a limiting case of portfolio margining (the two positions are perfectly negatively correlated). Portfolio margining is generally *not* used across asset classes, although this could change.

Once margin is computed for a position, margin can be held by the broker or clearinghouse depending upon whether there is gross or net margining.

5.3.2   OTC Margin Practice

Under Dodd-Frank, margin treatment in the OTC market should closely resemble that for clearinghouses, with the dealer bank serving as the clearing entity. Prior to Dodd-Frank, however, margin practice in the OTC market typically differed from that in clearinghouses.[11]

The OTC market is illustrated on the right-hand side of figure 5.1. Suppose that customers C and D enter into offsetting positions in an OTC version of the same contract that A and B are holding. The OTC dealer is counterparty to each, effectively serving the same role as the clearinghouse. The customers are exposed to the dealer, and the dealer is exposed to each customer. Prior to Dodd-Frank, it would have been possible that none of the participants in figure 5.1 would have posted maintenance margin.[12] Typically, the dealer would compute the independent amount (analogous to maintenance margin) for a counterparty and then the party with the larger independent amount (typically the customer) would post collateral equal to the difference in the independent amounts. This is in contrast with the situation at a clearinghouse, where the two clearing members would both post margin for their positions. Another difference is that OTC margin calculations for different asset classes may cover different horizons: several days, for example, rather than one day.

As with a clearinghouse, OTC dealers make use of portfolio margining but only for closely related assets.

5.4   Using Margin to Assess Risk

Margin requirements attempt to measure risk in a precise way, so systematic reporting of margin, broken down by asset class, reported by market participants, would provide potentially valuable information to regulators, analysts, and other market participants. One could imagine a reporting scheme in which derivatives would be broken out into standard asset class categories; for example, equity, index, fixed income, energy, agricultural

---

11. OTC margining is discussed in detail in appendix A of Brunnermeier and Pedersen (2009). One issue pertaining to OTC margining that I do not address is the effect of nonstandardized contracts and illiquid markets for the underlying asset.

12. Under proposed rules, the SEC and CFTC would designate large dealer firms as "covered swap entities." These firms would be required to collect margin from one another.

commodities, metals, and foreign exchange. Derivative margin by such categories would be reported by clearinghouses, swap clearing entities, dealers, and corporate end users.

Major market participants such as clearinghouses and swap clearing entities could report margin broken down by asset class, with and without incorporating the effects of cross margining. This number could be divided by two in order to compare directly to open interest.

- Clearinghouse rules might leave substantial customer margin held by clearing members (for example, if the clearinghouse uses net margining). In this case, the margin in the custody of clearing members could be reported as well.
- Covered swap entities could report margin, by asset class, for noncleared swaps.
- For users subject to the end-user exemption, margin that would have been otherwise required would be reported by asset class.

To illustrate the role of margin in measuring economic exposure, table 5.2 summarizes a series of transactions undertaken by different entities. The transactions illustrate three issues in assessing derivatives risk:

1. The existence of partial offsetting positions between two counterparties (transactions 1 and 2, group A)
2. Cyclical transactions, where individual firms face exposure that could be netted, but is not (transactions 3, 4, and 5, group B)
3. Nonstandard derivatives (transactions 6 and 7, group C)

Note that none of the positions in table 5.2 are exactly offsetting with respect to both the contract and the counterparty. The notional amounts for oil swaps in the table are based upon a price of $100 per barrel and settlement

Table 5.2   Hypothetical oil derivatives positions among six dealers (D1–D6) and one customer (C)

			Outright		
Group	Item	Description	Long	Short	Margin ($)
A	1	$125 1.25-year swap	D1	D2	6.25
	2	$150 1.5-year swap	D2	D1	7.50
B	3	$100 1-year swap	D3	D4	5.00
	4	$100 1-year swap	D4	D5	5.00
	5	$100 1-year swap	D5	D3	5.00
C	6	$100 1-year exotic levered swap	C	D6	20.00
	7	$100 1-year swap	D6	C	5.00

Notes: All swaps are based on 83,333 barrels per month, and outright margin is assumed to be 5 percent of notional for standard swaps. All dollar amounts are millions.

based on 83,333 barrels per month. The stated notional amount is the total barrels over the life of the swap times price. We assume that the margin is $5 per barrel or $5 million on a $100 million swap and $20 million for the exotic swap. The measured total notional derivatives positions implied by table 5.2, as well as the amount and location of risk exposures, will depend upon whether the trades are cleared.

5.4.1   Clearinghouse Treatment

Suppose first that trades are centrally cleared. Table 5.2 illustrates the original trades, but assume that the ordinary swaps have been presented to the clearinghouse and novated. For the purpose of this discussion it does not matter whether the dealers are clearing members.

In transactions 1 and 2, D1 and D2 have partially offsetting positions in swaps. Because each party is both long and short closely related contracts, margin on the net position is that of a spread, reflecting the remaining exposure in months sixteen through eighteen. The margin in this example would be about $1.25 million for each counterparty.[13]

Transactions 3, 4, and 5 illustrate the netting function of a clearinghouse. Each dealer is both long and short the same contract, albeit with a different counterparty. Novation of the contracts makes the clearinghouse a counterparty to all three contracts, eliminating the positions and therefore the exposure of the dealers.

Finally, transactions 6 and 7 again represent partial offsets for the customer, who is long oil via an exotic swap and short oil with an ordinary swap, with dealer 1. Assuming the exotic swap cannot be cleared, the customer owes $5 million margin to the clearinghouse for the ordinary swap and $20 million margin to the dealer for the exotic swap. The ordinary swap is novated, resulting in the dealer and customer both having a standard cleared contract.

Summarizing, with a clearinghouse, the transactions in table 5.2 would result in reported notional amounts of $475 million (transactions 3, 4, and 5 vanish due to novation) and margins of $1.25 million for transactions 1 and 2 (counting one firm's margin) and $25 million for transactions 6 and 7.

Margins thus reveal low risk associated with the $275 million notional amount of transactions 1 and 2, and the very high risk associated with the $200 million notional of transactions 6 and 7. Transactions 3, 4, and 5 do not exist.

---

13. Margin in this case would reflect the different notional amounts and also the different maturities. Presumably there would be a positive but small margin for equal notional amounts in the two contracts, and an additional margin for the residual $25 million, whence the assertion that margin would be "about" $1.25 million.

5.4.2   OTC Treatment

Suppose now that all of the transactions in table 5.2 are OTC, and therefore not centrally cleared.[14] Both open interest and margins are different due to differences in netting with and without central clearing.

Transactions 1 and 2 should result in the same margin as with central clearing. As the counterparties are the same, only net exposure matters and both sides are margined.

Transactions 3 to 5 are treated quite differently with and without central clearing. In the OTC market there is no novation; all bilateral transactions remain in place with the original counterparties. Therefore the transactions, which net to zero with central clearing, will remain outstanding. This increases total notional amounts by $300 million. Further, under Dodd-Frank, all dealers will post margin with their counterparties. (This creates a powerful incentive to identify and unwind such transactions, achieving the same outcome as novation.)

Finally, with the standard swap receiving OTC treatment, it is possible for dealer 1 and the customer to net the exotic and ordinary swap, transactions 6 and 7. The same notional amounts would be outstanding for these transactions, but the amount of margin is reduced from $25 million when cleared to $15 million when the exotic and ordinary swaps are not cleared.

Without clearing, notional amounts outstanding increase to $775 million and required margins increase by approximately $5 million. This takes account of the increase of $15 million from transactions 3 to 5 and the reduction of $10 million from transactions 6 and 7. The increase in OTC margin relative to clearinghouse margin in this example reflects the increase in counterparty credit risk from the inability to novate in an OTC setting.

5.4.3   Discussion

The examples illustrate how margin measures the net exposure to a given counterparty, providing a convenient and consistent measure of exposure to a given asset class. The aggregate notional amount of derivatives outstanding is quite different in the cleared and uncleared case, but margin is almost the same. The examples illustrate one case where margin is the same in a cleared and noncleared system (transactions 1 and 2), one case where margin and risk are both reduced in the cleared system (transactions 3, 4, and 5)—albeit because derivatives positions are eliminated by clearing—and one case where margin declines in the uncleared system (transactions 6 and 7). In each case, margin shows who is bearing risk and how it is distributed.

---

14. The examples here would also apply if there were multiple clearinghouses for the same product. The examples illustrate the incentive to consolidate trades in an asset class at a single clearinghouse.

Note that it would be difficult to obtain this risk exposure information in other ways. One possibility would be to acquire precise information about the terms and counterparties of derivatives claims outstanding, but assessing risk would require valuing these claims and computing net exposure to each counterparty. With margin, the counterparties have performed this calculation. The requirement of consistent margin reporting is thus a decentralized form of regulation: margin is computed by agents with economic stakes, rather than by a central entity.

In addition to margin, there are at least two other leading natural measures of derivatives usage and exposure applicable both to OTC and cleared positions.

- *Notional amount* measures the notional dollar value of contracts outstanding, with no adjustment for risk or offsetting positions. In table 5.2, notional amounts with clearing are $475 and without clearing $775, but the aggregate margin is almost the same. As discussed in the introduction, notional amount takes no account of the different risks of positions or whether there are offsetting positions. It is inherently difficult to interpret the economic significance of notional amounts.
- *Value at risk (VaR)* measures the firm's specific exposure. As discussed in section 5.2, margin is conceptually similar to value at risk. The difference is that value at risk may be zero in circumstances where margin would be positive. For example, in Group B without clearing, each of the three firms would show zero VaR, whereas under the rules proposed by Dodd-Frank, each would post margin for both positions. The positive margin amount would indicate that there is a chain of uncleared obligations, which is indicative of systemic risk.

The implementation questions for a margin reporting system include the following:

- How finely should asset classes be subdivided? It is common to subdivide products as equity, interest rates, credit, foreign exchange, and commodities. Finer subdivisions would include splitting equity and interest rates by currency of denomination, and commodities into agriculture, energy, and metals.
- How fine grained should entity-level reporting be? Two objections to fine-grained reporting by dealer banks would be the costs of reporting and the possibility of releasing proprietary information. Presumably regulators will be receiving detailed information, so the issue of cost should be moot. The issue of proprietary information is potentially more problematic.
- How frequent should reporting be? Under Dodd-Frank, OTC derivatives trades are to be publicly reported on a near real-time basis, and

dealers presumably will be performing margin calculations at least daily. Daily or weekly margin reporting should be feasible.

- Does portfolio margining raise special issues? If portfolio margins were sensitive to correlation assumptions, margins could change abruptly at the onset of a crisis. One could require reporting of margins with and without portfolio margining. This is probably not important with current practice, but could be a significant issue if the scope of portfolio margining were to increase.

5.5   The End-User Exemption

The exception to the requirement to post margin under Dodd-Frank is the proposed "end-user exemption" for nonfinancial firms. Specifically, under the Treasury's proposed margin and capital requirements for covered swap entities (Department of the Treasury et al. 2011),

> a covered swap entity would not be required to collect initial or variation margin from a nonfinancial end-user counterparty as long as the covered swap entity's exposures to the nonfinancial end-user were below the credit exposure limits that the covered swap entity has established. (25)

Note that under this proposed rule, because the trigger is credit exposure to the dealer, an exempt end user could avoid posting margin by splitting positions among multiple dealers.

The end-user exemption has been controversial because it exempts a large class of traders from the requirement to post explicit margin. Large end users lobbied for the exemption on the grounds that their hedging transactions are implicitly offsetting risk on nonfinancial assets and the margin requirement would make such transactions more costly. Nevertheless, large derivative positions would expose counterparties to credit risk. Large firms would take derivatives positions correlated with their business, so failure of the end user would be correlated with failure to pay on the contract. If failure occurs due to losses in the line of business associated with the hedged asset, this correlation would be negative. But if failure occurred due to systemic stresses, it is possible that failure of the business and failure to pay on the contract could occur simultaneously. In any event, the end-user exemption creates the economic equivalent of an off-balance sheet transaction between the dealer and end user. The exemption also creates an incentive for end users to use noncleared, nonstandard contracts in order to obtain the exemption.

Suppose an end user enters into an exchange-traded contract. The resulting hypothetical balance sheet, including margin and financing, is depicted in table 5.3. Margin posted by the end user, M_E, is assumed to be debt financed. This captures the idea that a failure to pay variation margin trig-

Table 5.3   **Hypothetical balance sheets for a firm transacting in a derivatives contract via a clearinghouse and posting margin for derivatives transaction that has a zero initial value**

End user			
Assets		Liabilities	
Risky asset	A	Financing	A
Derivative	0	—	—
Cash (margin)	M_E	Debt	M_E

Notes: Firm has preexisting assets and financing of A. Assumes that margin is debt financed.

gers default. For example, suppose the firm has A of assets and financing, and posts margin of M_E. If the firm suffers a loss on the position of λM_E, it is obligated to pay that amount, or else it is in default. Entering into a derivative is analogous to a firm issuing short-term debt of M_E and investing the proceeds in a risky asset. Any failure to pay the loan due to a loss on the invested value would trigger default.

Table 5.4 generalizes table 5.3 to the case where there is an OTC contract and both the firm and dealer post margin. Both issue debt to finance margin. Each has an off-balance sheet asset, margin posted by the other, to offset exposure to the other. The resulting conceptual balance sheet is in table 5.4.

Finally, consider the case whether neither firm posts margin. Each has credit exposure to the other and thus, implicitly, each has made a loan to the other. The end-user exemption, by allowing firms to avoid posting margin, effectively permits off-balance sheet financing of the margin amount. (See table 5.5.)

The upshot is that the end-user exemption creates an obligation resembling an off-balance sheet loan that finances an implicit margin deposit. Exempt firms could report the amount of margin they would have posted in the absence of the exemption. This would permit consistent analysis of entity exposures and aggregate measures of derivatives activity.

5.6   Conclusion

The Dodd-Frank Act was intended to reduce systemic risks. A central goal of the legislation was to increase clearing of derivatives transactions, but at this point no one knows the consequences of new rules. In particular, we do not know

- how large clearinghouses will be,
- how many clearinghouses there will be,
- how international integration and resolution will function,
- how empirically important the end-user exemption will be, and

Table 5.4   **Hypothetical balance sheets for a firm and dealer transacting in an OTC derivatives contract, with both posting margin for a derivatives transaction that has a zero initial value**

Assets		Liabilities	
End user			
Risky asset	A	Financing	A
Derivative	0	—	—
Cash (margin)	M_E	Debt (3rd party)	M_E
Dealer margin	M_D	Exposure to dealer	M_D
Dealer			
—	—	Derivative	0
Cash (margin)	M_D	Debt (3rd party)	M_D
End-user margin	M_E	Exposure to end user	M_E

Note: Assumes that margin is debt financed.

Table 5.5   **Hypothetical balance sheets for a firm and dealer transacting in an OTC derivatives contract, with neither posting margin for a derivatives transaction.**

Assets		Liabilities	
End user			
Risky asset	A	Financing	A
Derivative	0	—	—
Margin	M_E	Debt (from dealer)	M_E
Loan to dealer (margin)	M_D	Exposure to dealer	M_D
Dealer			
—	—	Derivative	0
Margin	M_D	Debt (from end user)	M_D
Loan to end user (margin)	M_E	Exposure to end user	M_E

Note: Implicitly, each lends to the other.

- how much market-making business will flee traditionally regulated entities (e.g., banks subject to Basel III).

Whatever the new configuration of firms and markets, the push to central clearing will likely create new systemically important clearinghouses or related financial utilities, some of which will be too big or interconnected to fail. A critical question is what information will be useful across different possible future configurations of activity.

Frequent, disaggregated, public reporting of margin provides a mechanism that should help regulators and market participants assess the risk of aggregate positions and the effects of changes in the level of risk. It should help to assess the risks borne by clearinghouses, dealers, and large market participants. Such reporting would reveal which asset classes have the greatest risk exposure and potentially, depending on the level of disaggregation, which sectors have exposure to which risks (e. g., insurance companies writing credit default swaps).

References

Bank for International Settlements (BIS). 2011. "OTC Derivatives Market Activity in the Second Half of 2010." Technical Report. BIS, Monetary and Economics Department. http://www.bis.org/publ/otc_hy1105.htm.

Bolton, P., and M. Oehmke. 2011. "Should Derivatives Be Senior?" Unpublished Manuscript, Columbia University.

Brunnermeier, M. K., and L. H. Pedersen. 2009. "Market Liquidity and Funding Liquidity." *Review of Financial Studies* 22 (6): 2201–38.

CME Group Inc. 2010. "Annual Report." http://www.cmegroup.com/investor-relations/annual-review/2010/.

Department of the Treasury et al. 2011. "Margin and Capital Requirements for Covered Swap Entities (Notice of Proposed Rule-making)." Technical Report. Department of the Treasury.

Duffie, D. 2011. "On the Clearing of Foreign Exchange Derivatives." Working Paper, Graduate School of Business, Stanford University. http://dx.doi.org/10.2139/ssrn.1869065.

International Swap Dealers Association (ISDA). 2011. "OTC Derivatives Market Analysis Year-end 2010." Technical Report. ISDA.

McDonald, R. L. 2013. *Derivatives Markets*, 3rd ed. Boston: Pearson/Addison Wesley.

6

A Transparency Standard for Derivatives

Viral V. Acharya

Derivatives exposures across large financial institutions often contribute to—if not necessarily create—systemic risk. During a crisis, lack of adequate understanding of such exposures often compromises regulatory ability to unwind an institution, inducing large-scale backstops and counterparty bailouts. It is often claimed—in spite of the massive assistance that was provided in this crisis to deal with derivatives exposures—that derivative contracts are well collateralized so that counterparty risk on derivatives exposures is not a significant issue. Documenting evidence that supports or refutes this claim beyond reasonable doubt is currently infeasible due to the poor quality—and lack of standardization—of derivatives disclosures by financial firms. Nevertheless, all available evidence points *against* the claim that counterparty risk in derivative exposures is always well collateralized.

In many important cases that contributed to the crisis, most notably but not exclusively the case of AIG Financial Products, collateralization was weak.[1] Some reports also suggest that the problem is probably of nontrivial magnitudes and that going forward derivatives exposures are likely to remain

Viral V. Acharya is the C. V. Starr Professor of Economics at the Stern School of Business at New York University and a research associate of the National Bureau of Economic Research.

This chapter is partly based on the chapter "Regulating OTC Derivatives," coauthored with Or Shachar and Marti G Subrahmanyam, in the book *Regulating Wall Street: The Dodd-Frank Act and the New Architecture of Global Finance* (NYU Stern and John Wiley & Sons, November 2010). The author is grateful to Melissa Johnston and John Yan for research assistance and comments from Or Shachar and participants at the NBER conference of the Measuring Systemic Risk Initiative (October 2010). For acknowledgments, sources of research support, and disclosure of the author's material financial relationships, if any, please see http://www .nber.org/chapters/c12511.ack.

1. For example, *The Financial Crisis Inquiry Report*, released in January 2011, reports: "In the housing boom, CDS were sold by firms that failed to put up any reserves or initial collateral or to hedge their exposure. In the run-up to the crisis, AIG, the largest US insurance company,

a potentially important contributor to systemic risk. For instance, using information from the 10-Q quarterly statements, the International Monetary Fund (IMF) reports estimate that the five key institutions that are active in the over-the-counter (OTC) derivatives market—Goldman Sachs, Citigroup, J.P. Morgan, Bank of America, and Morgan Stanley—were jointly carrying almost $500 billion in OTC derivative payables exposure as of 3Q09.[2] The report also estimates that the five largest European banks—Deutsche Bank, Barclays, UBS, Royal Bank of Scotland (RBS), and Credit Suisse—had about $600 to $700 billion in undercollateralized risk (measured by residual derivative payables) as of December 2008. This residual exposure arises for two reasons, as per the IMF report. First, sovereigns, as well as AAA-rated insurers, corporations, large banks and multilateral institutions "do not post adequate collateral since they are viewed by large complex financial institutions as privileged and (apparently) safe clients." Second, dealers have agreed in their bilateral contracts not to mandate adequate collateral for dealer-to-dealer positions whereby creditworthy dealers often post no collateral to each other for these contracts.

These reports raise several pertinent questions:

- What is the true potential exposure on derivatives dealings of large institutions?
- How much of this exposure is collateralized?
- Is the collateral posted adequate under some conservative requirements of maximum counterparty risk in case of system-wide stress when besides the emergence of counterparty risk, positions become illiquid, hard to replace, and may have to be unwound at short notice?
- Are derivatives being deployed in an undercollateralized manner to undertake significant maturity transformation and taking on attendant liquidity risks?[3]

The chapter addresses these questions by examining the theoretical justification for a transparency standard for derivatives positions. To demonstrate that such a standard is implementable, the chapter shows examples of existing disclosures from large dealer firms in their quarterly filings. These disclosures often contain useful firm-level data on derivatives, but due to a lack of standardization, these are not aggregation friendly for assessing the risk to the system. The chapter highlights the important role for tracking of

---

would accumulate a one-half trillion dollar position in credit risk through the OTC market without being required to post one dollar's worth of initial collateral or making any other provision for loss. AIG was not alone."

2. Singh (2010).

3. In terms of "risk topography," derivatives can be considered the mechanism to build contingent exposures—across states of nature and over time—which when not adequately collateralized or capitalized, lead to liquidity risk. Thus, derivatives facilitate complex forms of "liquidity mismatch," discussed in greater detail in chapter 7 of this volume by Markus Brunnermeier, Gary Gorton, and Arvind Krishnamurthy.

a "margin coverage ratio" (MCR), namely the ratio of a derivatives dealer's cash (or liquidity, more broadly) to its *contingent* collateral or margin calls in case of a significant downgrade of its credit quality. Finally, the chapter discusses the implications of such a possible standard for the Office of Financial Research (OFR) to be set up under the Treasury as per the Dodd-Frank Act in the United States.

6.1 Case for Regulatory *and* Market Disclosure of Standardized Derivatives Reports

It is useful to understand theoretically the market failure in the provision of information in derivatives markets. Acharya and Engle (2009) and Acharya and Bisin (2010) formalize this idea under the notion of a "counterparty risk externality."[4]

To illustrate the idea, suppose that counterparty A agrees to pay B. Then, A turns around and sells a similar contract to C. The addition to A's position from the contract with C dilutes the payoff on its contract with B in the case that A turns out ex post to not have adequate funds to repay both B and C. Thus, B's payoff dependency on what else A does represents a negative payoff externality on B due to A's counterparty risk. The key efficiency question is whether B can adequately reflect this risk in charging price or adopting risk controls (e.g., margins or overall position limits) on A. Clearly, B's ability to do so depends upon whether B can observe what A does.

Now, if markets are organized over the counter (OTC) as with many derivatives contracts, there is opacity at the level of derivatives positions of a financial firm. As a result of this opacity, counterparty risk externality described earlier cannot be adequately reflected in price and collateral arrangements. More broadly, since generating information about each firm's derivatives positions requires its cooperation but benefits the system at large, the firm may not fully internalize the social benefits of transparency. This theory predicts, thus, that there will be too little production of private information in settings that involve counterparty risk externality. Acharya and Engle (2009) and Acharya and Bisin (2010) present several proposals to address this market failure.

One proposal is that central clearing and margining on exchanges get around this failure (at least when viewed in the realm of a particular clearinghouse or exchange). Central counterparty or trade-guaranteeing body or exchange can observe end-of-day (or even intraday) positions, and set position limits, concentration limits, and margin calls accordingly. This arrangement works best if the same clearing entity clears most products. Yet, many markets, especially for complex and customized derivatives, will almost necessarily remain OTC. They cannot easily be standardized if their

---

4. Acharya and Engle (2009) and Acharya and Bisin (2010).

primary purpose is to provide customized hedging to some end users, and the system may not find it profitable to incur transaction costs in setting up clearinghouses or exchanges for these products if their volumes are thin. For these remaining derivatives, some regulators have proposed addressing counterparty risk directly by limiting leverage (charging adequately high margin requirements) against them. Still, regulatory attempts to design such instrument-specific requirements have failed miserably in the design of capital requirements even on simpler instruments such as mortgages, loans, and lines of credit.

A second proposal, not necessarily exclusive of the first one, is to rely more on markets' transparency at large. Suppose information on the derivatives position of a financial firm was made available to market participants. This would enable better pricing and managing of counterparty risk by markets themselves. This way, dealers would be incentivized to lower their counterparty risks in an efficient manner. With a market-wide standard, dealers would also be incentivized to provide transparency about their own management of counterparty risk, a move that would benefit them the most in times of significant aggregate uncertainty when customers tend to leave business with riskier counterparties, triggering a "franchise value run," as witnessed by Goldman Sachs and Morgan Stanley around the collapse of Lehman Brothers, and instead "fly to quality."

A common argument against such public transparency of positions and counterparty level data is that it reduces the economic benefits of undertaking these positions in the first place and could reduce risk-sharing gains for the economy. A compromise would be to provide market transparency with a reasonable lag, so that price impacts for trading parties are minimized, and yet the lagged information is useful for counterparty risk assessments.

Finally, it is highly likely that an efficient transparency standard for derivatives will in turn produce an efficient information system at each financial firm that aggregates its own derivatives positions in different subsidiaries, markets, and countries. This could improve a firm's own risk management by providing timely information to senior management and chief risk officers about enterprise-wide risks.

6.2   A Transparency Standard for Derivatives and Counterparty Risk

What might a transparency standard for derivatives look like? Here is an example. All dealers, as well as large swap players, provide to a centralized data repository frequent (for example, weekly or biweekly) risk reports on their derivatives positions as follows:

Classification of exposures into

- product types (such as single-name CDS, index CDS, interest rate swaps, currency swaps, commodities, equities, etc.),

- by major currency categories,
- maturity (buckets) of contracts,
- type of counterparty (bank, broker-dealer, corporation, government-sponsored enterprise, monoline, insurance firm, etc.), and
- credit rating of counterparties.

Size of exposures could be reported as[5]

- gross (maximum notional exposure),
- in fair-value terms (to account for mark-to-market changes),
- net (taking account of bilateral netting arrangements), and
- *uncollateralized net* (recognizing collateral posted by counterparties).

Uncollateralized net exposures could be disclosed also as *potential exposures* based on *stress tests*[6] that take account of

- several notches of ratings downgrade of a counterparty and its ability to post additional collateral, and
- counterparty default and replacement risk for the exposures assuming severe market conditions such as replacement time of two to four weeks.[7]

To facilitate the understanding of *contingent* or *potential* exposures and for deriving implications for systemically risky exposures, all dealers, as well as large swap players, could also provide two important and novel reports:
Margin call reports that list the additional collateral liabilities of the firm as

- total additional liability in case the firm was to experience one, two, or more (say, up to six) notch downgrades, and
- largest such liabilities aggregated by different counterparties (say, ten largest).

Concentration reports that provide the above-mentioned information for the entity's largest counterparty exposures (say, the largest ten) or accounting for at least a substantial proportion (say, 75 percent) of the total exposure.
When aggregated across firms, the standardized firm-level reports aggre-

---

5. The crucial item here is "uncollateralized," as without knowledge of collateral backing the contracts, there is the risk of overstating the derivatives exposures, but more importantly, it would create the uncertainty about magnitude of risk in the first place.

6. The focus of the standard considered here is on stress tests based on counterparty risk. Nevertheless, stress tests based on macroeconomic scenarios, as discussed in Darrell Duffie's chapter 3 in this volume, "Systemic Risk Exposures: A 10-by-10-by-10 Approach," could also be augmented to the standard.

7. In particular, the current disclosure of level 1, level 2, and level 3 of assets' underlying value might also be enhanced to report potential illiquidity and opacity of positions (not just for derivatives), so that an asset could be level 1 in normal times, but the disclosure would also state whether it is likely to be level 1, level 2, or level 3 in reasonable stress scenarios.

Table 6.1   Outcome of the possible transparency standard for derivatives

Disclosure	Firm 1	Firm 2	. . .	Firm n
Exposures				
Product type				
Maturity bucket				
Counterparty type				
Counterparty credit rating				
Value				
Maximum loss ("potential exposure")				
Uncollateralized net				
Net of collateral				
By currency categories				
Collateral posted				
Margin Report: Additional collateral to post				
One notch downgrade				
Two-notch downgrade				
Multinotch downgrade				
Concentration Report: Firms, percentage of exposure				

gate to a "map" of derivatives positions and their risks (mark-to-market risk, counterparty risk, and liquidity risk) as shown in table 6.1.

Although such a transparency standard appears at first to involve a large amount of information gathering, the costs of such disclosure are not likely to be that onerous. Sophisticated investment banks already maintain such information for their internal risk management purposes, and they do publish some of it in their quarterly reports (though in a highly nonstandardized and less granular manner, as explained later). Therefore, it is unlikely to be a significant additional burden for them to disclose such information to regulators in a standardized format at frequent intervals. Some aggregated versions that respect customer confidentiality can then be made transparent to markets at large, say on a monthly or at least quarterly basis, to help enhance market discipline against the buildup of uncollateralized exposures.

6.3   What Do Financial Firms Currently Do and Do Not Disclose?

The 10-Q filings of financial firms, as for any firms regulated by the Securities and Exchange Commission (SEC) in the United States, require disclosure of all materially relevant information. In case of financial firms, given their increasingly large presence in derivatives markets, these filings also contain information on positions—and on their risks—in these markets. A few examples to follow help illustrate what is useful in the current reports, and what changes would be necessary to adhere to a transparency standard such as the one outlined earlier.

Consider for example the reporting of credit protection sold by Citigroup and J.P. Morgan Chase, shown from their 10-Q filings in tables 6.2 and 6.3. Citigroup reports its positions by industry, product, and credit rating of underlying reference entity, whereas J.P. Morgan reports them by maturity and credit rating of underlying entity. While it is possible to draw some relative conclusions about average credit rating of entities they write protection against (Citigroup wrote more risky protection than J.P. Morgan), other aspects of disclosures are not comparable. Nevertheless, the table reveals that financial firms could report these data in a standardized manner if required to do so.

Next, consider tables 6.4 and 6.5 that show Goldman Sachs and J.P. Morgan Chase's reporting of counterparty credit risk in their over-the-counter (OTC) derivatives positions. Goldman Sachs reports the positions as well as their value net of collateral by credit rating of counterparty, by risk types, and by maturity buckets. In this case, J.P. Morgan's reporting provides similar information as that of Goldman Sachs, facilitating a straightforward comparison. One can easily reach the conclusion that overall, in terms of percentage of overall exposures, J.P. Morgan's counterparty credit risk profile is safer than that of Goldman Sachs, as 40 percent of J.P. Morgan's OTC derivative credit exposure is with counterparties at a AA and higher level versus around 20 percent for Goldman Sachs.

Table 6.2   **Citigroup's reporting of credit derivatives as protection seller**

In millions of dollars as of September 30, 2009	Maximum potential amount of future payments	Fair value payable[a]
By industry/counterparty		
Bank	$860,437	$46,071
Broker-dealer	301,216	17,661
Monoline	—	—
Nonfinancial	2,127	96
Insurance and other financial institutions	151,326	12,753
Total by industry/counterparty	$1,315,106	$76,581
By instrument		
Credit default swaps and options	$1,314,282	$76,383
Total return swaps	824	198
Total by instrument	$1,315,106	$76,581
By rating		
Investment grade	$759,845	23,362
Noninvestment grade	422,865	33,231
Not rated	132,396	19,988
Total by rating	$1,315,106	$76,581

Note: This table summarizes the key characteristics of the company's credit derivative portfolio as protection seller (guarantor) as of September 30, 2009.

[a] In addition, fair value amounts receivable under credit derivatives sold were $23,324.

Table 6.3   **JPMorgan Chase's reporting of credit derivatives as protection seller (protection sold—credit derivatives and credit-linked notes ratings/maturity profiles[a])**

December 31, 2008 (in millions)	< 1 year	1–5 years	> 5 years	Total notional amount	Fair value[c]
Risk rating of reference entity					
Investment grade					
(AAA to BBB−)[b]	$(177,404)	$(1,767,004)	$(713,555)	$(2,657,963)	$(215,217)
Noninvestment grade					
(BB+ and below)[b]	(121,040)	(992,098)	(428,895)	(1,542,033)	(244,975)
Total	$(298,444)	$(2,759,102)	$(1,142,450)	$(4,199,996)	$(460,192)

Note: This table summarizes the key characteristics of the company's credit derivative portfolio as protection seller (guarantor) as of December 31, 2008.

[a] The contractual maturity for a single-name CDS contract generally ranges from three months to ten years, and the contractual maturity for index CDS is generally five years. The contractual maturity for CLNs typically ranges from three to five years.

[b] Ratings scale is based upon the firm's internal ratings, which generally correspond to ratings defined by S&P and Moody's.

[c] Amounts are shown on a gross basis, before the benefit of legally enforceable master-netting agreements and cash collateral held by the firm.

Table 6.4   **Goldman Sachs's reporting of OTC derivatives counterparty exposure**

Credit rating equivalent	0–12 months	1–5 years	5–10 years	10 years or greater	Total	Netting[b]	Exposure	Exposure net of collateral
AAA/Aaa	$1,482	$3,249	$3,809	$2,777	$11,317	$(5,481)	$5,836	$ 5,349
AA/Aa2	6,647	12,741	7,695	9,332	36,415	(20,804)	15,611	11,815
A/A2	31,999	46,761	29,324	31,747	139,831	(111,238)	28,593	24,795
BBB/Baa2	4,825	7,780	5,609	8,190	26,404	(12,069)	14,335	8,041
BB/Ba2 or lower	3,049	13,931	2,903	1,483	21,366	(5,357)	16,009	9,472
Unrated	666	1,570	387	148	2,771	(224)	2,547	1,845
Total	$48,668[a]	$86,032	$49,727	$53,677	$238,104	$(155,173)	$82,931	$61, 317

Note: OTC derivative credit exposure (in millions) as of September 2009.

[a] Includes fair values of OTC derivative assets, maturing within six months.

[b] Represents the netting of receivable balances with payable balances for the same counterparty across maturity categories and the netting of cash collateral received, pursuant to credit support agreements. Receivable and payable balances with the same counterparty in the same maturity category are netted within such maturity category, where appropriate.

Notably, *no data on concentration of exposures in derivatives are currently revealed* in any of the 10-Q filings. This creates a significant challenge in assessing systemic risk based on current public disclosures of financial firms.

In contrast, there is some useful information on potential margin calls. Table 6.6 illustrates that different financial firms report their margin liabili-

Table 6.5   **JPMorgan Chase's reporting of OTC derivatives counterparty exposure**

Rating equivalent	2008		2007	
December 31 (in millions, except ratios)	Exposure net of all collateral ($)	Percentage of exposure net of all collateral	Exposure net of all collateral ($)	Percentage of exposure net of all collateral
AAA/Aaa to AA−/Aa3	68,708	48	38,314	57
A+A1 to A−/A3	24,748	17	9,855	15
BBB+/Baa1 to BBB−/Baa3	15,747	11	9,335	14
BB+/Ba1 to B−/B3	28,186	20	9,451	14
CCC+/Caa1 and below	5,421	4	357	—
Total	142,810	100	67,312	100

Note: Ratings profile of derivative receivables MTM.

ties in the case of their own downgrades with varying levels of granularity and "stress." J.P. Morgan's report historically appears the best in a relative sense in that it includes margin liabilities for one-notch downgrade and up to six-notch downgrade. Goldman Sachs, however, reports margin liabilities only up to two notches, and the second notch is disclosed only since the crisis. It is immediately apparent from this report that J.P. Morgan's liquidity risk from one- to six-notch downgrade is far smaller in terms of multiplier on the required margin than it is for Goldman Sachs.

No discussion of contingent liquidity risk related to margin calls can be complete without a discussion of AIG. Table 6.7 shows that AIG reported only a one-notch downgrade risk up until 3Q 2008, and in that last quarter, reported up to two notches. From one to two notch, its collateral liability increased by a factor of six, a valuable piece of information in assessing the system's counterparty risk to AIG that was *not* available in their reports until 2Q 2008.[8] As it turned out, while Moody's and Fitch downgraded it by two notches, Standard & Poor's did so by three notches, resulting in collateral liability of $20 billion, which was compounded upward eventually to

8. This information, too, was not available in a well-tabulated form in AIG's 10-Q of 3Q 2008, but in the body of the text: "Credit ratings are important to AIG's business, results of operations and liquidity. Downgrades in AIG's credit ratings could increase AIG's borrowing costs and could adversely affect its competitive position and liquidity. With respect to AIG's liquidity, it is estimated that, as of the close of business on April 30, 2008, based on AIGFP's outstanding municipal guaranteed investment agreements (GIAs) and financial derivative transactions at that date, a downgrade of AIG's longer−term senior debt ratings to 'Aa3' by Moody's Investors Service (Moody's) or 'AA−' by Standard & Poor's, a division of the McGraw−Hill Companies (S&P) would permit counterparties to call for approximately $1.8 billion of collateral, while a downgrade to 'A1' by Moody's or A+ by S&P would permit counterparties to call for approximately $9.8 billion of additional collateral. Further downgrades could result in requirements for substantial additional collateral, which could have a material adverse effect on how AIGFP manages its liquidity. The actual amount of collateral that AIGFP would be required to post to counterparties in the event of such downgrades depends on market conditions, the fair value of outstanding affected transactions and other factors prevailing at the time of the downgrade. Additional obligations to post collateral would increase the demands on AIGFP's liquidity."

Table 6.6   Contingent collateral liabilities for JPMorgan and Goldman Sachs collateral (credit risk-related contingent features in derivates)

	JP Morgan			Goldman Sachs	
	Collateral posted ($ billions)	Additional collateral ($ billions) in case of downgrade AA to BBB: 6 notch	Additional collateral ($ billions) in case of downgrade AA to AA−: 1 notch	Additional collateral in case of one-notch downgrade ($ millions)	Additional collateral in case of two-notch downgrade ($ millions)
2006-Q4	26.6				n/a
2007-Q1	27.0	2.6	0.1	607.0	n/a
2007-Q2	28.3	2.9	0.2	598.0	n/a
2007-Q3	32.8	3.2	0.3	752.0	n/a
2007-Q4	33.5	2.5	0.2	595.0	n/a
2008-Q1	48.5	3.4	0.3	957.0	n/a
2008-Q2	58.2	3.5	0.6	785.0	n/a
2008-Q3	60.1	4.3	0.9	669.0	n/a
2008-Q4	99.1	6.4	2.2	897.0	2,140
2009-Q1	82.3	4.9	1.4	941.0	2,140
2009-Q2	67.7	4.0	1.2	763.0	1,930
2009-Q3	66.0	4.4	1.5	685.0	1,700
2009-Q4					

Table 6.7   Contingent collateral liabilities of AIG ($ millions)

	2007-1	2007-2	2007-3	2007-4
Marginal call reports				
Additional collateral for one-notch downgrade rating	$902	$847	$830	$1,390
Additional collateral for two-notch downgrade rating				
Additional collateral for three-notch downgrade rating				
Additional collateral for multinotch downgrade rating				

	2008-1	2008-2	2008-3	Actual
Marginal call reports				
Additional collateral for one-notch downgrade rating	$1,800	$1,200	$1,800	
Additional collateral for two-notch downgrade rating			$9,800	Moody's and Fitch downgrade
Additional collateral for three-notch downgrade rating			−$20,000	S&P downgrade
Additional collateral for multinotch downgrade rating			−$32,000	Market risk adjustment

$32 billion, given mark-to-market or fair-value adjustments due to deteriorating market conditions.

Finally, it is instructive to use these margin call reports in conjunction with the cash position of these firms to assess their margin coverage ratios (MCR). In 4Q 2008, J.P. Morgan Chase had cash-equivalent assets of $26 billion, so that its MCR was over four, since its margin call for a six-notch downgrade is $6.3 billion. Goldman Sachs had cash assets (its "total global core excess") of over $100 billion, giving it an MCR of around 50 for a margin call of $2.14 billion at a two-notch downgrade. That is, while Goldman Sachs's liquidity risk due to collateral calls is substantial, it also holds a lot of unencumbered cash to deal with this risk. In contrast, AIG had cash assets of just around $2.5 billion in 2008, giving it an MCR of between 1 and 2 for its $1.8 billion margin call at one-notch downgrade. Once it revealed its two-notch downgrade risk in August 2008, its MCR for two-notch downgrade was just around 0.25 as its (hitherto undisclosed) margin call exposure was up at $9.8 billion with a two-notch downgrade. AIG's margin risk was simply not well covered for a "stress" downgrade scenario by its holdings of cash assets. Importantly, for a multinotch downgrade, this was not at all transparent based on its 10-Q's prior to August 2008.

The purpose behind reporting these data from 10-Q filings is twofold. One, to make it clear that financial firms can, and do, report much of the possible standard discussed in this chapter for derivatives reporting. Second, to illustrate that standardized data can support and enhance the assessment of counterparty risk in derivatives markets using simple analytical tools such as the margin coverage ratio (MCR) that is analogous to the interest coverage ratio employed by credit rating analysts in their assessment of nonfinancial corporations' liquidity risk.

We now examine how a transparency standard like that described earlier would affect the degree to which the objectives of the recent financial reforms legislated in the United States could be achieved.

6.4 Implications for the Dodd-Frank Reforms and the Office of Financial Research

The "Wall Street Transparency and Accountability" part of the Dodd-Frank Act of 2010 requires that

- all existing derivative positions (both cleared and uncleared swaps) be reported to a swap data repository within 180 days of its enactment;
- all new positions—cleared or uncleared—be reported starting ninety days after the enactment (or an alternative legislated period);
- the repository be tasked with providing data to the regulatory agencies—including foreign and international agencies, if applicable—to minimize systemic risk;

- the repository be tasked with publishing aggregate market information (trading and clearing in major swap categories, participants and developments in new products) to the public twice a year;
- there be *real-time public reporting*, meaning to report data relating to a swap transaction, including price and volume, as soon as technologically practicable after the time at which the transaction has been executed; and
- such public reporting, however, not include counterparty or customer information, and also have a delay exemption for "block trades" (to be defined by rule makers), taking account of the impact of disclosure of such trades on liquidity.

While these attempts to improve transparency in the derivatives markets are commendable, there are also several notable omissions:

- Prices of new trades are often not sufficient to mark old positions, since derivatives are often struck at terms so as to be at zero fair value to both involved parties. It is essential to have for derivative trades their *potential exposure* and *collateral risk*, not just current mark-to-market values. However, such risk management variables are not required by the act to be collected by a data repository. Indeed, there is no required reporting of collateral information of any trades, precluding analysis of potential counterparty risk.
- While clearinghouses will clearly collect required counterparty information for trades they clear and will (hopefully) set adequate initial and variation margins to counterparties, several complex derivatives positions will still remain OTC. Understanding the counterparty risk in these OTC positions is crucial for margining on clearinghouses as well as in broader assessments of credit risk and systemic risk.
- Legislating counterparty risk transparency for regulators may have some favorable effects. Extending such transparency in some lagged form to markets might help reinstitute market discipline as a buffer against regulatory failures to contain risks adequately.

All of these omissions can be addressed by a possible transparency standard, as explained in this chapter.[9] Although there will remain private data repositories such as the Depository Trust and Clearing Corporation (DTCC), it is beyond doubt that over time the Office for Financial Research (OFR), which is required by the Dodd-Frank Act to be set up under the Treasury for collecting, analyzing, and disseminating systemic risk-relevant information and early warnings, will require derivatives counterparty risk

---

9. Indeed, the current hedge-accounting standards could also be possibly employed to make it clear what proportion of the exposures are for hedging purposes and to account for hedging effects in reported values and risks of positions.

information. An adequate, standardized, and self-reported but audited disclosure of derivatives positions and risks by the largest financial firms would be invaluable in such an exercise. The Financial Stability Oversight Council (FSOC), representing heads of regulatory agencies in the United States, formed as per the Dodd-Frank Act and charged with the task of identifying systemically important financial institutions (SIFIs) and regulating them, would also find such standardized reporting on derivatives of direct use as this would reveal information about which firms are currently—or potentially—too interconnected to fail. Academics, regulators, accounting boards, and derivatives dealers and large banks could come together to refine and implement the standard.

6.5   Conclusion

In summary, enhancing market discipline and regulatory intelligence about counterparty risk in derivatives markets likely requires a new transparency standard. This standard could be layered on top of the current quarterly disclosures of derivatives positions and risks by financial firms, but with a greater frequency for regulatory reports. Of particular importance is position-level transparency of large derivatives players, not just in a static sense, but also as potential exposure to stress scenarios, margin call exposure in case of their credit quality deterioration, and concentration exposure for assessment of systemic interconnections. Such transparency would facilitate tracking valuable counterparty risk indicators, most notably the margin coverage ratio (MCR) that compares a firm's cash position to its margin call exposure under stress scenarios.

References

Acharya, Viral V., and Alberto Bisin. 2010. "Counterparty Risk Externality: Centralized versus Over-the-Counter Markets." Working Paper, New York University-Stern.

Acharya, Viral V., and Robert Engle. 2009. "Derivatives Trades Should All Be Transparent." *Wall Street Journal*, May 15.

Singh, Manmohan. 2010. "Collateral, Netting and Systemic Risk in the OTC Derivatives Market." IMF Working Paper 10/99, International Monetary Fund, Washington, DC.

III

Liquidity and Leverage

7

Liquidity Mismatch Measurement

Markus Brunnermeier, Gary Gorton,
and Arvind Krishnamurthy

Policymakers and academics recognize that liquidity is central in the dynamics of a financial crisis, and that measurement of liquidity is critical in evaluating and regulating systemic risk.[1] The proposed Basel liquidity coverage ratio, for example, calls for banks to maintain a sufficient buffer of liquid assets to cover outflows over the next thirty days.

Systemic risk depends primarily on the endogenous response of market participants to extreme events. Brunnermeier, Gorton, and Krishnamurthy's (2012) "Risk Topography" approach takes explicitly endogenous responses into account when collecting data on the value and liquidity factor exposure of major institutions. The liquidity measure is a key response indicator. Market participants react to the same shock very differently depending on whether they face a lack of liquidity or they are flush with liquidity. In addition, aggregate liquidity measures are important to detect a buildup of systemic risk in the background during a run-up phase.

The academic literature on liquidity has identified many different aspects

Markus Brunnermeier is the Edwards S. Sanford Professor of Economics at Princeton University and a research associate of the National Bureau of Economic Research. Gary Gorton is the Frederick Frank Class of 1954 Professor of Management and Finance at Yale School of Management and a research associate of the National Bureau of Economic Research. Arvind Krishnamurthy is the Harold L. Stuart Professor of Finance in the Kellogg School of Management at Northwestern University and a research associate of the National Bureau of Economic Research.

For acknowledgments, sources of research support, and disclosure of the authors' material financial relationships, if any, please see http://www.nber.org/chapters/c12514.ack.

1. Duffie (chapter 3, this volume) highlights liquidity risk, in addition to solvency and counterparty risk, in his 10-by-10-by-10 framework for assessing systemic risk. Acharya (chapter 6, this volume) and McDonald (chapter 5, this volume) evaluate approaches to measuring liquidity risk based on collateral/margins on derivative contracts.

of liquidity that are important in crises, ranging from a bank's reliance on short-term debt, to its overall funding liquidity, to the market liquidity of its assets. The purpose of this chapter is to examine the measurement of liquidity in light of the academic research on liquidity. That is, the liquidity in a given academic paper is often a highly stylized concept. The questions we seek to answer are the following:

1. What is the practical and measured counterpart of the theoretical concept of liquidity suggested by models?
2. If one is interested in a liquidity measure that is informative about systemic risk, what measure does the academic research suggest?

Answers to these questions can inform regulatory thinking on liquidity regulations as well as further academic research in empirically testing models of liquidity and crises.

We propose a liquidity (risk) measure that looks at the worst x percent of the stress scenarios. For each stress scenario and for each asset and liability a cash equivalent dollar value is assigned assuming that all counterparties withdraw as much funds as possible in this scenario.

7.1 Liquidity in Theoretical Models

Diamond and Dybvig (1983) is the canonical model emphasizing the importance of "funding liquidity" for understanding financial crises. In this model, it is not the borrowing or leverage of the financial sector that is salient, but rather the proportion of debt that is comprised of short-term demandable deposits. More broadly, the banking literature concludes that when the financial sector holds illiquid assets financed by short-term debt, the possibility of run behavior emerges and, in turn, can precipitate a crisis.

Brunnermeier and Pedersen (2009) model the interaction between an institution's ability to raise funds (funding liquidity) and the liquidity of the assets when it sells them (market liquidity). Here, when funding liquidity falls the institution provides less liquidity in the assets it trades, reducing the market liquidity of the assets. When these assets themselves serve as collateral for the loans taken on by the institution, the situation can precipitate an adverse feedback loop as decreased market liquidity tightens funding liquidity conditions, and vice versa. The literature also describes a feedback mechanism between capital problems and liquidity problems. See, for example, Allen and Gale (2004). When the financial sector runs into liquidity problems, triggered by runs by lenders, the sector sells assets whose prices then reflect an illiquidity discount. The lower asset prices lead to losses that deplete capital, further compromising liquidity. The critical point that emerges from this literature is that the liquidity of assets is endogenous, while in the Diamond and Dybvig analysis the market illiquidity of assets held by banks is taken to be fixed. This leads to the important conclusion, namely, that it can be misleading to measure the liquidity of assets during a quiescent period if one is interested in a liquidity measure that can be informative about financial crises. Importantly, it is the liquidity mismatch that matters, the market liquidity of the assets, that is, their price impact in times of crisis, relative to the maturity structure of the liabilities. Note the difference to the maturity mismatch concept. Holding thirty-year Treasury bonds financed overnight involves an extreme maturity mismatch, but the liquidity mismatch of such a position is limited as US Treasuries typically appreciate in times of crisis.

Gorton and Pennacchi (1990) point out that the function of the banking system is to issue (informationally insensitive) liquid short-term debt claims against illiquid assets. That is, functionally banks produce liquidity in much the same way that utilities produce electricity. Bank equity holders earn a liquidity premium on production of this liquidity. From this perspective, any accounting of financial sector liquidity should have the property that the sector has a negative aggregate amount of liquidity.

Holmström and Tirole (1998) and Caballero and Krishnamurthy (2004) offer a macroprudential analyses of aggregate liquidity. Both papers ask the question of whether the private sector will produce the socially efficient amount of aggregate liquidity, and both offer a negative answer. In an international context, Caballero and Krishnamurthy show that generally the private sector will go too far in liquidity production—issue too many short-term debt claims—because individual actors do not internalize the effects of their actions on the probability of a macroeconomic crisis. Holmström and Tirole show that the state can play a beneficial role by itself issuing liquid claims, against its taxing power, in effect acting as a financial intermediary. Both of these analyses highlight the importance from a regulatory standpoint of measuring liquidity in a fashion that can be aggregated across the financial sector and hence shed light on macroeconomic risks.

To summarize, liquidity is constrained by financial frictions often in the form of limited pledgeability of future cash flows due to asymmetric information. The theoretical literature offers the following lessons regarding liquidity:

1. It is important to measure the liquidity of a given economic unit using data both on the market liquidity of its assets and on the liquidity promised through its liabilities. The measures need to explicitly condition on a possible stress event.

2. Liquidity is also a "response indicator." It reveals firms' or a sector's reaction to shocks and whether they potentially lead to adverse feedback loops in the form of liquidity spirals. A situation where the financial sector has promised more liquidity than it has is what we should expect as the natural state of the financial sector. On the other hand, this natural state gives rise to the possibility of financial crises.

3. Measuring the aggregated liquidity of the financial sector can be informative for macroprudential policy.

7.2   Liquidity in Practice

We next turn to the practical issues in liquidity measurement. In practice, liquidity does not match up neatly with representations of stylized models. We illustrate the issues through a series of examples.

Liquidity mismatch. Consider a bank with $20 of equity and $80 of debt, where half the debt is overnight repo financing at 1 percent and the other half is five-year debt at 4.5 percent. The bank buys one agency mortgage-backed security (MBS) for $50 (which is financed via repo at a zero haircut) and loans $50 to a firm for one year at an interest rate of 5 percent.

What if the bank cannot renew the repo financing, and is forced to liquidate some of its assets? Standard measures, such as leverage, will not capture this liquidity risk. That is, they will treat the overnight debt and the five-year debt symmetrically. One could construct a leverage measure that focuses on the maturity mismatch in this example—for instance, a short-term leverage measure—but this too may prove inadequate. For example, suppose that instead of the agency MBS, the bank owned $50 of private-label MBS, which is less liquid than the agency MBS. Now this bank has more of a liquidity mismatch, stemming from the asset side. Thus, it is clear that a liquidity measure needs to incorporate information from both the asset side of the balance sheet and the liability side, that is, both market liquidity and funding liquidity.

Rehypothecation. The bank lends $100 to a hedge fund for one day and receives a bond with a market value of $100 as collateral (a reverse repo). The bank then uses the bond as collateral to borrow $100 in the overnight repo market. (Whatever else the bank is doing we ignore for purposes of the example.)

This bank, despite having a liability structure comprising of short-term debt, does not have liquidity risk. Suppose that the repo lender to the bank does not renew this repo. Then, the bank can also choose not to renew its repo loan to the hedge fund and thus unwind the debt position. Again, this example illustrates that it is important to use information from the asset side to measure liquidity. Note instead that if the reverse repo loan to the hedge fund is for three days, then the bank will have some liquidity mismatch.

Derivatives. Consider a firm with $20 of equity and $80 of debt; half the debt is overnight repo financing at 1 percent and the other half is five-year debt at 4.5 percent. The firm buys $100 of US Treasury securities and writes protection (using credit default swaps [CDS]) on a diversified portfolio of 100 investment-grade US corporates, each with a notional amount of $10, so there is a total notional of $1,000. The weighted-average premium received on the CDS is 5 percent.

Derivatives trade under the International Swaps and Derivatives Association master agreement. This agreement usually has a credit support annex (CSA), a legal document, which sets forth the conditions under which each party must post collateral. Suppose that in this example the CSA has collateral-posting requirements based on the market value of the CDS position. If the marks widen, that is, when it is more likely that a firm or firms in the portfolio will default, this firm will have to post collateral to the counterparty. It has a Treasury bond, which could be posted, but which would then reduce the amount of asset liquidity held by the firm. In the extreme, imagine that the entire Treasury holding is posted so that the firm no longer has any liquidity. Then, the only remaining asset the firm has is the CDS portfolio.

As another example of a liquidity event triggered by derivatives, consider the effect of a ratings downgrade. The CSA often prescribes that if the bank is downgraded during the term of the derivative contract, it will have to post more collateral, which again uses liquidity. Moreover, if the firm had written many derivative contracts—the CDS as in the example, plus interest rate derivatives—the need for liquidity will apply to all derivative contracts. Thus, the downgrade is potentially a significant liquidity risk that arises when firms use derivatives.

Credit lines. The bank has $20 of equity and $80 of five-year debt. The bank buys $100 of US Treasuries and offers a credit line to a firm to access up to $100.

In this example, as with the derivatives example, the bank has no illiquidity problem currently. However in the event that a firm draws down the credit line, the $100 of Treasuries will convert into a less liquid bank loan. Thus, this bank has acquired liquidity risk.

Forwards versus futures. A (Brazilian) sugar producing firm writes a forward contract to deliver X amount of sugar after the harvest. Alternatively, the firm could have also bought a large futures contract on the exchange that is marked to market on a daily basis.

In this example, the firm is naturally hedged against sugar price fluctuations, as it is a major sugar producer. Locking in the price via a forward creates no liquidity risk or fundamental risk for the firm. However, if the firm opts for an exchange-traded futures contract instead, it is subject to margin calls as the sugar price varies. Hence, the firm has to hold large cash reserves for this case.

Currency mismatch. A European bank has (euro) $2 equivalent of equity, $40 equivalent of euro retail deposit funding, and $40 of US overnight commercial paper. The bank owns $100 of ABS.

In this example, the bank is running a currency mismatch, owning dollar assets funded by retail euro deposits as well as dollar wholesale funding. Suppose that money market funds refuse to roll over the commercial paper. In this case, the bank will not be able to keep its ABS position.

Note that the real issue here is the maturity of the dollar debt and not the currency mismatch. That is, if the firm had long-term dollar debt, the firm would have no liquidity risk.

7.2   The Liquidity Mismatch Index (LMI)

We next present a theoretical liquidity measure, informed by the academic literature on liquidity, and analyze its benefits in terms of assessing liquidity risk both from a firm and macroprudential perspective.

There are two dates. Date 0 is the ex ante date at which each firm makes risk and liquidity decisions by choosing cash assets and cash liabilities, as well as derivative positions and off-balance sheet positions. Derivative positions may have a market value of 0 at date 0, but are sensitive to the risk factors. At date 1 a state $\omega \in \Omega$ is realized, one of which may be a systemic crisis, depending on what decisions firms have made. We will define a liquidity index for each state as well as a summary liquidity index for date 0.

Firm i chooses assets A^i and liabilities L^i. The assets are a mix of cash, repo lending to other firms, derivative exposure, outright asset purchases, and so forth. Liabilities include short-term debt, long-term debt, secured debt, equity, and others. We also consider hybrid contracts such as credit lines extended, which alter the firm's assets when they are drawn down.

7.2.1   Liquidity Risk Exposure and Cash Liquidity

We determine "liquidity risk exposure" at date 0 in two steps: First, we derive for each state at date 1 the cash-equivalent value of each asset and liability. Second, the liquidity risk measure at date 0 focuses on the, say, 5 percent worst draws of nature. In this sense our $t = 0$ liquidity risk measure follows the same method as standard risk measures like value at risk (VaR) or expected shortfall.

Cash liquidity for a given stress scenario. More specifically, the cash equivalent value in a specific state $\omega \in \Omega$ after nature has moved to realize a particular stress event for the firm is the value of the firm assuming that:

- *Counterparties act most adversely.* That is, parties that have contracts with the firm act to extract as much cash as possible from the firm under the terms of their contracts. This defines the liquidity liability.
- *The firm computes its best course of action*, given the assumed stress event, to raise as much cash against its balance sheet as it can to withstand the cash withdrawals. That is, the firm computes how much cash it can raise from asset sales, preexisting contracts such as credit lines,

and collateralized loans such as repos backed by assets currently held by the firm. The computation assumes that the firm is unable to raise unsecured debt or equity (following, see how to account for access to equity markets at some time in the future). The total cash raised is the liquidity asset.

The net of the liquidity asset and the liquidity liability is the LMI for that state. For each "relevant" state $\omega \in \Omega$ or stress scenario the LMI is calculated. Examples of stress scenarios are: the firm is downgraded, the haircuts on the firm's assets rise, the market for securitized assets turn illiquid, all credit spreads rise, and so forth.

Liquidity risk. The date 0 liquidity risk measure focuses on the worst stress scenarios. If one uses expected shortfall liquidity risk measure then one considers the x, say 5 percent, worst scenarios. Each of the worst scenarios gets the same weight. The value-at-liquidity risk is determined by the scenario that is closest to the x percent worst scenario.

In short, we assume that in each state $\omega \in \Omega$ counterparties take the worst action and the firm finds the best response (defense action) after nature's choice of ω. With regard to the choice of nature we focus on the worst x percent.

Our liquidity measure captures well the liquidity risk of all positions, including derivatives positions. Indeed, our measure is related to the margin dollar amount that McDonald (chapter 5, this volume) and Acharya (chapter 6, this volume) propose. In this sense our liquidity measure provides a unified approach across various asset classes and liabilities.

One attractive feature of our measure is that it can be expressed in terms of dollars like standard risk measures. This has the advantage that it can be aggregated across various institutions in a meaningful way. Note practitioners often use the maximum time an institution can survive without raising new funds in an environment in which counterparties and nature move against them. While this measure is useful for a single institution, it cannot be easily aggregated across institutions.

Before delving into the LMI analysis we provide (a) some examples, (b) details about how cash equivalent liquidity λ-weights are chosen, (c) some guidance as to how relevant stress scenarios ω are picked, and (d) steps on how the date 0 liquidity risk measure is determined.

Here are some examples to ground this definition:

1. If a firm has $100 of risk-free overnight debt, then the cash equivalent of this debt is $100 because the debtor can extract $100 by refusing to roll over the debt. Note that this $100 liquidity liability applies in all states, because the $100 from overnight debt can be extracted in all states of the world.

2. If a firm has a CSA that allows counterparties to extract more cash collateral if the firm is downgraded, then only in the downgrade state is there

a liquidity liability for the firm (equal to the maximum amount of collateral posted, as stipulated by the contract).

3. If a firm has $100 of Treasury securities, then the cash-equivalent value of these securities is $100 because we assume that Treasuries are always liquid.

4. If a firm has $100 of MBS with a repo haircut in a good state of 5 percent and a repo haircut in a bad state of 15 percent, then the cash-equivalent value in the good state is $95, while it is $85 in the bad state.

5. If a bank has written a $100 credit line to another firm that is uncontingent, then the "worst-case" computation means that the credit line is fully drawn down, resulting in a $100 liquidity liability. Now, the best response for the firm may be to take the resulting loan and raise cash against it (in the simplest case with cash from the same bank, or in more complicated cases through loan sales). Suppose that the firm raises $80 of cash against the loan, then the $80 of cash raised is offset against the $100 credit line drawn to give a liquidity mismatch of –$20.

Liquidity weights. The way we implement the LMI is to assign a liquidity weight λ_ω^j to each asset and liability for each state of the world. Assets are indexed with positive j, while liability j takes on a negative value. We normalize super-liquid monetary assets such as bank reserves and Treasuries to have a λ_ω^{money} of one across all states. For something like a mortgage-backed security (MBS), we can imagine measuring λ_ω^{MBS} as one minus the repo haircut on that MBS in state ω. Alternatively, λ_ω^{MBS} could measure the price discount that firm i has to accept if it immediately wanted to convert the asset into cash. The weights λ_ω^j measure the cash-equivalent value of asset j, as just described as the answer to the question, what is the maximum amount of cash that can be raised against a given asset? Aggregating liquidity across the asset side, one obtains firm i's asset liquidity $\Lambda_\omega^{A,i}$ for the different states of the economy. We also measure the liquidity of the liabilities as $\lambda_\omega^j < 0$. Overnight debt has liquidity of -1 in all states. A derivatives contract has a weight $-1 < \lambda_\omega^{DER} < 0$, in the state where the firm is downgraded or loses money on the derivative. The weight here reflects the maximum collateral posted in that state. If the margins/haircuts of a collateralized position can be increased from say 10 percent to 50 percent at the discretion of the financier, then essentially 40 percent of the position is financed by overnight debt. A credit line that is uncontingent has a weight that is the net between the liquidity lost when the line is drawn (weight $= -1$) and the asset liquidity from the loan made (weight > 0). This net number will be negative so that we consider it a liquidity liability. Common equity is $\lambda_\omega^{equity} = 0$ for all states ω. The same applies to long-term debt. Overall, firm i's liquidity position is $\Lambda_\omega^i \equiv \Lambda_\omega^{A,i} - \Lambda_\omega^{L,i}$, which we note is a function of the state ω.

An important consideration that arises with the liquidity weights is how to account for government insurance. For example, is it appropriate to include liquidity that can be obtained from the discount window? How should one handle the fact that government insurance of retail deposits makes such deposits far less run prone? We are interested in a measure of liquidity that can indicate when a systemic crisis is more likely. Since a crisis is an equilibrium outcome of an economy with government insurance, it is appropriate to take measurements that include government insurance. Thus, the best response of a firm accounts for the possibility of borrowing from the discount window. One can imagine a stress scenario in which discount window haircuts doubled, were subject to increased stigma, and so forth. However, the appropriate calculation for the LMI should still assume the existence of the discount window. Second, we assume that retail deposits pose no liability liquidity risk. This latter assumption comes from a great deal of evidence that in a macrostress event, the banking sector receives deposits in a flight to safety (see Gatev and Strahan 2006). Note that pure microliquidity risk considerations may lead one to consider that retail deposits are a liquidity liability, but that is an inappropriate perspective from a systemic risk standpoint.

One further conceptual issue in this computation is the *time* dimension. The LMI can only be defined for some time period. An overnight LMI is a computation that assumes only overnight contracts are not rolled over, and that after that the firm is able to raise equity. A thirty-day LMI is a computation that assumes that all debt maturing in the next thirty days is not rolled over, and that after the thirty days, the firm is able to raise equity to cover further obligations. How should time be handled and what is the relevant time frame for the liquidity measurement? We try to incorporate the time dimension by adjusting the λ-liquidity weights.

For the first question, we proceed as follows. Suppose that having free access to liquidity (e.g., being able to access equity markets) follows a Poisson process. There is a probability θ that the firm is able to raise equity in any given day (in principle θ can be a different number tomorrow, the day after that, etc.). Then, the LMI is based on the expected liquidity outflow going forward. Define the function $f(t,\theta) \in [0,1]$, where $t = 1$ corresponds to "one day" and $t = 30$ is thirty days, as the probability that the firm is unable to access free liquidity by date t. The probability is decreasing in t at a decay rate governed by the parameter θ. All liability contracts with payments due at date t have $\lambda_\omega^{j,t}$ equal to $f(t,\theta)$ times the λ_ω^j for the same contract if its payments were due at date $t = 1$. Thus, thirty-day debt has $\lambda_\omega^{j,30} = -1 \times f(30,\theta)$. This discounting structure has the property that standing at any date $t > 0$ where the firm is still liquidity constrained, the liquidity of a given contract is the same as at date 0.

The next question is how should one choose θ? We turn back to the academic literature. Models such as Diamond and Dybvig (1983) and Gorton and Pennacchi (1990) identify that the financial sector creates liquidity by issuing short-term debt claims. We would like measures to be informative of how much of this liquidity production is being done by the financial sector. The theoretical models imply that the relevant short-term debt carries a liquidity premium. Thus to map the models to practice, we need to identify what maturities of short-term debt carry a sizable liquidity premium. Greenwood, Hanson, and Stein (2010) document that Treasury bills with less than three months to maturity carry a liquidity premium. On average, over a sample from 1990 to 2006, the premium on the one-week bill relative to the six-month bill is 32 basis points. The premium is a nonlinear function of time, rising quickly and hitting about 5 basis points for the three-month bill.

Thus, consider fitting the function $f(t,\theta)$ to the liquidity premium evidence from the Treasury bill market, so that the function is near zero by $t = 90$. Note that the parameter θ can be part of the stress event (i.e., the state ω), so that, in systemic risk states where market measures of liquidity premia at all maturities rise, the measure naturally extends to incorporate more time into the construction of liquidity liabilities. However, the baseline can reflect the average liquidity premium evidence as captured in the Treasury bill market.

The determination of the liquidity weights is also primarily an empirical question. There is a large empirical finance literature on liquidity that can provide some guidance to setting the liquidity weights. For example, this approach will be closest to Krishnamurthy and Vissing-Jorgensen (2010) who measure the liquidity convenience of assets based on bond market spreads. For some security markets, another alternative would be to use repo haircuts. For other assets, bid-ask spreads, price impact measures, or trading volume can be used as guides for the liquidity weights.

However the base case is determined, different liquidity scenarios correspond to different specifications of weights, shocking one or more at a time. Here again, the empirical finance literature can be used to guide the exercise. There is a large literature that documents the time-series variation in liquidity measures such as bond-market spreads and stock market liquidity, as well as the covariances of these measures with aggregate risk factors. These patterns can guide the choice of liquidity scenarios. Consider an ω macro state described by movements in some underlying factors. From historical empirical work, we know the covariance between the factors and the aggregate liquidity measures. Thus, we can consider percentage deviations from the base-case set of liquidity weights based on moves in the aggregate liquidity measures.

Scenarios. The dimensions of the Ω state space that describes a firm's asset, liability, and liquidity positions can be huge. For practical reasons, suppose that liquidity measurements only focus on states s within an S-dimensional factor space, a subspace of Ω. Factors consist of certain prices (risk factors) or liquidity/funding conditions (liquidity factors).

Some examples of a liquidity risk scenario are the following:

- Firms are unable to access the market to raise new cash for one month, three months, and six months.
- Repo haircuts on some asset classes rise.
- The syndicated loan market, or the securitization market, shuts down for some period.

Once again, these are just examples, and the actual scenarios will depend on prevailing economic conditions.

Date 0 liquidity. The previous computations describe Λ_ω^i, that is, in a particular stress event. In practice, it is infeasible to compute a complete state-contingent vector Λ_ω^i. We are also interested in computing a single LMI at date 0 to summarize the liquidity position of the firm.

The following example illustrates our main consideration in defining the date 0 measure. Consider a highly rated firm that engages in an OTC interest rate swap contract that currently requires no collateral to be posted. From a liquidity standpoint, there will be states at date 1 where the firm will lose liquidity, but the firm at date 0 does not lose liquidity. Now consider an exchange-traded futures contract with the same risk profile as the swap contract. In this case, the firm posts collateral at date 0, which results in a loss of liquidity. We describe a measure that ensures that the possibility of the liquidity loss at date 1 in the derivatives case leads to a liquidity liability at date 0 commensurate to the margin posted on the futures contract. This example is similar to the forwards versus futures example we discussed earlier.

We measure the expected liquidity loss in the x percent (e.g., 5 percent) worst case for the derivatives contract. This computation is analogous to the expected shortfall measure common in risk management. Then the liquidity liability at date 0 for the derivative contract is this expected liquidity loss. For each state and asset/liability, we compute this expected liquidity loss. The overall LMI weighs all of these scenarios.

This appears complicated because it requires one to compute each LMI for each scenario. However, note that the LMI computation is linear so that it is equivalent to computing the expected shortfall for each stress separately and then simply aggregating across the stress events.

We denote the liquidity position at date 0 as Λ_0^i For each ω, we can define $\Delta\Lambda_\omega^i \equiv \Lambda_\omega^i - \Lambda_0^i$ as the change in liquidity for that firm due to that particular state or scenario.

7.3 Analyzing the LMI

The LMI measure incorporates the ideas from the academic literature on liquidity. First, it explicitly accounts for asset and liability liquidity, as many papers have emphasized. Second, since liquidity is measured conditional on a given ω macro state, the LMI explicitly accounts for liquidity risk—that is, the possibility that asset and liability liquidity are state dependent. Finally, as we discuss next, the LMI can be aggregated across firms and sectors. This is important for a macroprudential assessment of systemic risk.

Liquidity aggregates. An interbank loan that is a liquid asset for firm i is a drain on liquidity for the borrower, firm j (i.e., negative liquidity weight). Aggregating across firm i and firm j, the interbank loan will net out. Consider the net liquidity index for firm i,

$$\Lambda^i = \Lambda^{A,i} - \Lambda^{L,i}.$$

Again consider the sum,

$$\sum_i^I \Lambda^i.$$

Summed across all sectors, the liquidity aggregate equals the supply of liquid assets: the λ-weighted sum across all relevant liquid assets. The aggregate measures are analogous to Barnett's (1980) Divisia indices for monetary aggregates. Barnett devised indices to weight different components of the money supply based on their usefulness as a transaction medium. The LMI index is similar but is based on both assets and liabilities, and has weights that reflect the financial liquidity of the asset and liability.

The aggregates are most interesting in describing the liquidity position of particular sectors. We may expect to find, for example, that the banking sector always carries a negative liquidity position, as suggested by Gorton and Pennacchi (1990), while the corporate sector or household sector carries a long liquidity position. The extent of liquidity transformation done by the banking sector may also be informative for diagnosing systemic risk. For example, in the period from 2000 to 2008, it is likely that the aggregate LMI grew substantially. However, for systemic risk purposes, what would have been most interesting is a diagnosis that the aggregate growth reflected an increasing mismatch between the banking sector and the other sectors in the economy.

Intermediation chains. Note that the aggregation of liquidity given a specific stress scenario ω only punishes long intermediation chains to the extent that λ-weights of the market liquidity of assets differ from the liability λ-weights. If the weights are symmetric, that is, in the case in which the weight of a loan from firm i (asset for that firm) is equal to the negative of the weight of that loan to firm j (liability for that firm), then aggregation over an intermediation chain is neutral. However, for asymmetric weights intermediation chains lead to a higher liquidity mismatch.

For the date 0 liquidity (risk) measure, total liquidity in the economy shrinks as the intermediation chain lengthens. To see this, consider the stylized case in which two financial institutions only write one derivatives contract on a specific asset. The worst x percent ω-scenarios for one institution are the states in which the underlying asset moves in one direction, while for the other institution the opposite scenarios are the bad scenarios. In other words, both institutions focus on different worst scenarios (and ignore their favorable scenarios). This reduces the aggregated liquidity measure as long as the derivative contract does not hedge other risks. More generally, longer intermediation chains significantly reduce our liquidity measure. This is a desirable property, as it is widely thought that financial fragility is created by the long chains of assets and liabilities that underlie the securitization model (i.e., household mortgage, packaged into MBS, further packaged into CDO, and then serving as collateral for a repo, which may be rehypothecated many times). The aggregate LMI can measure this fragility.

Systemically important institutions. New banking regulations require greater oversight and higher capital requirements for systemically important institutions. One cut at judging who is systemically important is to rank institutions by size of assets. However, this type of ranking suffers from the same shortcomings as relying on balance sheet entries for asset holdings, which we discussed earlier. Economically, it is more meaningful to judge firms in terms of their magnitude of their risk exposures and liquidity exposures. Thus, the LMI index at the firm level can provide guidance on which institutions should be judged systemically important.

7.4   Conclusion

We have described and analyzed the benefits of the LMI, a liquidity metric. Since liquidity plays a central role in systemic crises, the LMI can be informative about systemic risks. Of course, the proof of the pudding will be in its empirical implementation. Early work in this regard appears promising (see Bai, Krishnamurthy, and Weymuller 2013). To close our theoretical discussion, we describe an important challenge in the use of the LMI to analyze systemic risk.

In practice, the liquidity weights λ_ω^j are endogenous to the state. For the purpose of measuring the risks for a firm, it is appropriate to take the λ_ω^j as exogenous; in a similar manner, it is appropriate to take market prices as exogenous when measuring the capital of a bank. However, for macroprudential purposes it is important to understand how λ_ω^j depends on the state. From a conceptual standpoint, we think of the λ_ω^j as akin to "market prices." The behavior of agents in the economy plus market clearing conditions describes the liquidity weights. For example, if the liquidity of assets is dependent on the financial health of a key set of financial intermediaries, then data on how the capital/liquidity of these financial intermediaries depends on the event ω can be useful in endogenizing the liquidity weights. From this standpoint, the LMI data needs to be fed into an economic model that endogenizes liquidity in order to fully describe systemic risk. We discuss the connection between measurement and modeling in Brunnermeier, Gorton, and Krishnamurthy (2012).

References

Allen, Franklin, and Douglas Gale. 2004. "Financial Intermediaries and Markets." *Econometrica* 72:1023–61.
Bai, Jennie, Arvind Krishnamurthy, and Charles-Henri Weymuller. 2013. "Measuring Liquidity Mismatch in the Banking Sector." Working Paper, Northwestern University.
Barnett, William A. 1980. "Economic Monetary Aggregates: An Application of Aggregation and Index Number Theory." *Journal of Econometrics* 14:11–48.
Brunnermeier, Markus, Gary Gorton, and Arvind Krishnamurthy. 2012 "Risk Topography." In *NBER Macroeconomics Annual 2011*, edited by Daron Acemoglu and Michael Woodford. Chicago: University of Chicago Press.
Brunnermeier, Markus, and Lasse Pedersen. 2009. "Market Liquidity and Funding Liquidity." *Review of Financial Studies* 22 (60): 2201–38.
Caballero, Ricardo, and Arvind Krishnamurthy. 2004. "Smoothing Sudden Stops." *Journal of Economic Theory* 119:104–27.
Diamond, Douglas, and Phillip Dybvig. 1983. "Bank Runs, Deposit Insurance, and Liquidity." *Journal of Political Economy* 91:401–19.
Gatev, Evan, and Philip Strahan. 2006. "Banks' Advantage in Hedging Liquidity Risk: Theory and Evidence from the Commercial Paper Market." *Journal of Finance* 61 (2): 867–92.
Gorton, Gary, and George Pennacchi. 1990. "Financial Intermediaries and Liquidity Creation." *Journal of Finance* 45 (1): 49–71.
Greenwood, Robin, Sam Hanson, and Jeremy Stein. 2010. "A Comparative Advantage Approach to Government Debt Maturity." Working Paper, Harvard University.
Holmström, Bengt, and Jean Tirole. 1998. "Private and Public Supply of Liquidity." *Journal of Political Economy* 106 (1): 1–40.
Krishnamurthy, Arvind, and Annette Vissing-Jorgensen. 2010. "The Aggregate Demand for Treasury Debt." Working Paper, Northwestern University.

Monitoring Leverage

John Geanakoplos and Lasse Heje Pedersen

8.1 Introduction

Systemic crises tend to erupt when highly leveraged financial institutions are forced to deleverage, sending the economy into recession; leverage is a central element of economic cycles and systemic risk. While traditionally the interest rate has been regarded as the single key feature of a loan, we argue that leverage is in fact a more important measure of systemic risk. We discuss how leverage can be monitored for assets, institutions, and individuals, and highlight the benefits of monitoring leverage. Our main conclusions are as follows:

- Monitoring leverage is "easy." Leverage at the asset level can be monitored by recording margin requirements, or, equivalently, loan-to-value ratios. This provides a model-free measure that can be directly observed, in contrast to other measures of systemic risk that require complex estimation.
- Monitoring leverage is monitoring systemic risk. Monitoring leverage provides information about how risk builds up during booms as

John Geanakoplos is the James Tobin Professor of Economics at Yale University, an external professor and member of the steering committee of the Santa Fe Institute, and a partner of Ellington Capital Management. Lasse Heje Pedersen is the John A. Paulson Professor of Finance and Alternative Investments at the Stern School of Business at New York University, professor in the Department of Finance and the Center for Financial Frictions (FRIC) at Copenhagen Business School, a research affiliate of the Centre for Economic Policy Research (CEPR), a principal at AQR Capital Management, and a research associate of the National Bureau of Economic Research.

We thank participants in the NBER systemic risk conference for helpful comments and suggestions. For acknowledgments, sources of research support, and disclosure of the authors' material financial relationships, if any, please see http://www.nber.org/chapters/c12549.ack.

leverage rises, and how crises start when leverage on new loans sharply declines.

- Monitoring leverage facilitates liquidity crisis management. Leverage data is a crucial input for crisis management and lending facilities, and for ascertaining the state of an indebted economy in the aftermath of a leverage crisis.
- Monitoring new versus old leverage is important. The leverage on new loans is a more timely measure of credit conditions and the beginning of a systemic crisis than the average leverage, but the average leverage signals the economy's vulnerability. The economy enters a crisis when leverage on new loans is low, and leverage on old loans is high, a deleveraging event that starts a liquidity spiral.

To understand the broad applications of these ideas, note that most loans are secured by some sort of collateral that can be confiscated by the lender in case of default. A house is a prime example of collateral. For example, a home owner may use a $100,000 house to collateralize borrowing $80,000. In this case, we say that the margin requirement (or down payment, or haircut) is 20 percent, the loan-to-value (LTV) ratio is 80 percent, and the leverage is 5 to 1. These ratios are all different ways of saying the same thing. These leverage numbers on individual loans and collateral are the building blocks out of which aggregate measures of asset leverage, institutional leverage, and household leverage can be most accurately and informatively constructed.

Before the crisis of 2007 to 2009, there had been absolutely no comprehensive monitoring of leverage aside from aggregate debt-equity ratios in a few markets. In particular, no effort had been made by the government to keep track of leverage ratios at the individual asset level. Though it would be a radical departure from past practice, our chapter discusses the potential benefits of collecting such data. Just as the Fed started collecting Treasury yields in the early twentieth century and other agencies started collecting macrodata for the national accounts, some government agency could begin to systematically collect leverage data at the level of individual loans backed by assets (such as houses and cars) and by securities (such as mortgages and mortgage derivatives in the repo market). Such leverage data would be very valuable input in monitoring and managing systemic risk.

For some agents, like designated financial entities, noncollateralized debt information could also be collected. All this individual loan data could then be aggregated up to give the leverage of financial institutions like banks, hedge funds, nonfinancial firms, the household sector in different geographical regions, and the government. Aggregated in different ways, the data could provide the average leverage on various assets and security types. The data could also be used to improve the flow of funds reports that the government currently releases.

We have a number of suggestions regarding data collection. We discuss how to collect leverage data for (a) real estate, (b) durable goods, (c) cash financial securities such as bonds, (d) exchange-traded derivatives such as futures, (e) over-the-counter derivatives such as interest-rate swaps and currency forwards, and (f) collateralized default swaps and other securities with asymmetric payoffs. To properly monitor leverage it is imperative to distinguish three numbers: leverage at origination on extant old loans, leverage offered on new loans, and current leverage on extant loans updated to reflect current collateral values and amortization of loan amounts. Current leverage on all existing loans is a barometer of vulnerability, while leverage on new loans is a barometer of current credit conditions. To see that, note that the current average loan-to-value ratio across all loans on assets of a particular kind (e.g., houses) signals how vulnerable the system is to shocks because this is the total debt that needs to be serviced relative to the aggregate equity (provided that the collateral value is measured at current market prices). For this purpose one should measure the aggregate loan-to-value ratio by taking the ratio of all outstanding loans on some asset class to the current value of all assets in that class, thus including in the composite number assets on which there is no borrowing. Similarly, the current average leverage of institutions and households measures the vulnerability in those sectors. These leverage numbers depend mostly on old loans and current asset values. The loan-to-value ratio on new loans has a small effect on the current leverage of all loans (since a flow only gradually affects the stock).

However, it is important to monitor the leverage on new loans since this reflects current credit conditions. As prices decline and lenders get more nervous and tighten credit, leverage on old loans will increase (because of dropping asset values) while leverage on new loans plummets (because of deteriorating credit conditions). Leverage on old loans and leverage on new loans thus often go in opposite directions. For example, Reinhart and Rogoff (2009) show that, on average, deleveraging begins two years after a crisis and lasts for many years. But they measure total debt/equity or debt/income, which is mostly leverage on old loans. If they had measured leverage on new loans, they would have found that new leverage falls just before the crisis; deleveraging is a key element of the crisis, not a lagged effect. Leverage on new loans reveals much more quickly the state of the economy. Of course leverage offered on new loans was not being monitored, so they could not have presented such data even if they had wanted to.

Leverage data on individual loans backed by individual collateral must also be properly aggregated and presented. Average (or median) leverage is one important statistic, but sometimes the distribution of leverage is also important. Obviously an economy is much more vulnerable if half the mortgage loans are at 100 percent LTV and half are at 0 percent LTV than if they are all at 50 percent LTV. Similarly, it is important to keep track of the distribution of leverage across buyers. For example, most home owners own one house. Many own two. Some own three or four or more, all bought by loans.

A sharp increase in the number of individuals with multiple loans on different houses would be an important signal of the rise of speculative buying.

An important advantage to collecting leverage data is that the investment community, as well as regulators, will find it extremely useful:

- An investor who learns that the other buyers are highly leveraged will understand that the market is more dangerous for him.
- Investors who leverage their way to profits will be exposed.
- Lending markets will be rendered more competitive.
- Regulators will be able to monitor the economic cycle and see early warning signals of rising systemic risk due to high levels of leverage.
- Central banks need leverage data to manage a liquidity crisis, including to set haircuts on the collateral they receive when they act as lenders of last resort.

The funding markets are opaque over-the-counter markets and, therefore, a governmental agency might need to use its authority if it were to collect this data. We discuss ways the data can be collected and published while imposing minimal revelation of proprietary information belonging to financial institutions; for example, by focusing on aggregated data from multiple institutions and delayed publication. Maintaining the enthusiastic support of the business community is crucial to this data collection program. The data must be kept secure, so that proprietary information is not leaked. And the collection process must be streamlined and coordinated so that financial firms do not feel they are spending half their time filling out questionnaires.

Further, we note that to ascertain an institution's true leverage, one must account for derivatives and off-balance sheet items in a meaningful way. Further, one must always include purchases made entirely by cash as "zero leverage loans," since such loans also provide information about leverage. Indeed, pure cash financing sometimes signals the extreme form of deleveraging where no credit is available for that collateral.

A solid theoretical foundation for the importance of leverage is emerging in the literature, though much more research is likely to follow as leverage data becomes available. Borrowing constraints can have significant effects on the real economy (Bernanke and Gertler 1989; Geanakoplos 1997; Holmstrom and Tirole 1997; Kiyotaki and Moore 1997), and bad news coupled with increased uncertainty can cause leverage and asset prices to plunge in a leverage cycle (Geanakoplos 2003, 2010a, b). Shocks to agent's funding conditions can also start liquidity spirals of deteriorating market liquidity, funding liquidity, and prices with spillover effects across markets (Fostel and Geanakoplos 2008; Brunnermeier and Pedersen 2009; and Pedersen 2009) and, just like the risk of a traditional bank run leads to multiple equilibria (Diamond and Dybvig 1983), so does the risk of a "collateral run" of increased margin requirements (Brunnermeier and Pedersen 2009). Leverage can rise to inefficient levels during booms (Lorenzoni 2008), while a clear piece of evidence that investors' leverage constraints become binding during crisis is that agents flee to assets that are more easily usable as collateral, causing, for example, violations in the law of one price (Fostel and Geanakoplos 2008; and Garleanu and Pedersen 2011). Theory and empirical evidence show that central banks' lending facilities alleviate leverage constraints during crisis (Ashcraft, Garleanu, and Pedersen 2010; Geanakoplos 2010b). Indeed, leverage/haircuts can be an important second monetary tool, complementing the traditional interest-rate tool (Ashcraft, Garleanu, and Pedersen 2010; Geanakoplos 2010a, b). Also, leverage effects can explain many features of emerging market economies, including issuance rationing (Fostel and Geanakoplos 2008). Investors' demand for leverage significantly affects the cross section of asset prices in equity, bond, and credit markets (Frazzini and Pedersen 2011) and creates a demand for securities designed to embed leverage (Frazzini and Pedersen 2012).

Margin requirements and down payments are not just abstract terms in our models. They are negotiated every day in a variety of markets. The data we discuss gathering exists. And it can be reported by two different and independent entities, the borrower and the lender. One just needs to collect it! It does not require model-based estimation (unlike many other systemic risk measures).

The chapter is organized as follows. Section 8.2 reviews the basic theory of leverage and macroeconomics, section 8.3 discusses how to monitor leverage in practice, and section 8.4 concludes.

8.2   Understanding Leverage and the Macroeconomy

8.2.1   Determinants of Leverage and Margin Requirements

Leverage tends to rise when there is substantial heterogeneity in outlook or risk tolerance in the population, when the volatility of the underlying asset prices is low, when liquidity is good so that seized assets can be quickly sold, when leverage can be hidden or disguised, when regulators relax their vigilance, when loans are guaranteed by third parties like the government, and when interest rates are low enough to induce investors to reach for yield.

Lower down payments allow new buyers to enter the market who previously could not raise enough cash to purchase (assuming a minimal indivisibility of the asset), and they allow existing buyers to buy more. When the asset supply is inelastic, because production is difficult or takes time, when short selling is difficult, and when there is substantial heterogeneity in the willingness of the population to pay for the assets, increases in leverage will lead to a change in the marginal buyer and therefore to an increase in the asset price.

Increased leverage makes asset owners more vulnerable, especially if the loans are short term, or subject to margin calls. Bad news for the asset lowers its price, and the highly leveraged owners might be forced to sell to meet margin calls just when they might desire to be even bigger buyers. Moreover, the losses from the asset declines fall disproportionately on the leveraged buyers, redistributing wealth away from those who value the assets the most to those who value them least. Often the bad news comes with increased volatility of economic fundamentals and the very vulnerability of the buyers creates more uncertainty. This leads lenders to demand more collateral, forcing deleveraging and more asset sales, and thus further price declines and a downward spiral.

In the crisis stage of the leverage cycle there tend to be many defaults, which are messy in and of themselves. Further, defaults often lead to chain reactions when borrowers are also lenders, and also to contagion when there are crossover investors between assets. Finally, the aftermath of the crisis can be marked by a long period when many agents are under water, or close to insolvent, and thus unable to borrow and unwilling to make productive investments.

Every stage of the leverage cycle can be monitored. We illustrate the subprime leverage buildup and crash in the housing market and the securities market in figures 8.1 and 8.2 (which are based on data from Ellington; see

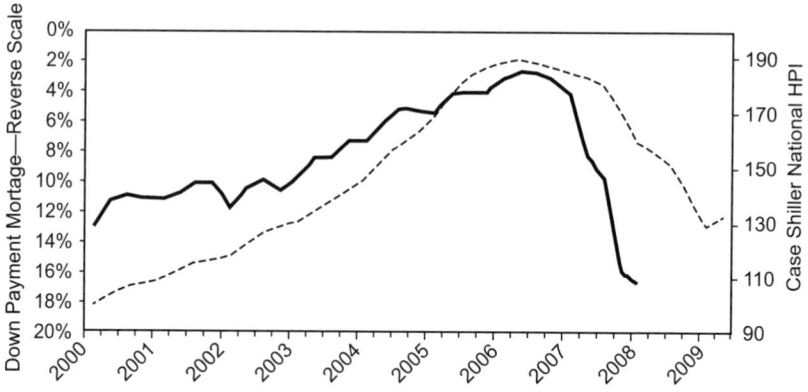

— Avg Down Payment for 50% Lowest Down Payment Subprime/AltA Borrowers

-- Case Shiller National Home Price Index (right axis)

Fig. 8.1   Housing leverage cycle

Notes: Margins offered (down payments required) and housing prices. Observe that the down payment axis has been reversed, because lower down payment requirements are correlated with higher home prices. For every AltA or subprime loan originated from Q1 2000 to Q1 2008, down payment percentage was calculated as appraised value (or sale price if available) minus total mortgage debt, divided by appraised value. For each quarter, the down payment percentages were ranked from highest to lowest, and the average of the bottom half of the list is shown in the diagram. This number is an indicator of down payment required: clearly many home owners put down more than they had to, and that is why the top half is dropped from the average. A 13 percent down payment in Q1 2000 corresponds to leverage of about 7.7-to-1, and a 2.7 percent down payment in Q2 2006 corresponds to leverage of about 37-to-1. Subprime/AltA issuance stopped in Q1 2008.

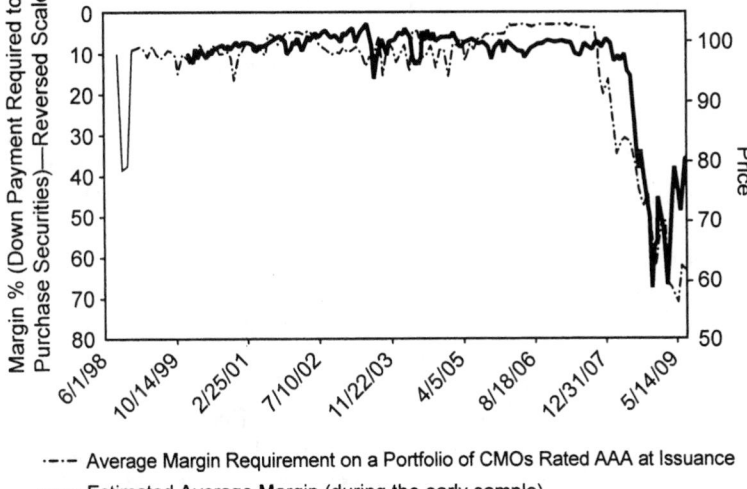

·—·— Average Margin Requirement on a Portfolio of CMOs Rated AAA at Issuance
———— Estimated Average Margin (during the early sample)
━━━━ Prime Fixed Prices (right axis)

Fig. 8.2   Securities leverage cycle

Notes: Margins offered and AAA securities prices. The chart represents the average margin required by dealers on a hypothetical portfolio of bonds subject to adjustments noted. Observe that the "Margin %" axis has been reversed, since lower margins are correlated with higher prices. The portfolio evolved over time, and changes in average margin reflect changes in composition as well as changes in margins of particular securities. In the period following August 2008, a substantial part of the increase in margins is due to bonds that could no longer be used as collateral after being downgraded, or for other reasons, and hence count as 100 percent margin.

also Geanakoplos [2010]). Had the Federal Reserve or other regulatory bodies been aware of these numbers, they may have considered more policy options before the crisis, and been in a better position to act during and after the crisis. We next discuss how leverage builds up during good economic times, how crisis can be detected and managed, and how to handle the aftermath of a crisis.

8.2.2   The Buildup of Systemic Risk

Investor leverage is central to the vulnerability of the system. A ten times leveraged institution loses ten times as much of its capital when asset values fall as an unleveraged institution holding the same type of assets; indeed, this is the origin of the word leverage. Furthermore, a shock to prices might force a highly leveraged firm to sell to meet margin calls, locking in losses and further depressing the asset price, just when the firm thinks the assets are most undervalued, whereas an unleveraged firm could hold onto its position. When the leveraged institutions are playing a central intermediation function, the losses are far more dangerous than losses to dispersed unleveraged investors. As a case in point, the spillover effects during the recent global financial crisis were far more severe than those around the burst of the Internet bubble.

The upshot is that to monitor the vulnerability of the financial system and the growth of potential bubbles, one should keep track of the distribution of asset leverage, the distribution of investor leverage (especially in the high tail), the concentration of buyers, and the prices and volatility of the underlying assets. If the loans of the leveraged buyers are guaranteed by the government or some other agency, then monitoring is still more important, because the lenders will not be vigilant.

While asset pricing bubbles are notoriously difficult to identify in real time, it is useful to recognize that they are often fueled via leveraged investments by a limited group of optimistic agents (or agents believing they can sell to greater optimists). Thus data on the distribution of leverage and haircuts on new loans, juxtaposed with data on prices and volatility (especially downward volatility), would provide an indication of emerging credit bubbles. The evolution of margins across asset classes provides indications of risk-taking behavior in different market segments. Rising prices, rising leverage, the concentration of assets in the hands of fewer or different buyers, and the absence of episodes of asset price declines are together a signal suggestive of a bubble. If the prevailing haircut is not large enough to cover a price drop equal in size to a recent price run-up, then the market is heading into dangerously leveraged territory prone to bubbles. What can go up can come down, and bubbles often arise when lenders forget this.

The publication of aggregate data on leverage can thus help reveal systemic risk, but it has other benefits as well. Once market participants recognize that a recent rise in prices is more likely a leveraged-fueled bubble than a strengthening of fundamentals, they may take precautionary risk management measures, which in turn might change market dynamics. Further, public data on investor leverage will also reveal that some investors are making money primarily through leverage, and not through astute investments. Finally, leverage data might also make the lending markets less opaque and more competitive.

8.2.3   Crisis Detection

According to the leverage theory, large price declines and reductions in market liquidity are often accompanied by, or anticipated by, rising margin requirements for new loans. This is evident in both the housing leverage cycle and the securities leverage cycle as illustrated by the two graphs of home owner leverage and repo leverage previously shown. The crisis can thus sometimes be identified early if the data shows that margin requirements are suddenly increasing.

There are several reasons that rising margin requirements may signal a crisis: First, more uncertainty makes nervous lenders ask for more collateral, and these lenders may be aware of impending problems before prices collapse (partly because an increase in uncertainty does not directly reduce the expected payoff). Second, margin requirements may partly reflect the lenders' own funding conditions (and risk tolerance), so rising margins could be the beginning of a tightening credit environment. Third, increasing margin requirements may endogenously start a downward liquidity spiral, leading to forced sales, falling prices, and increasing liquidity risk. For detection purposes, it is crucial to have frequent margin requirement data on new loans at a granular level and to keep track of volatility.

8.2.4   Crisis Management

From at least the time of Irving Fisher in the early 1900s, it has been commonly supposed that the interest rate is the most important variable in the economy. When the economy slows, the public clamors for lower rates, and the Fed usually obliges. In this latest crisis, the Fed has been pumping out billions of dollars in bank loans and, in December 2008, the Fed lowered the fed funds rate to zero. But sometimes in crises, leverage and margin requirements are more important. Said simply, for many investors and individuals, it becomes a question of getting a loan, not the loan's interest rate. Hence, leverage/haircuts is a very important second monetary tool to manage liquidity crisis as well as limiting the risk buildup before the crisis.

A liquidity crisis can be managed by reversing the three main causes of the price collapse and the drop in market and funding liquidity:

1. Reducing the uncertainty that paralyzes lenders and investors. The growing uncertainty during the crisis is partly caused by doubts about who is solvent; if investor leverage for important financial entities were accurately reported, these doubts would be much reduced.

2. Injecting equity. Part of the collapse of asset prices stems from the loss of wealth of the most optimistic buyers. The government could counter this by injecting equity directly into these firms or into the market as a buyer; but it cannot know the scale of the necessary injections without knowing how much wealth was lost and how much these optimists were buying.

3. Stemming the rising margin requirements and deteriorating credit environment. During a crisis, required down payments (or margin requirements) drastically rise. A central bank can counter this by lending directly to investors on margins below what the market is offering (rather than at interest rates below what the market is offering) as exemplified by the lending facilities during the recent crisis. (For theory and evidence of the effect of this monetary tool, see Ashcraft, Garleanu, and Pedersen 2010, and for a discussion about how to manage such facilities see Geanakoplos 2010b.) This helpful method of crisis management can be facilitated far more easily and more prudently with a clear record of what margins had been and what they became. Indeed, central banks need to impose haircuts that are large enough to provide adequate protection to the central bank and low enough

to address the funding crisis. To find this reasonable level of haircuts, data on market haircut practices are essential.

8.2.5   Managing the Aftermath of a Crisis

After bad systemic crises, many investors and households find themselves underwater or close to it. Those agents will not take costly investments to increase value. A home owner who is well underwater will not spend $20,000 to increase the value of his house by $50,000 if he thinks he will lose the house in foreclosure at some point anyway. And even if he did want to undertake the investment, nobody would lend him the money to do it. If he is slightly underwater, but nonetheless endeavors to make his mortgage payments to avoid default, then he will not be able to move to take a job in a different state, unless he defaults after all.

To get a handle on how serious these kinds of problems are, for businesses as well as home owners, it is again essential to monitor current leverage at current market values. Here appraisals and home price indexes at the zip code level are helpful.

8.3   How to Monitor Leverage in Practice

8.3.1   Asset Leverage: Margin Requirements and Haircuts

A new data set on asset leverage across a wide spectrum of assets would be of tremendous usefulness, we believe. In particular, asset leverage could be measured in the main asset classes as follows:

1. For real estate, leverage can be monitored by collecting data on down payments or LTV ratios. Indeed, the down payment on a house is the flip side of leverage as it is the capital provided by the owner of the house.

2. Similarly, for cars and other durable goods, down payments data can be collected.

3. For cash financial securities such as bonds, leverage is measured as the margin requirement or haircut on a collateralized loan such as a repo contract.

4. For exchange-traded derivatives such as futures, the futures exchanges charge margin requirements and it would be helpful to consolidate this margin data for all the major exchanges and keep track of how they evolve over time.

5. For over-the-counter derivatives margin requirements are more difficult to collect, especially for exotic bespoke products, but it should be feasible to collect margin requirements for the large markets for standardized products such as interest-rate swaps and currency forwards.

6. For collateralized default swaps (CDS) one can again get haircut data. The party that writes the insurance is in effect in the position of an owner of the asset (losing value if it goes down), and so the CDS margin can be

recast in exactly the same terms as the leveraged purchase of the asset. When margin requirements are different for long and short positions, as they are in CDS, both these margins should be collected.

In addition to keeping the history of origination leverage for all the above-mentioned assets each time a loan is taken, leverage on outstanding loans must be regularly updated to reflect changes in the underlying collateral values and amortization of the loan amounts.

It is also important to keep track of which assets are being borrowed against and which are not. If certain securities are suddenly not accepted as collateral, no loans with these assets will be recorded. In this case, the margin requirement is effectively 100 percent and this is useful information about the credit environment. Only considering assets that are actively being used as collateral is a selection bias. In figure 8.3, we compute the average margin requirement in two ways (based on data from Ellington): one by giving the average leverage on a portfolio of loans backed by assets that could still be used for repo loans, and another average computed by including assets that could no longer be used to obtain repo loans. The difference is large.

To collect asset leverage data, it is useful to ask both lenders and borrowers to report the margin requirement as well as other terms like interest rate and maturity. Having both borrowers and lenders report the loan terms makes it easier to verify the accuracy of the data and makes it more difficult for market participants to misreport this data. Monitoring asset leverage also has the advantage in that it may be less subject to political pressure.

Once margins or LTVs are collected at the level of all individual collateralized loans, they must be aggregated. To get the average loan to value on

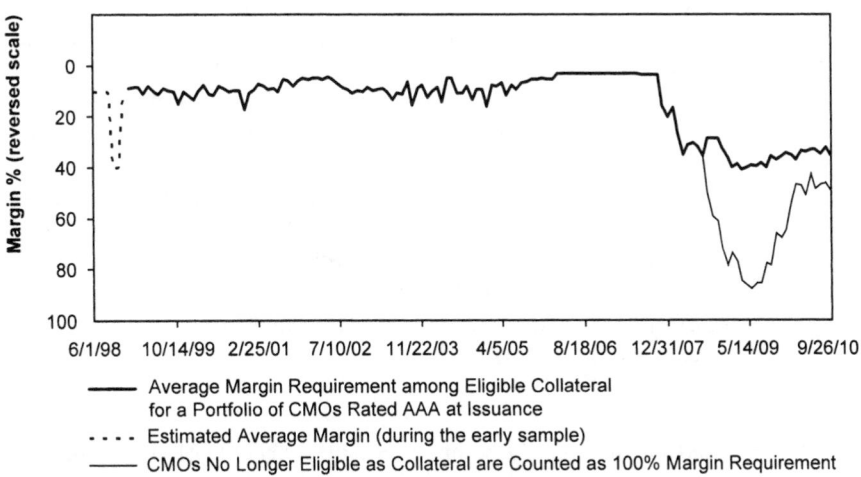

Fig. 8.3   **Leverage (LTV) taking account of assets no longer allowed on repo**

an asset, one can simply add up the total value of the asset in everybody's hands, and then divide that into the total size of all the loans using that asset as collateral. It will usually be more informative to get the distribution of LTV. For example, one might look only at the instances of the asset that were leveraged in the top decile, and then find the aggregate LTV ratio for that group. In the home owner leverage data presented in figure 8.1, homes were ranked according to how much their purchase was leveraged, and then the average LTV ratio was computed for the top half.

At present, both the Treasury and the Fed have initiated programs to collect leverage data. But to the best of our knowledge, these are proceeding via questionnaires sent to both lenders and borrowers including questions like, What is the average LTV ratio you have taken out on the mortgage securities you currently hold? While useful to be sure, this kind of question does not go nearly far enough, and in fact can mislead. The question does not get at loan-level information. It lumps loans of different kinds together. It makes it impossible to cross-check answers between borrower and lender on the same loan. It does not distinguish between repo margins negotiated three months ago (but still held today) from the repo margins being negotiated on new loans. It does not reveal the quantity of loans taken out, and is therefore of no help in computing the investor leverage of the institution, or in aggregating different margins across different lenders and borrowers. And, it falls prey to the selection bias by ignoring the possibility that the borrower drops loans when their margins get tighter and substitutes other higher-leveraged loans.

8.3.2   Leverage of Institutions and Individuals

It is also useful to continue and to improve the collection of data on the leverage of financial institutions and individuals. The advantage of borrower-level leverage data is that it is ultimately each borrower's ability to repay the loans that determine whether default occurs and financial crisis unfolds. For instance, even if a financial institution holds certain assets at a high LTV ratio, this may not create much risk if the firm simultaneously holds large cash reserves. In short, investor leverage needs to be kept as well as asset leverage.

However, it is worth noting that measuring the overall leverage of a complex financial institution can be difficult and is subject to accounting decisions and can be affected by moving things off the balance sheet, and so forth. Another issue is that overall borrower leverage does not distinguish the leverage of old loans from new loans and thus may not be a timely indicator of increase risk of a crisis.

8.3.3   Public Data

We believe that there could be many potential benefits of providing an extensive public data set of leverage. First, making leverage data public makes the agency that collects the data accountable and researchers and market participants can independently test if the data appears correct. Second, if each market participant can see that the overall leverage in the system is rising to unsustainable levels, then the market participant can start reducing his own leverage before the problem grows too large. Third, a greater transparency can possibly make funding markets more efficient. Fourth, firms that make large profits simply because they leverage more than others will be exposed, even in good times. Fifth, a public leverage data set will likely spur lots of new research that can further our understanding of how systemic risk arises and can be contained.

To achieve these benefits, it would be very useful to publish an easily accessible panel data set of margin requirement for each asset and time period. For instance, one data point would be that the median margin requirement for new loans with AAA corporate bond collateral made in June 2011 was X percent, where X is the number to be collected. The data set would have these margin requirement numbers for AAA corporate bonds for each month, as well as margin requirements for each of the other assets. In addition to the median (or average) margin requirements, it would be interesting to provide data on the dispersion of margin requirements (e.g., the interquartile range).

Similarly, it would be useful to provide aggregate data on the leverage of each borrower type, ranging from individuals, banks, and so on. For designated financial institutions, we believe it would be useful to publish firm-level leverage numbers.

Despite these advantages of public leverage data, certain market participants may have an interest in keeping funding markets opaque for several reasons. Leverage data may be proprietary, and the lender and borrower's interest could be respected when appropriate by keeping the public data anonymous by only making aggregate averages public, not loan-level data, and possibly by releasing the data with a time lag (though regulators should observe the data in real time). Also, an increased transparency may increase competition among lenders, but this is no reason not to release leverage data publicly.

There is much precedent for making economic data publicly available. Central banks have been collecting data on Treasury yields for a century and already monitor banks, and macrodata is being collected in the national accounts by the Bureau of Labor Statistics and others. Recently, the TRACE data introduced posttrade transparency for over-the-counter corporate bond trades, reducing transaction costs.

To understand how leverage evolves in a historical perspective, and to test the effects of leverage expansions and contractions, it would be helpful to have a data set of historical leverage at the asset level and at the borrower level. While this is surely not an easy task, perhaps it is possible with detective work in finding data sets and piecing them together.

8.4   Conclusion

Traditionally regulators, central banks, and researchers have focused on interest rates, not leverage. This is akin to controlling car safely by regulating gasoline prices without monitoring how fast people drive. Risk rises when everyone starts driving faster, and a crisis may start when someone gets scared and starts hitting the brakes on a crowded highway where speeding drivers keep little distance.

Systemic crises often arise when a highly leveraged financial system is hit by a shock that starts a downward spiral of deleveraging, forced selling, dropping prices, and economic contraction. While the global financial crisis of 2008 to 2009 is the most recent case in point, history contains a long list of prior examples such as the Great Depression and the S&L crisis. A central aspect in these crises is the extent to which leverage built up before the crisis, how leverage dropped during the crisis, and the central bank's ability to facilitate its role as lender of last resort. Monitoring leverage is therefore necessary to control how risk builds up, to detect early signs of crisis, and to manage an evolving crisis.

Leverage and margin requirements play a key role in models of financial frictions in finance economics, general equilibrium economics, macroeconomics, and monetary economics. To apply these models in mitigating systemic risk, leverage must be monitored. However, monitoring leverage does not rely on these models; leverage is a fundamental measure of systemic risk that is model free. Monitoring leverage is simply a matter of collecting the data. As the availability of leverage data grows, much new research will unquestionably follow.

References

Ashcraft, A., N. Garleanu, and L. H. Pedersen. 2010. "Two Monetary Tools: Interest Rates and Haircuts." In *NBER Macroeconomics Annual 2010*, vol. 25, edited by Daron Acemoglu and Michael Woodford, 143–80. Chicago: University of Chicago Press.
Bernanke, B., and M. Gertler. 1989. "Agency Costs, Net Worth, and Business Fluctuations." *American Economic Review* 79 (1): 14–31.
Brunnermeier, M., and L. H. Pedersen. 2009. "Market Liquidity and Funding Liquidity." *Review of Financial Studies* 22:2201–38.
Diamond, D., and P. Dybvig. 1983. "Bank Runs, Deposit Insurance, and Liquidity." Journal of Political Economy 91 (3): 401–19.
Fostel, A., and J. Geanakoplos. 2008. "Leverage Cycles and the Anxious Economy." *American Economic Review* 98 (4): 1211–44.
Frazzini, A., and L. H. Pedersen. 2011. "Betting Against Beta." Working Paper, New York University.
———. 2012. "Embedded Leverage." Working Paper, New York University.

Garleanu, N., and L. H. Pedersen. 2011. "Margin-Based Asset Pricing and Deviations from the Law of One Price." *Review of Financial Studies* 24 (6): 1980–2022.

Geanakoplos, J. 1997. "Promises, Promises." In *The Economy as an Evolving Complex System II*, edited by W. B. Arthur, S. N. Durlauf, and D. A. Lane, 285–320. Reading, MA: Addison Wesley Longman.

———. 2003. "Liquidity, Default, and Crashes: Endogenous Contracts in General Equilibrium." In *Advances in Economics and Econometrics: Theory and Applications, Eighth World Congress 2000*, Vol. II, Econometric Society Monographs, 170–205. Cambridge: Cambridge University Press.

———. 2010a. "The Leverage Cycle." In *NBER Macroeconomics Annual 2009*, vol. 24, edited by D. Acemoglu, K. Rogoff, and M. Woodford, 1–65. Chicago: University of Chicago Press.

———. 2010b. "Solving the Present Crisis and Managing the Leverage Cycle." *Federal Reserve Bank of New York Economic Policy Review* August: 101–35.

Holmstrom, B., and J. Tirole. 1997. "Financial Intermediation, Loanable Funds, and the Real Sector." *Quarterly Journal of Economics* 112 (1): 35–52.

Kiyotaki, N., and J. Moore. 1997. "Credit Cycles." *Journal of Political Economy* 105 (2): 211–48.

Lorenzoni, G. 2008. "Inefficient Credit Booms." *Review of Economic Studies* 75 (3): 809–33.

Pedersen, L. H. 2009. "When Everyone Runs for the Exit." *International Journal of Central Banking* 5: 177–99.

Reinhart, C., and K. Rogoff. 2009. *This Time is Different*. Princeton, NJ: Princeton University Press.

IV

Financial Intermediation and Credit

Repo and Securities Lending

Tobias Adrian, Brian Begalle, Adam Copeland, and Antoine Martin

9.1 Introduction

The markets for repurchase agreements (repos) and securities lending (sec lending) are part of the collateralized US-dollar-denominated money markets. The markets for repos and sec lending are crucial for the trading of fixed-income securities and equities.[1] Repos are especially important for allowing arbitrage in the Treasury, agency, and agency mortgage-backed securities markets, thus enhancing price discovery and market liquidity. Securities lending markets play key roles in allowing shorting, both in fixed-income and equity markets. Given the essential role of these markets to the functioning and efficiency of the financial system, it is important to better understand and monitor repo and sec lending.

Tobias Adrian is a senior vice president and the head of the Capital Markets Function at the Federal Reserve Bank of New York. Brian Begalle is an assistant vice president at the Federal Reserve Bank of New York. Adam Copeland is a senior economist in the Money and Payments Studies Function at the Federal Reserve Bank of New York. Antoine Martin is a vice president and the head of the Money and Payments Studies Function at the Federal Reserve Bank of New York.

The authors thank Markus Brunnermeier, Michael Fleming, Ken Garbade, Frank Keane, Jamie McAndrews, and Arvind Krishnamurthy for constructive comments on earlier versions of this chapter. The views expressed in this chapter are those of the authors and do not necessarily reflect those of the Federal Reserve Bank of New York or the Federal Reserve System. For acknowledgments, sources of research support, and disclosure of the authors' material financial relationships, if any, please see http://www.nber.org/chapters/c12515.ack.

1. Krishnamurthy, Nagel, and Orlov (2012) offer a detailed comparison of these collateralized money markets. See Covitz, Liang, and Suarez (2013) for an excellent overview of the market for asset-backed commercial paper, which constitutes another important secured money market.

- The key question addressed in this chapter is, what are the data requirements for monitoring repo and sec lending markets so as to inform
policymakers and researchers about firm-level and systemic risk?
- One conclusion emerging from the chapter is the need to better understand the institutional arrangements in these markets.
- To that end, we find that existing data sources are incomplete. More
comprehensive data collection would both deepen our understanding
of the repo and sec lending markets and facilitate monitoring firm-level
and systemic risk in these markets.
- Specifically, we argue that, at a minimum, six shared characteristics
of repo and sec lending trades would need to be collected at the firm
level: (a) principal amount, (b) interest rate (or lending fee for certain
securities loan transactions), (c) collateral type, (d) haircut, (e) tenor,
and (f) counterparty.
- In addition, we believe there would be value in collecting data at the firm
level on the instruments in which securities lending cash collateral are
invested. The reinvestment of cash collateral as practiced by securities
lending agents potentially introduces a source of risk in addition to the
"run" risk that also exists in repo markets.

These data would create a complete picture of the repo and sec lending
trades in the market, allowing for a deeper understanding of the institutional
arrangements in these markets and for accurate measurement of firm-level
risk. Further, these data would allow for measures of the interconnectedness
of the repo and sec lending markets, which would allow for better gauges
of the systemic risk in these markets. The involvements of custodians, sec
lending agents, and tri-party repo banks contribute to the riskiness of each
transaction.

9.2   Background on Repurchase Agreements and Securities Lending

A repurchase agreement is the sale of securities coupled with an agreement to repurchase the securities, at a specified price, at a later date (see
Duffie 1996; Garbade 2006). Securities lending agreements are economically
similar to repo agreements.[2] Both agreements resemble a collateralized loan,
but their treatment under the US bankruptcy law is more beneficial to cash
lenders: In the event of bankruptcy, cash lenders can typically sell their collateral, rather than be subject to an automatic stay as would be the case for
a collateralized loan.

A repo or sec lending trade consists of six key variables: the size of the

---

2. For a detailed comparison of repo and sec lending agreements from a legal perspective,
see Ruchin (2011). In practice, repos are used more often to finance fixed-income securities,
while securities lending is used more often to obtain equities.

transaction, the interest rate, the type of eligible collateral, the haircut, the maturity date, and the counterparties. The haircut corresponds to the difference between the value of the cash and the value of the collateral and is generally expressed as a percentage. For example, if $100 of securities collateralizes a loan of $98, the haircut is 2 percent. The level of haircut will typically reflect the quality of the collateral but may also vary by counterparty, reflecting the collateral provider's creditworthiness. The haircut can thus limit the counterparty credit risk exposure in secured borrowing transactions.

Repo and sec lending trades are conducted in over-the-counter markets that intermediate between borrowers and lenders, facilitating the exchange of securities and cash.[3] Given that these are collateralized money markets, each transaction features a collateral provider and a cash lender. The motivation behind a specific repo or sec lending transaction can be either cash or security driven. A cash-driven transaction is one where the collateral provider is seeking to borrow cash. In such cases, the securities backing the transaction are typically "general collateral," meaning that they are part of a class of acceptable securities rather than a specific one. A security-driven transaction is one where the cash lender is seeking to borrow securities. In such cases, the security is usually specific.

Among the financial intermediaries that participate in repo and sec lending markets, two sets of institutions are crucial. First, clearing banks and custodial agents are primarily involved in the operations of the repo and sec lending markets. Second, security dealers are both lenders and borrowers owing to their role as market makers. In contrast to the repo market, custodians play a unique role in sec lending transactions.

A schematic of the US repo markets, provided in figure 9.1, highlights the extensive intermediation role played by securities dealers.[4] For example, securities dealers intermediate between financial institutions that are long in cash, such as money market mutual funds, corporate treasuries, and custodial agents, and those institutions that are short in cash, such as hedge funds and other dealers. Repo markets are also used to reallocate securities both among securities dealers and between securities dealers and hedge funds, asset managers, and other financial institutions. The role of the clearing banks is hidden in figure 9.1—they provide the operational support for the tri-party repo market (see the following section for details on that market).

Securities dealers also intermediate in the sec lending markets. In these markets, securities dealers are often borrowing securities from custodial agents and lending these same securities to hedge funds and other financial

---

3. Sec lending agreements can accommodate the exchange of securities for securities. In the United States, however, most sec lending transactions exchange securities and cash. This article focuses on this more common case.

4. See also Copeland, Davis, et al. (2012).

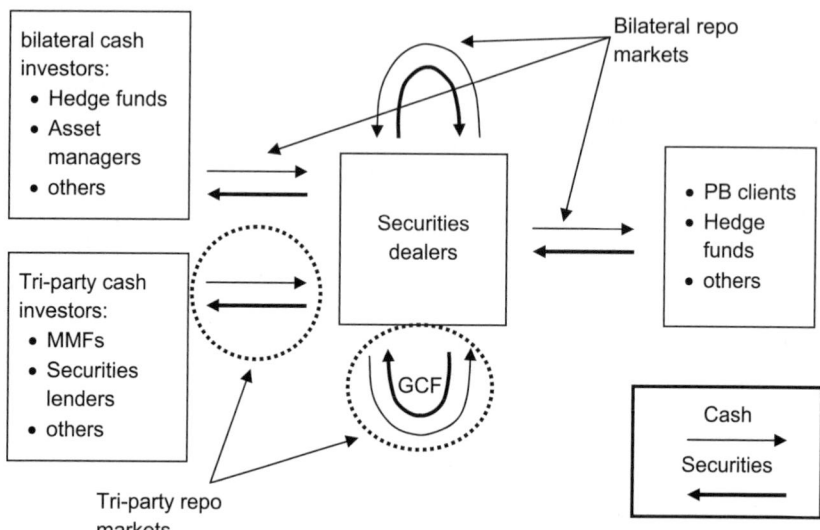

Fig. 9.1   US repo markets

Source: Copeland, Duffie, et al. (2012).

Notes: MMFs are money market mutual funds and PB is prime brokerage. GCF is the General Collateral Financing Repo® market run by the Fixed Income Clearing Corporation; this repo market is discussed in detail in section 9.3.3.

institutions. Part of the cash collateral that custodial agents acquire in the sec lending market is typically invested in the repo markets, creating an important link between the two markets. The custodial business is fairly concentrated: A few large players dominate the market as suppliers of general collateral and specific securities. Consequently, custodial agents are also large cash lenders in the market for repos.

While repo and securities loans may be open or term, most sec lending transactions are open. An open loan has an overnight tenor, but continues until one of the counterparties decides to cancel it. In particular, if the borrower returns the securities, the lender must return the cash collateral.

9.3   The US Repo Markets

9.3.1   Overview

It is useful to separate two broad classes of repos, distinguished by the way they are settled: bilateral and tri-party. Bilateral repos are repurchase agreements between two institutions where settlement typically occurs on a "delivery versus payment" basis. More specifically, the transfer of the collateral to the cash lender occurs simultaneously with the transfer of the cash to the collateral provider. Hence, the cash lender must have back-office capabilities to receive, track, value, and account for the securities.[5]

In a tri-party repo transaction, a third party provides a suite of collateral management and settlement services, such as settling the repos on its book, valuing the collateral, and making sure that the collateral adheres to the lender's eligibility requirements. Because settlement occurs on the books of a third party to whom collateral management has been outsourced, the cash lender does not need the back-office capability to take possession of the collateral.

Currently, the US tri-party repo market is set up to facilitate cash-driven transactions against general collateral. The services provided by the clearing banks make such repos less expensive for most investors than bilateral repos. In contrast, bilateral repos are usually used to obtain specific securities and raise cash against such securities, as the tri-party mechanism is not set up to facilitate the use of specific collateral.

9.3.2   The Bilateral Repo Market

The bilateral repo market provides for the exchange of cash and securities directly between collateral and cash providers. Use of this market may be preferable to other repo markets when two parties want to interact directly with each other, rather than through an agent, or if specific collateral is desired. Dealers use bilateral repos to provide cash to hedge funds, real estate investment trusts, banks, and other institutions, primarily through their prime brokerage activities. The collateral that dealers obtain in this fashion can in many cases be used as collateral in other repo markets (i.e., the collateral is "rehypothecated"), notably the tri-party repo market.

Bilateral repos are also common in the interdealer market, either as a source of funding or as a way to obtain specific securities. Dealers often serve as the custodian for their prime brokerage clients. In such cases, they settle bilateral repos through which they provide cash to these clients on their books. Interdealer bilateral repos are typically settled on the Fedwire Securities Service or through the Fixed Income Clearing Corporation (FICC).[6] One of the benefits of settling with FICC is that the settlement of a dealer's repos, reverse repos, buy-sell transactions, and auction awards are netted (see Garbade and Ingber 2005).

9.3.3   The GCF Repo® Market

The GCF Repo® market is a blind-brokered interdealer market for Fedwire-eligible securities run by FICC. This is the market where most interdealer repo transactions occur.[7] Fleming and Garbade (2003) provide

---

5. The cash lender can also hire its custodial bank to perform these services.
6. For more information on the FICC, see http://www.dtcc.com/about/subs/ficc.php.
7. For further information, see http://www.dtcc.com/products/fi/fixed_income_gsd/gcf _repo.php.

an overview of the GCF Repo® market, which is part of the tri-party repo market because it settles on the books of the clearing banks. The FICC guarantees settlement as soon as it receives the data from the broker and compares the transaction.

To participate, dealers must be netting members of FICC's Government Securities Division. The GCF Repo® service enables dealers to trade general collateral repos based on rate, term, and underlying product, throughout the day without requiring intraday, trade-for-trade settlement on a delivery-versus-payment basis, which shifts settlement risk to the FICC netting members in aggregate.

9.3.4   The Tri-party Repo Market

The US tri-party repo market is set up to facilitate cash-driven transactions and serves as a key source of funding for securities dealers. Hence, the main collateral providers in the tri-party repo market are securities dealers—in particular, primary dealers. Some large hedge funds and other institutions with large portfolios of securities also borrow in the tri-party repo market, but they represent a small share of the total volume.

The cash lenders are more numerous and diverse than collateral providers. More than 4,000 individual firms are active as cash lenders. However, despite this large number, there is some concentration among cash lender types as money market mutual funds represent between a quarter and a third of the cash invested in the tri-party repo market, and securities lenders represent an additional quarter of cash invested. Securities lenders use the tri-party repo market to reinvest some of the cash collateral received from lending securities.

In the United States, the role of the third party is played by the two government securities clearing banks: J.P. Morgan Chase and the Bank of New York Mellon, which we also call tri-party agents.[8] In addition to providing collateral management and settlement services, the clearing banks finance the dealers' securities during the day under current market practice.[9] The intraday credit exposure results in high concentration risk of the clearing banks vis-à-vis tri-party repo borrowers. Specifically, clearing banks "unwind" the tri-party repo trades each day. The unwind consists of sending cash back to the lenders' cash accounts and the securities back to the collateral providers' securities accounts, respectively, on the balance sheet of the clearing bank. This exchange results in the clearing banks extending intraday credit to the collateral providers, since the securities are no longer

---

8. The number of US government securities clearing banks has decreased from nine in the early 1980s to two. This is likely due to economies of scales in this business that provide incentives for concentration.

9. Reforms are currently under way to reduce or eliminate this intraday exposure. See http://www.newyorkfed.org/banking/tpr_infr_reform.html.

financed by the tri-party cash lenders. The unwind facilitates the settlement of repos at the end of the day (Copeland, Duffie, et al. 2012).

9.4   The US Securities Lending Market[10]

9.4.1   Overview

In US equity markets, securities lending is driven primarily by the prohibition on "naked" short selling, which is a short sale by an institution that does not hold the security and therefore cannot complete delivery.[11] The ban on naked short selling creates a role for securities lending, which allows an institution that wants to sell a security short to borrow it.

In US fixed-income markets, securities lending is used not only for short selling, but also for other borrowing transactions such as security-for-security arrangements. An institution may also want to borrow a security to hedge risk through the use of derivatives or to avoid "failing" on a delivery. Institutions also borrow securities to trade the repo rate itself; that is, if a Treasury security is trading special and a participant expects it to gain more specialness value, it will borrow that collateral for term and lend it overnight, hoping that the average overnight special repo rate is more attractive (lower) than the special repo rate it pays to borrow the security for term.

In the United States, most securities lending is done against cash collateral. Typically, the lender of a security pays an interest rate to the borrower for the cash collateral. The scarcer the security, the lower the interest rate paid by the securities lender. In addition to the return potentially generated through the lending transaction, lenders of securities seek to earn an additional return by investing the cash collateral. It should be noted that yield enhancement strategies embedded in the sec lending markets tend to be fundamentally different from plain repo transactions. In the sec lending markets, cash collateral is frequently invested in assets with characteristics that are very different from GC repo collateral, thus creating potential liquidity risk exposures.

The main lenders of securities are beneficial asset holders, such as pension plans, mutual funds, hedge funds, or insurance companies. These institutions typically own the securities outright and view sec lending as a way to enhance the yield of their security portfolios. Because the borrowing of securities is mainly for short selling, derivative hedging, or avoiding fails, the main borrowers are hedge funds, asset managers, option traders, and market makers.

---

10. Lipson, Sabel, and Keane (1990a, b) provide a comprehensive overview of the securities lending market.

11. For SEC regulation SHO, see http://www.sec.gov/divisions/marketreg/mrfaqregsho1204.htm.

Custodian banks typically provide securities lending services (lending of securities as well as cash collateral reinvestment) to their clients, although some large beneficial asset holders may conduct these activities themselves. There are also some noncustodian third-party providers of these services. Prime brokers usually facilitate transactions for borrowers of securities.

9.5   Crises in the Repurchase and Securities Lending Markets

During the recent financial crisis, both the repo and sec lending markets experienced runs. This section describes what is known about these runs, highlighting the additional data required to better understand them.

9.5.1   US Repo Markets

Both the bilateral and tri-party repo markets experienced runs, but they were different in nature. In a repo market, an increase in haircuts can force a borrower to delever because a smaller amount of cash is raised with the same amount of securities. Hence, a repo market can experience a run if haircuts for all collateral classes increase by a large amount.[12] Similarly, an asset class can experience a run if the haircuts for that particular asset class increase. A run on one or several asset classes seems to have happened in some bilateral repo markets during the crisis.

A different kind of run can occur in a repo market if haircuts do not increase. An institution that relies on a repo market for its funding may be forced into bankruptcy if its creditors refuse to extend repo financing. This seems to have happened to Bear Stearns and Lehman Brothers in the tri-party repo market during the crisis, as lenders reacted to the perceived creditworthiness of the counterparty as opposed to the quality of the collateral.

Our knowledge of the events in these markets comes from recent empirical studies: Gorton and Metrick (2012) analyze haircuts in the bilateral market, while Copeland, Martin, and Walker (forthcoming) and Krishnamurthy, Nagel, and Orlov (2012) focus on the haircuts in the tri-party repo market.

These studies suggest that haircuts in the bilateral and tri-party markets behaved differently during the crisis. In the bilateral market, Gorton and Metrick show that haircuts increased rapidly and reached high levels.[13] Hence, these authors argue that there was a generalized "run" on this repo market that reduced the amount of cash that could be raised by borrowers. Corroborating evidence for Gorton and Metrick's hypothesis is the high number of hedge fund failures due to margin calls. On July 31, 2007, two hedge funds operated by Bear Stearns filed for bankruptcy protection.

---

12. In addition, Adrian and Shin (2009), Brunnermeier and Pedersen (2009), and Ashcraft, Garleanu, and Pedersen (2010) suggest that haircuts are state variables for aggregate economic activity.

13. Different counterparties may have faced different haircuts in this market, but data are not available to support this view.

Both were highly levered mortgage funds that were funded primarily in the repo markets. A closely related bankruptcy occurred on March 5, 2008, when Carlyle Capital Corporation failed to meet margin calls as a result of increases in repo haircuts. In the fall of 2008, many more hedge funds and shadow banks failed when they were unable to meet margin calls. These instances are labeled "repo runs" by Gorton and Metrick, though one could alternatively view them as forced deleveraging.[14]

In contrast, haircuts barely moved in the tri-party repo market, as documented in Copeland, Martin, and Walker (forthcoming). The difference between the haircuts in the bilateral and tri-party repo markets increased during the fall of 2008, peaked sometime in the first half of 2009, and fell back close to the level of July 2008 by the beginning of 2010.

This evidence suggests no generalized run on the tri-party repo market, although Krishnamurthy, Nagel, and Orlov (2012) argue that there was a run on repo backed by nonagency MBS/ABS collateral. However, it appears that Bear Stearns and Lehman Brothers did experience runs, and the loss of funding in the tri-party repo market contributed to their difficulties. So in the case of the tri-party repo market, stress seemed to affect specific counterparties rather than the broad collateral classes, except perhaps the nonagency MBS/ABS.

Understanding the differences in behavior between the bilateral and the tri-party repo markets is important. Rising haircuts, while problematic in their own right, can be viewed as an equilibrating phenomenon (Martin, Skeie, and von Thadden, forthcoming). Indeed, increasing haircuts reduce the amount of funding borrowers can obtain, but this does not shut them out of the market altogether. In addition, if the increase in margins is gradual, it may give institutions time to adapt or find other sources of funding. In the tri-party repo market, the reduction in funding was precipitous, leaving little time for the firms to adapt.

Another difference between the bilateral and tri-party repo markets during this time was the creation of the Primary Dealer Credit Facility (PDCF) by the Federal Reserve following the Bear Stearns crisis of March 13, 2008 (see Adrian, Burke, and McAndrews 2009). The PDCF was created to backstop dealers funding in the tri-party repo market, and the set of eligible collateral was broadened over time. The PDCF may have prevented some runs on securities dealers, although it could not prevent the trouble experienced by Lehman. While the PDCF is designed to provide liquidity, it cannot prevent credit events due to solvency problems.

While the empirical studies discussed above present compelling evidence of the variety of behavior that occurs in repo markets, they also highlight

14. Adrian and Shin (2010) show that there is generally a close connection between repos and leverage of broker-dealers. The increase of haircuts in the bilateral market thus maps into the deleveraging of the broker-dealer sector following the Lehman bankruptcy and the concurrent decline of outstanding repos.

the lack of comprehensive data. Gorton and Metrick (2012) analyze data on one firm's activities in one repo market segment, and Copeland, Martin, and Walker (forthcoming) describe quantity and haircut data on the tri-party repo market. Krishnamurthy, Nagel, and Orlov (2012) have collected firm-level data on all six elements of the repo transactions, but, as they explain in their paper, these data are limited by their scope and frequency. This lack of data hinders a deep understanding of the drivers behind the different run dynamics observed in repo markets. Furthermore, the lack of data makes it much more difficult to evaluate the effectiveness of policy actions, such as the PDCF.

9.5.2   US Securities Lending Markets

As in the repo markets, aspects of the securities lending market behaved differently during the recent crisis. A broad deleveraging took place, creating liquidity stress and, in some cases, losses for securities lenders as they were forced to return the cash collateral to the borrowers of the securities. The liquidity stress and the losses were typically commensurate with the degrees of credit risk and liquidity transformation associated with the investment of cash collateral. Excessive speculation in cash reinvestment created extreme asset-liability mismatches, in what could have been a boring and safe activity (that is, investing only in Treasury GC repo).

The crisis surrounding AIG offers an example. Like many other large insurance companies, AIG engaged in securities lending. Before the financial crisis, its loans were mostly open and its pool of cash collateral was invested in particularly long-term and illiquid assets. This meant that AIG was performing considerable liquidity transformation, which can result in liquidity stress. This investment strategy yielded high returns before the crisis; however, it contributed to AIG's liquidity squeeze during the crisis. The firm experienced something similar to a run as borrowers of its securities sought to return them as part of the general market deleveraging that took place. The need to liquidate some illiquid assets to accommodate this return of securities contributed to a sizable share of AIG's losses. Maiden Lane II LLC was created to alleviate capital and liquidity pressures on AIG associated with the securities lending portfolios of several regulated US insurance subsidiaries of AIG.[15]

9.6   The Economics of Collateralized Short-Term Lending and Data Needs

The runs described in the previous sections suggest that understanding the fragility of repo and securities lending markets requires a good understanding of the institutional arrangements under which these contracts are

---

15. See http://www.newyorkfed.org/markets/maidenlane.html for more details.

traded. This means that disaggregated data are particularly useful to understand market participants' reactions under stress.

Liquidity transformation is one of the key functions of financial intermediation. In general, intermediaries tend to be funded with short-term debt and tend to hold longer-term, relatively illiquid assets. This liquidity mismatch can give rise to fragility, as pointed out in the seminal contribution by Diamond and Dybvig (1983). However, the inefficiencies arising in this simple setup can be solved with a variety of policies or financial innovations. More recently, a rapidly growing literature has been focusing on fragility that is due to rollover risk (see Acharya, Gale, and Yorulmazer 2011; Brunnermeier and Oehmke 2013; and He and Xiong 2012).

The key concerns related to the repos and securities loans described in our examples are associated with the possibility of runs, which arise from liquidity transformation and their potential spillover, which can occur when institutions are interconnected. This suggests that data on the degree of liquidity transformation being performed, notably the tenor of repos and securities loans, are particularly important. The tenor of instruments in which cash collateral is reinvested is of additional importance, as is information about the interconnectedness of the participants engaged in these markets.

In addition to providing insights about the amount of maturity transformation, information about the tenor of an institution's funding can serve as an early warning system. Difficulty in renewing long-term funding typically signals that an institution is under stress. Longer-term funding gives the institution more time to find alternative sources of funding or to take other measures to improve its odds of survival. A longer-duration maturity profile also gives regulators more time to prepare for a potential rescue of the firm or an orderly unwind.

Repos are an important part, but not the only source, of funding for dealers. Getting a better picture of the various sources of dealer funding and how dealers are passing this funding on is important for our understanding of the sources of dealer fragility. For example, Duffie (2010) suggests three potential sources of "runs" on dealers: OTC derivative counterparties trying to reduce their exposure to dealers, loss of prime brokerage business, and a run on secured financing, including repo. Disclosure of cash management holdings could mitigate the potential for creating hidden vulnerabilities in the securities lending markets.

It is helpful to gauge the availability of different funding sources in times of stress and to know the extent to which different funding sources are substitutable. Understanding the differences in behavior between bilateral and tri-party repos contributes to that knowledge. In addition, understanding the extent to which financial market participants are interconnected can help us draw conclusions about the possible propagation of stress throughout the financial system.

Another potentially interesting source of data is the type of collateral being financed in repo markets. This information may provide some insights into the risk appetite of the institutions that fund dealers. Changes in the type of assets serving as collateral, or the introduction of new asset classes, can offer insights into the evolution of funding markets.

In addition to these data, information about rates and haircuts would also be useful—particularly information about interest rates and haircuts faced by dealers, given the critical intermediating role they play. Owing to the behavioral differences between the tri-party repo market and the bilateral repo market, interpreting those data could be difficult. Nevertheless, the data could help us understand these markets better and also provide interesting cross-sectional information about different dealers. Making cross-sectional data public, however, could raise disclosure issues.

9.7   Existing Data and Data Gaps

Both repo and securities lending transactions can be characterized by six pieces of information: principal, interest rate, collateral, haircut, tenor, and counterparty. For regulatory purposes, all six pieces of information are crucial for properly gauging systemic and firm-level risk. For example, in response to a rise in the perceived risk of a dealer seeking to finance its securities, cash lenders might ask for higher interest rates, higher-quality collateral, increased haircuts, shorter maturities, or all of these. Because they are heterogeneous, there is no standard response by cash lenders when faced with increased counterparty risk. As such, knowing a financial institution's counterparties is essential to understanding that firm's risk level.

Furthermore, counterparty information would allow regulators and researchers to measure the interconnectedness of a repo or securities lending market. An important goal for regulators is to understand how difficulties arising in a firm will impact other firms in the market, but this cannot be accomplished without information on counterparties. In addition, information about the cash reinvestment strategies of sec lending cash lenders is an important ingredient for assessing the riskiness of these transactions. This is in contrast to GC repo transactions, where counterparty information is less relevant owing to the liquidity of the collateral.

A number of data sources provide information on the six characteristics of repo and sec lending trades previously described. Following, we review which types of data on these characteristics are generally available to the public and discuss which additional data would need to be collected.

9.7.1   Interest Rates

A number of sources offer average interest rates on repo or sec lending transactions, conditional on the type of collateral offered and the tenor of the trade. Bloomberg, for example, provides daily averages of interest rates by tenor and collateral type for general collateral repo trades. Data Explorer offers similar average interest rate data based on sec lending transactions.

These public sources report interest rate data at the aggregate level and therefore do not provide the rates paid by individual firms. But interest rates often reflect the perceived risk level of the financial institution borrowing the cash. As such, we argue that collecting interest rate data for repo and sec lending trades at the firm level is important to understanding the risks in these markets.

A source of firm-level interest rate data is the SEC N-Q report filed by publicly traded money market mutual funds (MMFs). Although these data are not reported in a standardized form, MMFs generally report, by type, the total value of securities they have accepted as collateral for repo transactions, as well as information on haircuts, maturity, interest rates, and counterparties. Hence, these data provide a fairly detailed snapshot of MMF repo activities. Krishnamurthy, Nagel, and Orlov (2012) have started to collect and organize these data for the larger MMFs, focusing on the years encompassing the recent financial crisis. These data are promising because they provide firm-level information on all six characteristics of repo trades.

Obtaining these data for all major repo and securities lending firms would provide enough information to accurately measure firm-level and systemic risk in repo and sec lending markets. Unfortunately, these data on MMFs are limited in their scope and frequency. MMFs are a large source of cash in US repo markets, but they are far from being a majority—for example, they account for one-quarter to one-third of total cash invested in tri-party repo. The snapshots of activity are also fairly infrequent, with new data on a MMF arriving semiannually. Furthermore, these snapshots may not be representative of normal activity because these money funds may take into account that their repo transactions will be included in their Securities and Exchange Commission (SEC) reports (in other words, these data may suffer from the window-dressing problem).

9.7.2   Principal and Collateral

There are a number of data sources on the value of securities used in repo and sec lending transactions (i.e., the amount of collateral posted). Data Explorer offers a wealth of detailed information on the daily quantity of securities lending trades. As with interest rates, these data are available only at the market level, making it difficult to use them for monitoring individual firms.

Additional data on the value of securities used in repo and sec lending transactions are available from regular balance-sheet filings with the SEC. Every publicly traded company has to file quarterly 10-Q and annual 10-K reports. For financial institutions that participate in repo and sec lending transactions, the 10-Ks and 10-Qs will report those transactions to the extent that they occur on the balance sheet. While the 10-K and 10-Q reports contain balance-sheet data at the consolidated holding company level, the SEC also collects balance-sheet data on the subsidiaries of securities dealers. The US flow of funds relies on these reports in aggregating balance-sheet information on broker-dealers.

In early 2010, the SEC required money market mutual funds to file N-MFP reports. The data captured by this form contain, among other things, information on the securities a MMF accepts as collateral for repo transactions—in particular, the name of the security's issuer, the maturity date of the security, the coupon or yield, and value of the security. The form also reports haircuts (the ratio of the collateral value relative to the repo value), the maturity of the repo as determined under rule 2a-7 (taking maturity-shortening provisions and maturity-date extensions into account), and the interest rate of the repo.

The N-MFP report collects its data in a standardized manner, and the report is filed in an XML-tagged data format. Consequently, it will be fairly straightforward going forward to collect and analyze data on the collateral that MMFs are accepting in their repo transactions.

Moreover, the Federal Reserve form FR2004 assembles information on market activity from primary dealers.[16] Primary dealers report the total value of securities purchased and sold through repo transactions by asset class. While the dealer-level data are confidential, aggregated information is made available to the public.

A relatively new source of information is provided by the Tri-Party Repo Infrastructure Reform website.[17] This source reports, by asset class, the total value of securities that are posted as collateral in the tri-party repo market on the seventh business day of each month. Also reported is the total value of securities, by asset class, posted in the GCF Repo® market.

The above-mentioned data essentially provide snapshots of activity at the aggregate or firm level. But although interesting, these data do not provide sufficient information to answer many important questions about the repo and securities lending markets.

9.7.3   Haircuts

Information on haircuts is limited. Beyond the aforementioned SEC data on money market mutual funds, there is *only* aggregate data on haircuts in the tri-party repo market. Specifically, the Tri-Party Repo Infrastructure Reform website provides information on the distribution of haircuts.

---

16. See http://www.federalreserve.gov/reportforms/reportdetail.cfm?WhichFormId=FR_2004. For more information on primary dealers, see http://www.newyorkfed.org/markets/primarydealers.html. Adrian and Fleming (2005) provide an overview of the FR2004 data.
17. See http://www.newyorkfed.org/banking/tpr_infr_reform.html.

9.7.4 Tenor and Counterparty

As far as we know, the only public source of information on tenor and counterparties is the aforementioned SEC N-Q report data filed by money market mutual funds.

In summary, a number of public data sources provide information on the interest rates and values of securities used in repo and securities lending trades. Much less is known about haircuts, tenor, and counterparties and the exact nature of cash reinvestment strategies in these markets. Unfortunately, it is often difficult or impossible to piece together the information at the firm level, and this is exactly the information needed to properly assess the risk level of a firm. While the overall amount of repo and sec lending trades of a firm is informative, the term structure of those trades is of first-order importance when assessing a firm's risk level. Similarly, counterparty, interest rate, and haircut information all significantly impact a firm's risk level. Consequently, it is important to collect this information at the firm level and in a comprehensive fashion.

In addition to the type of data just described, insight into the use of cash collateral provides value. As previously mentioned, cash collateral is frequently provided against securities lending transactions in the US market and that cash is reinvested to earn an additional return. Individual lenders determine the degree of reinvestment risk they desire; therefore, investments can be across a broad range of instruments of varying credit quality and tenor. Collection of data related to instrument type, credit rating (if applicable), and tenor can help identify the degree to which securities lending cash collateral is supporting other markets, as well as the degree of associated risk.

9.8 Conclusion

In a September 2012 speech, "Implications of the Financial Crisis for Economics," Federal Reserve Chairman Ben Bernanke distinguished between economic science, economic engineering, and economic management:[18]

> *Economic science* concerns itself primarily with theoretical and empirical generalizations about the behavior of individuals, institutions, markets, and national economies. Most academic research falls in this category. *Economic engineering* is about the design and analysis of frameworks for achieving specific economic objectives. Examples of such frameworks are the risk management systems of financial institutions and the financial regulatory systems of the United States and other countries. *Economic*

18. The speech can be found at http://www.federalreserve.gov/newsevents/speech/bernanke 20100924a.htm.

management involves the operation of economic frameworks in real time—for example, in the private sector, the management of complex financial institutions or, in the public sector, the day-to-day supervision of those institutions.

Chairman Bernanke goes on to add, "With that taxonomy in hand, I would argue that the recent financial crisis was more a failure of economic engineering and economic management than of what I have called economic science."

Our argument in this chapter is consistent with the Fed chairman's view and suggests that we need both better data and a better understanding of the institutional arrangements and the economic engineering by which key economic actors operate. The two go hand in hand. Good data help illuminate market functioning and can be useful for detecting changes in market practices that could increase risk. A good understanding of institutional arrangements may be necessary to make sense of the patterns identified by the data and can suggest the need for new data as market infrastructure evolves.

Better data are particularly important for understanding repo and securities lending markets and monitoring developments that may indicate stress. Such early warning signals can be the basis for policy decisions that aim at stabilizing the financial system. These are the money markets at the heart of the market-based financial system. While repo markets primarily enhance the efficiency of fixed-income markets, securities lending markets play central roles for both fixed-income and equity markets. Repo and securities lending markets are especially important for allowing arbitrage in the Treasury, agency, and agency MBS markets, thus enhancing price discovery, efficiency, and market liquidity. Securities lending markets play crucial roles in the shorting of securities. However, both markets also perform liquidity transformation roles and are thus exposed to the drying up of liquidity.

In the securities lending markets today, the degree of liquidity transformation is not reported in any transparent or systematic fashion, even when transactions involve large amounts of liquidity transformation. The repo market experienced liquidity shortages in the week prior to the Bear Stearns crisis, and the securities lending portfolio in Maiden Lane II illustrates the risk in liquidity mismatches of securities lending. The differences in behavior between the tri-party repo market and the bilateral repo market underscore this point. In the bilateral market, stress manifested itself in the form of a large and rapid increase in haircuts, creating a generalized run on the market. In the tri-party repo market, haircuts barely moved but some firms experienced dramatic decreases in the amount of financing they obtained in this market. Hence, the structure of each market, and the nature of their participants, appears to have an impact on how stress manifested itself. Understanding these differences remains important.

References

Acharya, V., D. Gale, and T. Yorulmazer. 2011. "Rollover Risk and Market Freezes." *Journal of Finance* 66 (4): 1175–207.

Adrian, T., C. Burke, and J. McAndrews. 2009. "The Federal Reserve's Primary Dealer Credit Facility." Federal Reserve Bank of New York *Current Issues in Economics and Finance* 15(4).

Adrian, T., and M. Fleming. 2005. "What Financing Data Reveal about Dealer Leverage." Federal Reserve Bank of New York *Current Issues in Economics and Finance* 11(3).

Adrian, T., and H. S. Shin. 2009. "Prices and Quantities in the Monetary Policy Transmission Mechanism." *International Journal of Central Banking* 5 (4): 131–42.

———. 2010. "Liquidity and Leverage." *Journal of Financial Intermediation* 19 (3): 418–37.

Ashcraft, A., N. Garleanu, and L. H. Pedersen. 2010. "Two Monetary Tools: Interest Rates and Haircuts." *NBER Macroeconomics Annual 2010*, vol. 25, edited by Daron Acemoglu and Michael Woodford, 143–180. Chicago: University of Chicago Press.

Brunnermeier, M. K., and M. Oehmke. 2013. "The Maturity Rat Race." *Journal of Finance* 68 (2): 483–521.

Brunnermeier, M. K., and L. H. Pedersen. 2009. "Market Liquidity and Funding Liquidity." *Review of Financial Studies* 22 (6): 2201–38.

Copeland A., I. Davis, E. LeSueur, and A. Martin. 2012. "Mapping and Sizing the US Repo Market." *Liberty Street Economics*, June 25. http://libertystreeteconom ics.newyorkfed.org/2012/06/mapping-and-sizing-the-us-repo-market.html.

Copeland, A., D. Duffie, A. Martin, and S. McLaughlin. 2012. "Key Mechanics of the US Tri-Party Repo Market." Federal Reserve Bank of New York *Economic Policy Review*.

Copeland, A., A. Martin, and M. W. Walker. Forthcoming. "Repo Runs: Evidence from the Tri-Party Repo Market." *Journal of Finance*.

Covitz, D., N. Liang, and G. A. Suarez. 2013. "The Evolution of a Financial Crisis: Panic in the Asset-Backed Commercial Paper Market." *Journal of Finance* 68 (3): 815–848.

Diamond, D., and P. Dybvig. 1983. "Bank Runs, Deposit Insurance, and Liquidity." *Journal of Political Economy* 91:401–19.

Duffie, D. 1996. "Special Repo Rates." *Journal of Finance* 51 (2): 493–526.

———. 2010. *How Big Banks Fail and What to Do About It*. Princeton, NJ: Princeton University Press.

Fleming, M., and K. Garbade. 2003. "The Repurchase Agreement Refined: GCF Repo®." Federal Reserve Bank of New York *Current Issues in Economics and Finance* 9(6).

Garbade, K. 2006. "The Evolution of Repo Contracting Conventions in the 1980s." Federal Reserve Bank of New York *Economic Policy Review* 12(1).

Garbade, K., and J. F. Ingber. 2005. "The Treasury Auction Process: Objectives, Structure, and Recent Adaptations." Federal Reserve Bank of New York *Current Issues in Economics and Finance* 11(2).

Gorton, G. B., and A. Metrick. 2012. "Securitized Banking and the Run on Repo." *Journal of Financial Economics* 104 (3): 425–51.

He, Z., and W. Xiong. 2012. "Rollover Risk and Credit Risk." *Journal of Finance* 67 (2): 391–429.

Krishnamurthy, A., S. Nagel, and D. Orlov. 2012. "Sizing up Repo." NBER Working Paper no. 17768, Cambridge, MA.

Lipson, P., B. Sabel, and F. Keane. 1990a. "Securities Lending, Part 1: Basic Transactions and Participants." *Journal of Commercial Bank Lending* 6:4–18.
———. 1990b. "Securities Lending, Part 2: Regulation, Pricing, and Risks Borne by Participants." *Journal of Commercial Bank Lending* 7:18–31.
Martin, A., D. Skeie, and E.-L. von Thadden. Forthcoming. "Repo Runs." *Review of Financial Studies*.
Ruchin, Andre. 2011. "Can Securities Lending Transactions Substitute for Repurchase Agreement Transactions?" *Banking Law Journal* 128 (5): 450–80.

10

Improving Our Ability to Monitor Bank Lending

William F. Bassett, Simon Gilchrist,
Gretchen C. Weinbach, and Egon Zakrajšek

Bank lending to households and businesses over the past several years was affected substantially by the turmoil that raged in the global financial markets during the 2007 to 2009 period. The successive waves of turbulence that ripped through the financial system during that period—especially the intensification of stresses that followed the bankruptcy of Lehman Brothers in the early autumn of 2008—exerted substantial pressure on both the asset and liability sides of banks' balance sheets. During the height of the crisis in the latter part of 2008, banks faced funding markets that were largely illiquid and secondary markets that were essentially closed to sales of certain types of loans and securities. Together with the slowdown in economic activity that set in at the end of 2007 and accelerated appreciably in late 2008, these financial disruptions caused banks to become significantly more cautious in the extension of credit and to take steps to bolster their capital and liquidity positions.

Throughout this period of financial market turmoil, policymakers were

William F. Bassett is deputy associate director of the Division of Monetary Affairs of the Board of Governors of the Federal Reserve System. Simon Gilchrist is professor of economics at Boston University and a research associate of the National Bureau of Economic Research. Gretchen C. Weinbach is associate director of the Division of Monetary Affairs of the Board of Governors of the Federal Reserve System. Egon Zakrajšek is associate director of the Division of Monetary Affairs of the Board of Governors of the Federal Reserve System.

We thank Hesna Genay for helpful comments and suggestions. Ben Rump (Federal Reserve Board) provided excellent research assistance. The views expressed in this chapter are solely the responsibility of the authors and should not be interpreted as reflecting the views of the Board of Governors of the Federal Reserve System or of anyone else associated with the Federal Reserve System. For acknowledgments, sources of research support, and disclosure of the authors' material financial relationships, if any, please see http://www.nber.org/chapters /c12554.ack.

greatly concerned about the availability of bank-intermediated credit to both households and businesses, as large reductions in the supply of bank loans had the potential to exacerbate the ongoing contraction in spending and production.[1] In addition to the usual problem of trying to disentangle the effects on bank lending of supply versus demand, the ability to measure the provision of credit by banks was greatly complicated by the lack of sufficient data on credit flows through the banking sector. In particular, the most widely used and comprehensive US data sources on banks' lending activities provide detailed information only on the *stock* of loans on banks' books at the end of the reporting period, along, in some instances, with the cumulative year-to-date amounts charged off.[2]

Importantly, changes in the outstanding stock of bank loans are a very noisy signal of banks' underlying loan origination activity, because such changes also capture other intermediation activities, including loan purchases, loan sales, and securitizations. Indeed, there is virtually no information available on the *flow of loan originations*, or factors other than charge-offs that affect the amount of outstanding loans. Moreover, because the banking system provides credit to households and businesses in two important ways—by originating new loans (on-balance sheet) and by providing lines of credit (off-balance sheet)—information on drawdowns, credit line expirations, and bank- or borrower-induced reductions or cancellations of

1. Empirical studies documenting the real side effects of adverse shocks to bank loan supply include, among others, Bernanke and Lown (1991), Peek and Rosengren (1997, 2000), Calomiris and Mason (2003), Ashcraft (2005), Lown and Morgan (2006), and Bassett, Chosak, Driscoll, and Zakrajšek (2014). Gilchrist and Zakrajšek (2011, 2012b), in contrast, employ secondary market prices on individual corporate bond issues to derive a broader measure of disruptions in the credit intermediation process—the so-called excess bond premium—and show that their measure of financial distress has significant effects on economic activity and asset prices; Gilchrist and Zakrajšek (2012a) show that shocks to the excess bond premium have a significant effect on bank lending.

2. By far the most comprehensive publicly available data on bank lending come from the quarterly Consolidated Reports of Condition and Income (Call Reports), which are submitted by insured US commercial banks and by US branches and agencies of foreign banks to the Federal Financial Institutions Examination Council (FFIEC). The Call Reports collect information on outstanding loan balances for a wide variety of loan categories, along with the flow of gross charge-offs and recoveries. The Call Reports do contain some information on loan originations and on the amount of loans purchased, but this information is limited to a few narrow loan categories, is available over a limited period of time, and is insufficient to track accurately the flow of credit through the banking sector. The Federal Reserve's weekly H.8 Statistical Release, "Assets and Liabilities of Commercial Banks in the United States," provides an estimated aggregate balance sheet for all commercial banks in the United States; the release also includes separate balance sheet aggregations for several bank-size groups. Based on items that are derived from the Call Reports, the H.8 release includes only the amount of loans outstanding for the major categories of loans to households and businesses—it does not, for example, include data on charge-offs. Similarly, the Flow of Funds Accounts of the United States, which are also based largely on Call Reports, include information on the aggregate amount of bank loans outstanding at quarter-end for the major categories of loans to households and businesses.

credit lines is also crucial to any effort that attempts to monitor banks' lending capacity during a cyclical downturn. The existing data sources, however, provide only limited information on the stock of banks' off-balance sheet—that is, unused—commitments to fund loans.

In this chapter, we highlight some of the difficulties that arise in measuring accurately the provision of credit by the banking sector during an economic downturn, such as the one experienced during the recent financial crisis. Specifically, we argue that existing bank regulatory reports provide insufficient detail to monitor banks' lending activities accurately.[3] We then outline a conceptual framework for measuring bank lending that could be used to improve the existing information on banks' on-balance sheet lending activities and the equally important information on banks' off-balance sheet credit line provision activities. The improved data would help address the following questions of concern to both economic researchers and policymakers, questions that cannot be readily answered with the existing data sources:

- Are banks making loans? If so, how much and to whom are they lending?
- Can the broad research community provide timely quantitative analysis about the relative contributions of the supply of, and demand for, credit that drive changes in banks' outstanding loan balances and unused commitments to fund loans?
- What adjustments to credit provision are banking organizations making in response to the enhanced regulatory capital and liquidity requirements that are pending as a result of the Dodd-Frank Act and the Basel III agreement?

We recognize that the literal adoption of our framework would increase banks' reporting burden. Our aim, rather, is to provide a detailed description of the kind of data that would significantly inform the analysis of credit flows and greatly enhance our ability to assess the availability of bank-intermediated credit. In practice, of course, discussions among all the members of the Federal Financial Institutions Examination Council (FFIEC), consideration of how the proposed new data items are stored in banks' reporting systems—if they are stored at all—and the costs associated with reporting new items on a regular basis would have to be carefully weighed to ensure that the marginal benefits of the additional information exceeded the associated reporting burden.

---

3. The existing data sources also made it difficult to assess the effectiveness of certain policies implemented by government agencies during the recent financial crisis; see, for example, testimony of Paul Atkins, member, Congressional Oversight Panel, before the House Financial Services Committee on May 18, 2010, available at http://www.house.gov.apps/list/hearing/financialsvcs_dem/atkins_5-18-10.pdf.

10.1   Bank Lending during the 2007–2009 Financial Crisis

To help frame our discussion, we use the quarterly Flow of Funds Accounts to examine the cyclical dynamics of bank lending to households and businesses, with a particular aim of providing some historical context for the 2007 to 2009 financial crisis. We consider the following four major categories of bank loans: home mortgages, commercial mortgages, consumer credit (i.e., credit card, auto, and other consumer loans), and nonfinancial business credit (i.e., commercial and industrial [C&I] loans extended to nonfinancial businesses).

We first converted each category of nominal loans outstanding to real terms by deflating it with the gross domestic product (GDP) price deflator. Because our focus is on cyclical fluctuations in bank lending, we detrended the resulting series by regressing the logarithm of each real loan aggregate on constant and linear and quadratic time trends over the 1952:Q1–2010:Q4 period. For each NBER-dated recession since 1952, we normalized the detrended series to equal zero at its respective business cycle peak. The thin black line in each panel of figure 10.1 depicts the average behavior of each bank loan category around NBER-dated business cycle peaks, calculated using data for all recessions since 1953 (excluding the 2007 to 2009 downturn), while the shaded band represents the corresponding range of outcomes. The thick black line in each panel shows the behavior of each series during the 2007 to 2009 financial crisis.

As shown in the top left panel, the collapse in housing market activity and a widespread drop in home prices—two distinct features of the 2007 to 2009 downturn—have left a significant imprint on home mortgage lending by commercial banks. Over the three years following the business cycle peak in 2007:Q4, (real) home mortgage debt on banks' books has fallen almost 30 percent relative to its trend growth, and the runoff in this loan category shows no sign of abating. The remaining three major loan categories, in contrast, share a similar, though noticeably different, pattern. Bank credit extended to consumers and bank loans to businesses (both C&I and loans secured by commercial real estate) increased relative to trend in the early stages of the 2007 to 2009 recession, peaking at the end of 2008, around the time of the bankruptcy of Lehman Brothers. A large part of this surge in lending to businesses and households undoubtedly reflects loans that were drawn down under previous commitments, though the magnitude of this important effect cannot be ascertained with the existing data sources.[4]

The emergence of the destructive feedback loop between the turmoil in

---

4. Ivashina and Scharfstein (2010) provide detailed corroborative evidence of this phenomenon using Reuters's DealScan database on syndicated lending. Unlike Call Reports, DealScan contains data on new loan originations, though the scope of the data is limited to large syndicated business loans, and the data fall well short of providing a comprehensive picture of banks' credit intermediation activities.

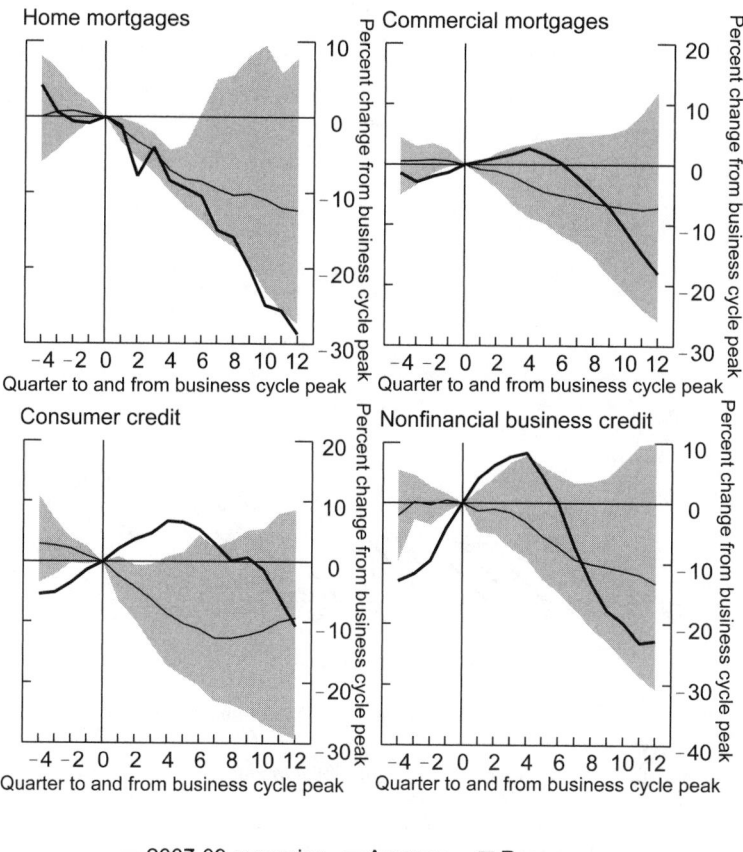

— 2007-09 recession — Average   ▒ Range

Fig. 10.1   Cyclical dynamics of household and business lending at commercial banks

Source: Authors' calculations using US Flow of Funds data.

Notes: The panels of the figure depict the behavior of the major categories of loans to households and nonfinancial businesses around NBER-dated business cycle peaks. Each category of loans outstanding is deflated by the GDP price deflator (2005 = 100). The logarithm of each real loan aggregate was detrended using linear and quadratic time trends. For each loan category, the average cyclical component (the black lines) and the range of cyclical components (the shaded bands) are based on data for recessions designated by the NBER since 1953, excluding the 2007–2009 downturn.

financial markets and the downturn in economic activity sparked by the collapse of Lehman exerted substantial pressure on both sides of banks' balance sheets. As a result, banks became significantly more cautious in the extension of credit, saw massive losses deplete capital, and relied more on the Federal Reserve—and less on the market—as a source of funding. Starting in late 2008, these factors, in combination with the reduced demand for credit, caused a significant contraction in commercial mortgages, con-

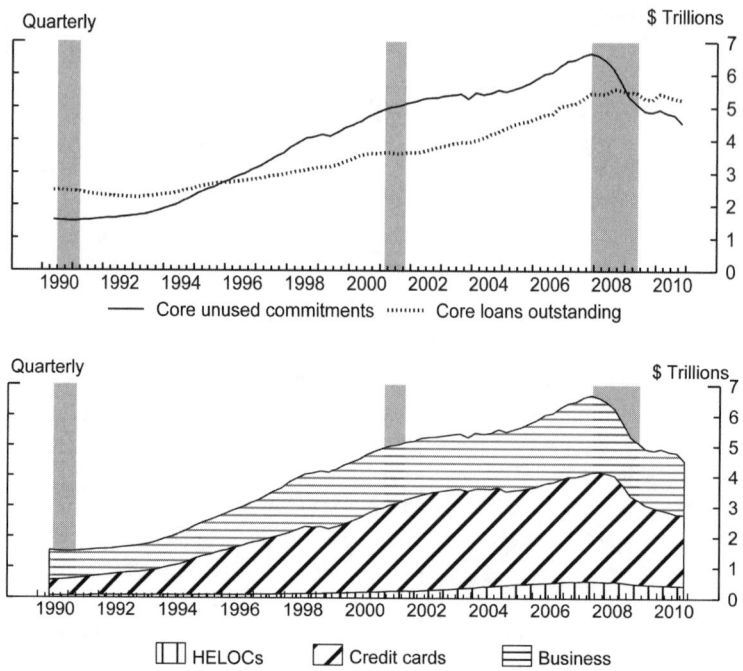

Fig. 10.2   Core loans and unused commitments at commercial banks

Source: Call Reports.

Notes: The solid line in the top panel depicts the dollar amount of core unused commitments, and the dotted line depicts the dollar amount of core loans outstanding at US commercial banks. Core loan categories include C&I, real estate, and consumer loans. The bottom panel depicts the composition of unused commitments. All series are deflated by the GDP price deflator (2005 = 100). Shaded vertical bars represent NBER-dated recessions.

sumer credit, and C&I loans on banks' books. Indeed, the runoff in both types of business loans outstanding during the 2007 to 2009 recession was considerably more severe and persistent compared with an average postwar recession.[5]

The fact that changes in bank loans outstanding—especially of C&I loans—are typically a lagging business cycle indicator reflects importantly the banks' unique role as a provider of credit in the form of credit lines. According to the top panel of figure 10.2, the dollar amount of unused commitments to fund loans to households and businesses—that is, core unused commitments—has, on average, exceeded the amount of core loans outstanding by a significant margin over the past two decades.[6] As shown

5. Although our analysis is focused on the commercial banking sector, we note that the general cyclical patterns of these four loan categories at banks are very similar to those at all depository institutions.

6. These data were added to Call Reports in 1990:Q2.

in the bottom panel, credit card commitments account for the majority of this off-balance sheet exposure, followed closely by business credit lines.[7]

Another distinct feature of the 2007 to 2009 economic downturn is the fact that core unused commitments contracted much earlier and by a substantially greater amount than core loans outstanding on banks' books. A portion of this decline, of course, reflects drawdowns on the existing lines by households and businesses, which mechanically boosts the amount of loans outstanding. A significant portion, however, also represents a reduction in the supply of bank credit lines, as banks, in response to capital and liquidity pressures, reduced their off-balance sheet credit exposures by reducing their customers' existing lines of credit.

Given the relative importance of banks' commitments to fund loans, we can define a broader measure of credit intermediation by commercial banks: *core lending capacity*, which attempts to capture the full potential of households and businesses to borrow from the banking sector over time, as measured by the sum of core loans outstanding (i.e., loans already extended) and corresponding commitments to fund such loans (i.e., promised extensions). The black line in figure 10.3 depicts the (annualized) quarterly growth rate of core lending capacity, while the shaded portions of the vertical bars represent the quarterly growth contributions of core loans outstanding and core unused commitments.

According to the figure, cyclical fluctuations in core lending capacity are driven importantly by changes in unused commitments, a pattern that was especially pronounced during the most recent crisis. Although the available data cover only the past three recessions, the dynamics in figure 10.3 indicate that changes in unused commitments are likely to provide a more timely signal regarding cyclical changes in credit availability, compared with changes in loans outstanding.

10.2   Information Needed to Measure Credit Flows

The analysis presented earlier highlights the inherent limitations faced by researchers and policymakers when assessing the availability of bank-intermediated credit during a cyclical downturn based on changes in outstanding loans and commitments. In particular, to help distinguish the relative contributions of supply and demand factors in driving changes in outstanding balances held on banks' books, considerably more detailed information about banks' lending and credit line provision activities would need to be collected. This information falls into the following four broad

---

7. It is important to note that what we label as "business lines" is recorded in Call Reports prior to 2010 as "other" unused commitments. More detailed data available since 2010 suggest that credit lines to businesses—both financial and nonfinancial—account for the vast majority of this category, which indicates that these data provide a useful proxy for unused credit lines to businesses.

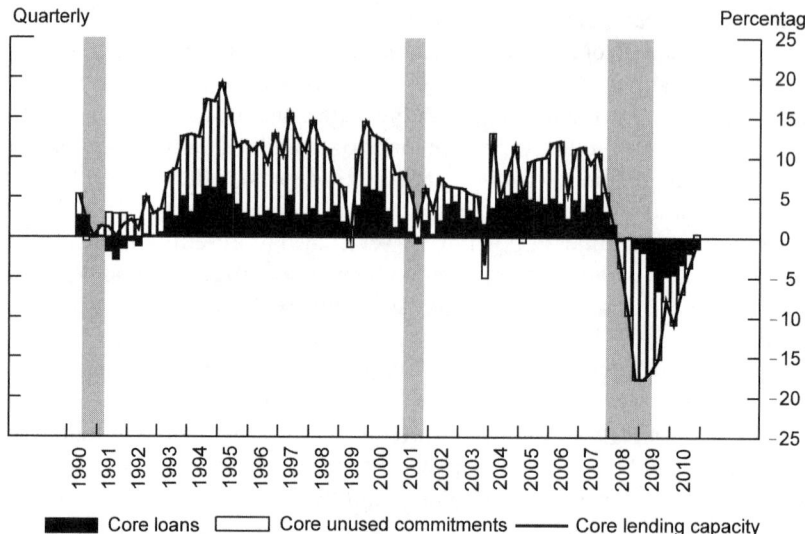

Fig. 10.3   Growth in core lending capacity at commercial banks

Source: Authors' calculations using Call Report data.

Notes: The thick solid line depicts the seasonally adjusted (annualized) quarterly growth rate of core lending capacity at US commercial banks; core lending capacity is defined as the sum of core loans outstanding and corresponding unused commitments. All series are deflated by the GDP price deflator (2005 = 100). Shaded vertical bars represent NBER-dated recessions.

categories: (a) credit extended under commitment versus credit extended not under commitment; (b) credit provided to new customers versus credit provided to existing customers;[8] (c) changes in credit flows owing to decisions by the bank versus changes in credit flows owing to decisions by the borrower; and (d) purchases and sales of credit products by the bank.

Separating loan originations made under commitment from originations not made under commitment, and more accurately measuring lending to new customers compared with existing customers, would likely yield significant insights into the relative contributions of supply and demand factors to lending flows. Because loans not extended under previous commitment typically embody the most recent lending standards and terms being applied by the bank, an expansion or contraction in such loans should be indicative of both current supply and demand conditions.[9] Likewise, newly established

8. By banks' new customers, we mean those that currently have no loans outstanding with a particular institution—that is, the bank currently has no credit exposure to that customer. If, as we argue later, data on new loan originations were to be collected by expanding the existing Call Report schedules, the "new customer" concept would be assessed at the bank level and not at the holding company level.

9. Indeed, as shown by Morgan (1998), changes in loans outstanding not made under commitment are more sensitive to changes in the stance of monetary policy than changes in loans made under commitment.

credit lines, or increases in existing credit lines, also reflect the confluence of supply and demand as embodied in the current economic landscape. In contrast, loans drawn down under previous commitment largely reflect lending policies that prevailed at the time the agreement was reached. As a result, changes in outstanding loan balances under existing credit lines may be most indicative of the demand for credit from firms with such credit lines.

The sources of loan growth—whether under commitment or not under commitment and whether from existing customers or new customers—can also contain important information for monitoring financial stability and can, therefore, inform macroprudential regulatory policies and responses (see Schularick and Taylor 2012). Growth in loans outstanding that is driven primarily by existing customers drawing down funds under standing lending commitments can be a sign of stress in credit markets and a signal that loan supply effects may be exerting a drag on economic growth. In contrast, strong growth in credit extended to new customers could signal an increase in demand for credit—and hence a pickup in economic activity—or it could suggest that banks have eased their lending standards.[10] The extent to which a step-up in credit growth is accounted for by increased lending to existing customers—whose risks are better known to the bank—or lending to new customers could provide supervisory authorities with potentially useful information regarding the safety and soundness of individual banking institutions.

In order to fully decompose lending flows, it is not only necessary to track credit extensions, but also credit that has been extinguished—for example, because it has been paid down or off, or because credit lines were reduced or cancelled, either at the request of the borrower or by the bank. In addition, information on purchases and sales of loans would greatly improve the ability of researchers and policymakers to better understand the creation of credit by the banking sector, as well as help monitor the buildup of risk and the web of interconnectedness among banks and nonbank financial intermediaries. As demonstrated by the recent financial crisis, a number of financial institutions purchased or sold certain types of loans without properly vetting borrowers or securing the appropriate documentation, a practice that contributed importantly to financial instability during the 2007 to 2009 period (see Shin 2009). Detailed data on purchases and sales of loans would allow supervisory authorities to monitor changes in the volumes of such transactions by particular institutions and help identify institutions with greater interconnectedness in those markets; such data would also facilitate

10. For example, Keeton (1999) and Igan and Pinheiro (2010) present evidence showing that rapid loan growth leads to higher-than-average subsequent losses. This result is consistent with the notion that rapid loan growth at an institution—relative to its peer group—is an indication that such an institution may have eased lending standards and terms, perhaps by more than is warranted by prevailing economic conditions.

rigorous analysis of the potential costs and benefits of those operations, which could enhance efficiency of rule making in this area.[11]

To measure accurately the provision of underlying credit over time, a substantial upgrade to currently available information would be required. Specifically, letting L(t) denote the amount of loans outstanding at the end of a reporting period t, equation (1) describes the possible ways that loans outstanding can change between periods $t - 1$ and t:

$$
(1) \quad L(t) = L(t-1) - M(t) - P_1(t) - P_2(t) - S(t) - W(t)
$$
$$
+ E_1(t) + E_2(t) + D(t) + N_1(t) + N_2(t) + A(t),
$$

where

- $M(t)$ = loans (or portions of loans) that matured and were not rolled over or extended during period t;
- $P_1(t)$ = loans (or portions of loans) paid off in advance of maturity during period t;
- $P_2(t)$ = loans (or portions of loans) paid off at maturity during period t;
- $S(t)$ = loans sold or securitized, with or without further obligation during period t;[12]
- $W(t)$ = loans charged off during period t;
- $E_1(t)$ = unpaid loans (or portions of loans) that matured and were rolled over or extended during period t;
- $E_2(t)$ = unpaid loans (or portions of loans) that became newly past due;
- $D(t)$ = amount of previously existing loan commitments newly drawn during period t;
- $N_1(t)$ = draws on new loan commitments that were finalized during period t;
- $N_2(t)$ = new loans that were not made under commitment during period t; and
- $A(t)$ = loans that were purchased or otherwise acquired during period t.

Of these items, only loans outstanding ($L(t)$) and loans charged off ($W(t)$) are systematically collected on Call Reports.

As discussed earlier, accurate monitoring of banks' capacity for credit intermediation over time requires a similar decomposition for unused com-

11. Detailed data on purchases of loans would serve an additional practical purpose. In the National Information Center (NIC) database—a central repository of data about banks and other institutions for which the Federal Reserve has a supervisory, regulatory, or research interest—a bank can purchase up to 95 percent of the assets of another institution before the transaction is recorded as a merger. When a transfer of assets involving less than 95 percent of the assets of the institutions occurs, it is recorded in the NIC database, but no information is recorded on the type or amount of assets acquired; and when less than 40 percent of an institution transfers ownership, no entry is made in the NIC database at all. The lack of data on these types of transactions results in substantial outliers when using changes in loans outstanding to analyze credit growth.

12. Further obligation includes the retention of servicing rights, recourse obligations, or other ongoing credit or liquidity enhancements.

mitments to fund loans. Specifically, letting $LC(t)$ denote the amount of unused commitments outstanding at the end of the reporting period t, equation (2) describes the evolution of this important off-balance sheet item over time:

$$(2) \quad LC(t) = LC(t-1) - MC_1(t) - MC_2(t) - MC_3(t) - SC(t) - D(t)$$
$$+ EC(t) + NC(t) + AC(t),$$

where

- $MC_1(t)$ = unused loan commitments that expired or matured during period t;
- $MC_2(t)$ = unused loan commitments reduced or canceled by the bank in advance of maturity during period t;
- $MC_3(t)$ = unused loan commitments reduced or canceled by the customer in advance of maturity during period t;
- $SC(t)$ = unused loan commitments sold or securitized during period t;
- $D(t)$ = amount of previously existing loan commitments newly drawn during period t (same as in equation [1]);
- $EC(t)$ = extensions of expired or matured unused loan commitments during period t;
- $NC(t)$ = unused portion of new loan commitments finalized during period t (i.e., new commitments during period t net of draws on those commitments); and
- $AC(t)$ = unused loan commitments purchased or otherwise acquired during period t.

Again, of the above-mentioned items, only the amount of unused commitments ($LC(t)$) is systematically collected on Call Reports.

From an operational perspective, the expansion of the FFIEC reporting forms 031, 041, and 002—the reporting forms that underlie the existing Call Report data for commercial banks—would provide the most natural way to collect quarterly information on the full scope of banks' lending activities.[13] The loan categories for which these data would ideally be collected would include, at a minimum, all of the major categories of lending to businesses and households that are currently being monitored via Call Reports. Data on the full spectrum of loan categories is important because, as discussed earlier and as evident from existing Call Report data, loan categories can behave quite differently over time, as conditions in relevant sectors of the economy and of various borrowers differ widely at times.

The pronounced and prolonged contraction in business loans on banks'

---

13. For consistency with the loan schedules in the Call Reports, each new flow item could be reported as the portion of the outstanding stock of loans on the Call Report date that owed to the given activity over the quarter that ended on the Call Report date. To reduce the reporting burden, an asset-based size test could possibly be used to exempt the smallest banks from having to report the additional items.

books over the past several years has also underscored the limited ability of researchers and policymakers to assess and analyze the availability of credit for small businesses, which are an important engine of economic growth.[14] In order to provide a window into the functioning of this important market, it would be most useful to obtain business loan originations (both C&I and commercial real estate) by the size of borrower. Specifically, the new data items listed previously, in combination with the existing Call Report schedules for outstanding loan balances and credit quality, could be disaggregated by firm size, using either the number of employees or revenues as the size criterion.[15] And lastly, there is a case for collecting all of this information from other depository institutions as well (e.g., savings banks, savings and loan associations, and credit unions), in order to obtain a comprehensive overview of credit intermediation in the US economy.

10.3   Conclusion

The recent financial crisis and its aftermath has highlighted the limited ability of policymakers and researchers to track and monitor accurately the provision of credit by the commercial banking sector. The data currently available are inadequate to monitor and analyze credit flows for the most important categories of lending to both businesses and households. This chapter outlined the type of data that would be needed to provide a more complete picture of banks' lending and credit line provision activities, information that would significantly improve our understanding of the credit intermediation process.

Even if such data were available, any analysis of the behavior of credit flows over the course of a business cycle is complicated by the fact that lending dynamics are determined by fluctuations in both the demand for and the supply of credit. While the proposed new data items would be helpful in disentangling the relative importance of demand and supply factors, fundamental identification problems are likely to remain. Accordingly, collecting information on borrower characteristics—for example, their income and balance sheet information—along with a more detailed and systematic information on lending standards and loan terms would also likely provide

14. See the Federal Reserve Board's Report to the Congress on the Availability of Credit to Small Businesses, available at http://www.federalreserve.gov/boarddocs/rptcongress/small businesscredit/sbfreport2007.pdf.

15. Small businesses are often classified as such on the basis of the number of employees, though there is no universally accepted employee threshold that defines a small business. For example, the US Small Business Administration's Office of Advocacy defines a small business as "an independent business having fewer than 500 employees." The Congress, in contrast, has in past legislation frequently defined small businesses as those that have no more than fifty employees. Institutions that lend to small businesses, however, are more likely to collect—for underwriting purposes—information on firms' revenues. As a result, a definition of a small business based on the firm's revenues may be more appropriate when collecting information on small business lending from banking institutions.

considerable insights regarding the role of bank-intermediated credit in the macroeconomy.

References

Ashcraft, A. B. 2005. "Are Banks Really Special? New Evidence from the FDIC-Induced Failure of Healthy Banks." *American Economic Review* 95 (5): 1712–30.

Bassett, W. F., M. B. Chosak, J. C. Driscoll, and E. Zakrajšek. 2014. "Changes in Bank Lending Standards and the Macroeconomy." *Journal of Monetary Economics* 62:23–40.

Bernanke, B. S., and C. S. Lown. 1991. "The Credit Crunch." *Brookings Papers on Economic Activity* 2 (2): 205–39.

Calomiris, C. W., and J. R. Mason. 2003. "Consequences of Bank Distress during the Great Depression." *American Economic Review* 93 (3): 937–47.

Gilchrist, S., and E. Zakrajšek. 2011. "Monetary Policy and Credit Supply Shocks." *IMF Economic Review* 59 (2): 194–232.

———. 2012a. "Bank Lending and Credit Supply Shocks." In *The Global Macro Economy and Finance*, edited by F. Allen, M. Aoki, N. Kiyotaki, R. Gordon, J. E. Stiglitz, and J.-P. Fitoussi, 154–76. New York: Palgrave Macmillan.

———. 2012b. "Credit Spreads and Business Cycle Fluctuations." *American Economic Review* 102 (4): 1692–720.

Igan, D., and M. Pinheiro. 2010. "Exposure to Real Estate in Bank Portfolios." *Journal of Real Estate Research* 32 (1): 47–74.

Ivashina, V., and D. S. Scharfstein. 2010. "Bank Lending During the Financial Crisis of 2008." *Journal of Financial Economics* 97 (3): 319–38.

Keeton, W. R. 1999. "Does Faster Loan Growth Lead to Higher Loan Losses?" *Federal Reserve Bank of Kansas City Economic Review* 84 (QII): 57–75.

Lown, C. S., and D. P. Morgan. 2006. "The Credit Cycle and the Business Cycle: New Findings from the Loan Officer Opinion Survey." *Journal of Money, Credit, and Banking* 38 (6): 1575–97.

Morgan, D. P. 1998. "The Credit Effects of Monetary Policy: Evidence From Using Loan Commitments." *Journal of Money, Credit, and Banking* 30 (1): 102–18.

Peek, J., and E. S. Rosengren. 1997. "The International Transmission of Financial Shocks." *American Economic Review* 87 (4): 625–38.

———. 2000. "Collateral Damage: Effects of the Japanese Bank Crisis on Real Activity in the United States." *American Economic Review* 90 (1): 30–45.

Schularick, M., and A. M. Taylor. 2012. "Credit Booms Gone Bust: Monetary Policy, Leverage Cycles, and Financial Crises, 1870–2008." *American Economic Review* 102 (2): 1029–61.

Shin, H. S. 2009. "Securitisation and Financial Stability." *Economic Journal* 119 (536): 309–32.

The Case for a Credit Registry

Atif Mian

11.1 Introduction

The banking sector is often blamed for exposing the economy to systemically important risks through either excessive credit creation and asset bubbles during episodes of credit boom, or excessive cut back in credit during slumps. The basic reasoning behind such arguments is that credit supply matters. For example, a relaxation in lending standards may lead to excessive credit creation during booms and large losses to capital may generate a deleveraging cycle that wipes out good credit during busts.

The concern that malfunctions in the credit supply process may generate unnecessary crises leads to calls for large scale policy intervention in credit markets. For example, central banks are advised to "lean against the wind" if credit is expanding due to lax lending practices. On the other hand, central banks and governments are urged to inject liquidity and capital in the banking system if credit is being cut due to a deleveraging process.

This chapter seeks to answer the following question:

What tools does a regulator or policymaker have at her disposal to judge whether changes in bank credit are driven by supply-side factors?[1]

Atif Mian is professor of economics and public policy at Princeton University and a research associate of the National Bureau of Economic Research.

I thank Asim Khwaja, Markus Brunnermeier, Arvind Krishnamurthy, and participants at the NBER conference on systemic risk in New York for comments and suggestions. Special thanks to Ramón Santillán at Banco de España for answering questions concerning the design of credit registry systems. Funding from the Coleman Fung Risk Management Center at Berkeley is gratefully acknowledged. For acknowledgments, sources of research support, and disclosure of the author's material financial relationships, if any, please see http://www.nber.org/chapters/c12553.ack

1. My focus here is on commercial lending to firms. A related question corresponding to consumer financing is discussed by Amir Sufi in "Detecting Bad Leverage" (chapter 14, this volume).

The question is important because if changes in bank credit were driven by genuine demand-side factors such as productivity shocks or shocks to expectations, then policy intervention based on the premise that the fault lies on the credit supply side can be counterproductive. Moreover, even if supply-side factors influence bank credit, these factors may not be too relevant for the economy if there are sufficient new and alternative sources of financing to pick up any slack created by misperforming banks.

I outline a methodology that can help policymakers better understand the extent to which supply-side factors generate aggregate fluctuations in credit. The methodology is based on the regulator having access to a timely and comprehensive *credit registry* that contains information on every business loan given out by the banking sector. While such credit registry data are available in many countries around the world, the United States does not currently have a comparable system. I discuss the design issues related to the building up a credit registry database in section 11.2. Section 11.3 outlines the methodology that can be applied to credit registry data to isolate the role of supply-side factors and section 11.4 provides real world examples. Section 11.5 concludes with a discussion of some of the limitations of the proposed methodology.

11.2   Credit Registry Design

I begin with a brief description of the design of credit registries (see World Bank [2011] for more details). There are four basic steps in the design of a credit registry system: data collection, data validation, data dissemination, and data usage.

Data collection. Credit registry data are collected from every commercial borrower in the banking system. The data contain identification information on borrower and lender, and may include details such as name, location, industry, and ownership information. Information on location, industry, and ownership is particularly useful for testing if credit is concentrated in certain regions, industries, or groups of companies and whether such trends have strengthened over time. A typical credit registry records both positive and negative credit information. Positive credit information includes total amount of credit issued, credit outstanding, maturity, and collateral value (if any). Negative credit information includes default rate (broken by thirty-day, sixty-day, etc.), recovery in case of default, and any legal actions against the borrower in the past. In certain countries there may be a sunset provision on negative information such that negative information is automatically deleted from the record after a predetermined number of years. It is common for credit registry data to be updated on a monthly basis. With the advancements in information technology, collecting credit registry data at a monthly frequency is not too cumbersome.

Data validation. An important step after data collection is its validation to minimize errors. Automated routines can be set up to check if the data are coded appropriately and whether individual data items add up to the consolidated version. Any significant discrepancy found in the validation stage can be sent back to the data collection stage for further verification. Random audits of loan-level data are also useful in strengthening data quality and incentivizing data collectors to monitor the process appropriately. Such audits not only help keep the data quality high but also improve transparency and reliability of the banking sector financial data.

Data dissemination. Every credit registry data must have appropriately designed rules on how data will be disseminated and who can get access to the data. There is a fundamental tension between maintaining proprietorship of data and making data accessible to a wider audience. Banks that rely on "relationship banking" may want to keep their portfolio confidential to maximize leverage and rents in their relationship. Doing so may—in theory—also be optimal ex ante to give incentives to banks to spend effort in adding first-time borrowers to the banking sector. However, such benefits of data proprietorship must be weighed against the broader benefits of data sharing. These include enabling banks to get a real time sense of the overall exposure of their clients (and related parties) with other banks and allowing regulators/researchers quick access to data for macroprudential purposes (as explained in the following sections).

Putting all this together, while it is important to create and share credit registry data, it is equally important to outline strict guidelines on who can access the data and how. It is imperative that everyone contributing to the credit registry data must have full confidence that the data will only be used for legitimate purposes.

Data usage. Once a credit registry data is put in place, an obvious use of the data is to help regulators and the banking sector use the data for prudential and risk-management purposes. The rest of this chapter explains how the data can also be combined with more scientific empirical methodologies to better identify the fundamental drivers of credit boom and bust. The accumulated knowledge can then help policymakers make more informed choices.

11.3 Methodology

The methodology outlined here was introduced by Khwaja and Mian (2008) and augmented by Jiménez et al. (2011). The basic purpose of the methodology is to test specific hypotheses about the role of supply-side factors in generating observed changes in bank credit. The methodology offers two advantages from an econometric standpoint. First, it provides an unbiased estimate of the supply-driven "bank lending channel" effect. Second, it takes into account general equilibrium adjustments made at the borrower level in reaction to the bank lending channel effect and provides a bias-corrected net effect of the bank lending channel at the borrower level. We briefly illustrate the methodology below.

Consider an economy with banks and firms indexed by i and j, respectively. Firm j borrows from n_j banks at time t, and assume that it borrows the same amount from each of the n_j banks. The economy experiences two shocks at t: a firm-specific credit demand shock η_j and a bank-specific credit supply shock δ_i. The variable η_j reflects changes in the firm's demand for credit driven by productivity or customer demand shocks. Variable δ_i reflects changes in the bank's funding situation, such as a run on short-term liabilities (a negative shock), or new opportunities to access wholesale financing (a positive shock.)

Let y_{ij} denote the log change in credit from bank i to firm j. Then the basic credit channel equation in the face of credit supply and demand shocks can be written as:

(1) $$y_{ij} = \alpha + \beta * \delta_i + \eta_j + \varepsilon_{ij}.$$

Equation (1) assumes that the change in bank credit from bank i to firm j is determined by an economy-wide secular trend α, credit supply and credit demand shocks, and an idiosyncratic shock ε_{ij}. While equation (1) is reduced form in nature, it can be derived as an equilibrium condition by explicitly modeling credit supply and demand schedules.

In a frictionless world (as in the Modigliani-Miller theorem), bank lending is independent of credit supply conditions and only depends on "fundamental" credit demand factors. Financial intermediaries in such scenarios have no impact on the economy and, hence, there is no bank transmission channel, that is, $\beta = 0$ in equation (1). The presence of financing frictions, however, may force banks to pass on their credit supply shocks δ_i to borrowing firms, making $\beta > 0$

Variable β is often referred to as the "bank lending channel," and is the key supply-side parameter of interest. Variable β can be estimated from equation (1) using ordinary least squares (OLS), giving us $\hat{\beta}_{OLS} = \beta + [Cov(\delta_i, \eta_j) / Var(\delta_i)]$. The expression implies that as long as credit supply and demand shocks are significantly correlated, $\hat{\beta}_{OLS}$ in equation (1) would be a biased estimate of the true β. For example, if banks receiving a positive liquidity shock are more likely to lend to firms that simultaneously receive a positive credit demand boost, then β would be biased upward. Khwaja and Mian (2008) resolve this issue by focusing on firms with $n_j \geq 2$, and absorbing out η_j through firm fixed effects. The estimated coefficient $\hat{\beta}_{FE}$ then provides an unbiased estimate of β.

However, $\hat{\beta}_{FE}$ does not give us a complete picture of the net effect of bank lending channel on the economy. In particular, individual firms affected by the local lending channel due to a positive β in equation (1) may seek funding from new banking relationships to compensate for any loss of credit. Jimenez et al. (2011) show that an unbiased estimate of the *net* (or aggregate) effect of supply-side banking shocks on borrower j can be estimated using the equation:

$$(2) \qquad \bar{y}_j = \bar{\alpha} + \bar{\beta} * \bar{\delta}_j + \eta_j + \bar{\varepsilon}_j,$$

where $\bar{y}_j$ denotes the log change in credit for firm j across *all* banks.[2] It is *not* a simple average of y_{ij} from equation (1), since a firm can start borrowing from new banks as well. Variable $\bar{\delta}_j$ denotes the *average* banking sector shock experienced by firm j at time t, that is, $\bar{\delta}_j = \Sigma_{i \in N_j} \delta_i / n_j$, where N_j represents the set of banks lending to firm j at time t. Variable $\bar{\varepsilon}_j$ is an idiosyncratic error term. The same credit demand shock η_j appears in both equations (1) and (2) under the assumption that the shock equally affects a firm's borrowing from all banks. The aggregate impact of credit supply channel is captured by the coefficient $\bar{\beta}$. If there is no adjustment at firm level in the face of bank-specific credit channel shocks, then $\bar{\beta} = \beta$.

How does one estimate $\bar{\beta}$? An OLS estimate of equation (2) yields $\hat{\bar{\beta}}_{OLS} = \bar{\beta} + [Cov(\delta_i, \eta_i) / Var(\bar{\delta}_j)]$.[3] While the variance of $\bar{\delta}_j$ can be estimated in data, the covariance term between credit demand and credit supply shocks is unobservable to the econometrician. However, a unique advantage of the preceding fixed-effects estimator at loan level is that it allows us to back out the covariance term. Since $\hat{\beta}_{FE}$ is an unbiased estimate of β, we can write $Cov(\delta_i, \eta_j) = (\hat{\beta}_{OLS} - \hat{\beta}_{FE}) * Var(\delta_i)$, where variance of bank credit supply shocks δ_i can be estimated directly from data. Thus the aggregate lending channel effect, $\bar{\beta}$, can be estimated as:

$$(3) \qquad \hat{\bar{\beta}} = \hat{\bar{\beta}}_{OLS} - \left(\hat{\beta}_{OLS} - \hat{\beta}_{FE}\right) * \frac{Var(\delta_i)}{Var(\bar{\delta}_j)}.$$

The second term on the right-hand side of equation (3) is the adjustment term that corrects for any bias in the OLS estimate of equation (2). The adjustment term corrects for the otherwise unobserved covariance between credit supply and demand shocks. The extra variance term in the denominator corrects for the fact that the variance of bank shocks averaged at the firm level may be different from the variance of bank shocks overall.

A key advantage of the proposed methodology is that it can be implemented in real time. In particular, for any given bank shock δ_i that is suspected of generating a transmission channel, run OLS and fixed effects (FE) versions of equation (1) to estimate $\hat{\beta}_{OLS}$ and $\hat{\beta}_{FE}$ respectively. Then estimate firm-level equation (2) using OLS to generate $\bar{\beta}_{OLS}$. Finally, plug these three coefficients in equation (3) to estimate the unbiased impact of credit supply channel at the firm level.

A second advantage of the proposed procedure is that it relies on credit registry data, which exists in most countries of the world with banking

---

2. Depending on data availability, it could include nonbank sources of credit as well.
3. This follows from the observation that $Cov(\bar{\delta}_j, \eta_j) = Cov(\Sigma_{i \in N_j} (\delta_i / n_i), \eta_j) = Cov(\delta_i, \eta_j)$.

supervision departments. We next provide three examples of the use of this methodology from Pakistan, Spain, and the United States.

11.4   Examples

11.4.1   Nuclear Tests and Dollar Deposit Run on Banks in Pakistan

The unexpected nuclear tests by Pakistan in May 1998 imposed stiff sanctions on the country that led to a serious balance of payment crisis. Consequently, the government defaulted on its obligation to pay back dollars that it had borrowed through the banking sector's "dollar deposit scheme." The default on dollar obligations led to a serious run by depositors on the banking sector. However the run was not uniform across banks, but concentrated on banks that were more reliant on dollar deposits as a funding source.[4]

Khwaja and Mian (2008) evaluate the credit supply consequences of the run on bank deposits. We estimate equation (1) with borrower fixed effects separately for each quarter t. Variable y_{ij} is defined as log change in loan from bank i to firm j. The change is computed from the quarter prior to the nuclear tests until quarter t. Variable δ_i is defined as the log change in deposits for bank i in the aftermath of the nuclear tests.

The set of estimated coefficients $\hat{\beta}_{FE,t}$ (one for each t) trace out the supply-side impact of the run on deposits. Each coefficient $\hat{\beta}_{FE,t}$ is computed using the within-firm difference in loan growth from banks with (relatively) high deposit growth versus banks with low deposit growth. Figure 11.1 plots this difference after classifying above and below median deposit growth as "positive" and "negative" liquidity shocks respectively.

There is no sign of a credit supply effect until the nuclear shock hits. Following the nuclear tests, we see a strong credit supply effect from the run on deposits. While there is a strong credit supply shock at the loan level, Khwaja and Mian (2008) show that this effect is completely neutralized by large firms (top 30 percent of firms by size) as they are able to borrow from new sources of funding. Thus the credit supply shock ends up affecting only smaller firms. Such an analysis can help policymakers understand the magnitude of the credit supply shock, and isolate the set of firms most in need of additional credit support.

11.4.2   Real Estate Securitization and Bank Credit in Spain

Jiménez et al. (2011) apply the aforementioned methodology to the case of Spain and test whether the boom in real estate securitization during the

---

4. Banks could not hold these dollar deposits themselves. They turned over the dollar deposits to the central bank in exchange for equivalent rupees under the promise that the central bank would return dollars on demand from the depositor.

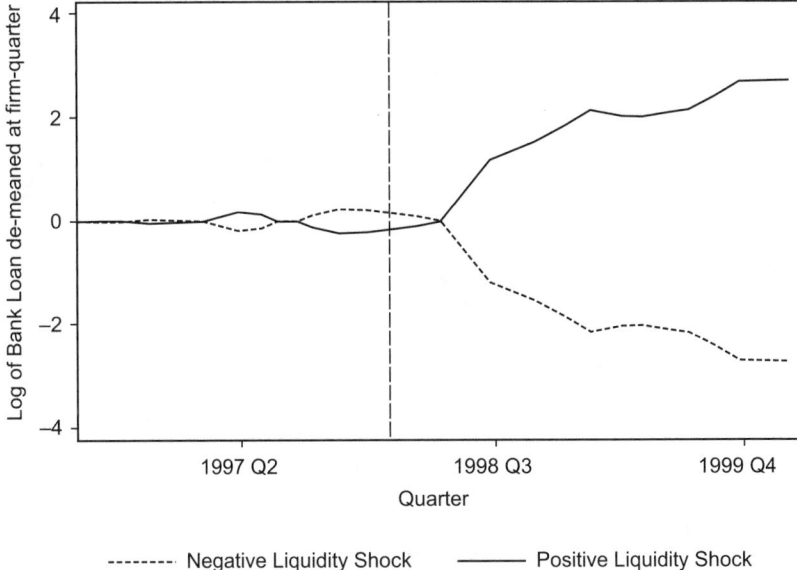

Fig. 11.1 Loan-level credit channel effect for Pakistan

Notes: The figure illustrates the credit supply effect due to the run on deposits in the aftermath of the May 1998 nuclear tests by Pakistan (dashed vertical line). It plots the change in credit within the same firm borrowing from two different types of banks—one that experiences a positive (above-median) growth in deposits and one that experiences negative (below-median) growth in deposits in the aftermath of the nuclear tests.

2000s enabled banks with large real estate assets to expand credit supply by securitizing their real estate portfolio. They estimate equation (1) with borrower fixed effects separately for each quarter t. Variable y_{ij} is defined as log change in loan from bank i to firm j. The change is computed from 2004Q4 until quarter t. Variable δ_i is defined as the ex ante (year 2000) variation in real estate holdings for bank i. Real estate exposure proxies for the capacity of banks to securitize assets during the securitization boom. The analysis utilizes a comprehensive quarterly loan level credit registry data from the Bank of Spain that covers a period from 1999Q4 to 2009Q4.

Figure 11.2 plots the firm fixed-effect estimate of the credit supply effect of real estate exposure, $\hat{\beta}_{FE,t}$. Starting in 2004 (when securitization in Spain shoots up), there is a strong positive credit supply effect for banks with real estate exposure due to improved access to wholesale financing. The positive credit supply effect turns negative in 2008, however, as the global securitization market shuts down.

Jiménez et al. (2011) show that despite a significant loan-level credit supply effect, the net (aggregate) impact of securitization at the borrower level is muted due to a "crowding out" effect. Nonetheless, there is a sig-

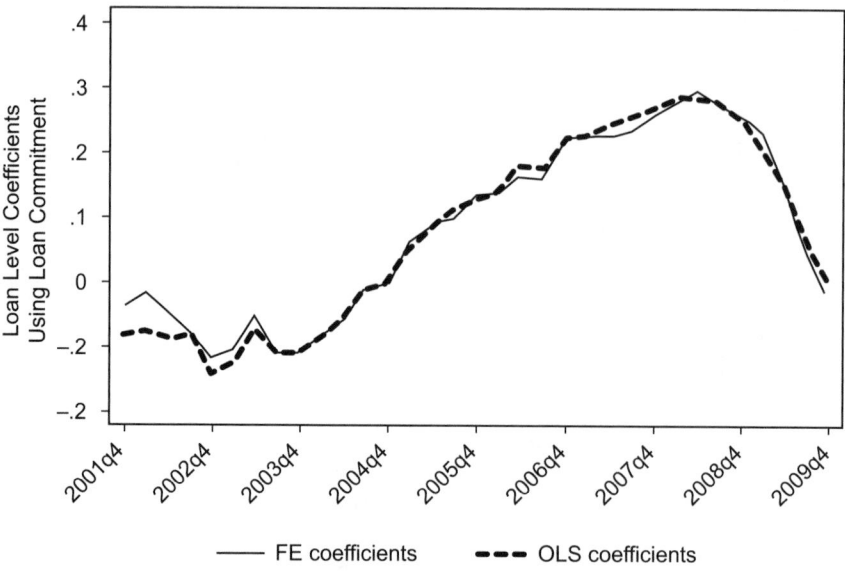

Fig. 11.2 Loan-level credit channel coefficients for Spain by quarter

Notes: The figure plots the coefficient estimates for β^t for the following specification for each quarter t: $y_{ijt} - y_{ij,04q4} = \alpha^t + \beta^t * REexposure_{i,2000} + \eta_{jt} + \varepsilon_{ijt}$, where y is the natural logarithm of loan commitment amount for firm j from bank i. $REexposure_{i,2000}$ is the share of loan portfolio exposed to real estate for bank i in 2000. The OLS coefficient estimates do not include the firm fixed effects term, η_{jt}.

nificant aggregate impact of the expansion in credit supply on the price of credit. Securitization also leads to a reduction in loan collateralization rates and lengthens the maturity of loans.

11.4.3   US Financial Crisis and Bank Credit Lines

Some observers argue that a reduction in the supply of credit to corporations was an important factor in precipitating the economic downturn during 2007 and 2008. Ivashina and Scharfstein (2010) show that corporations drew down on their lines of credit significantly during this period, and especially more so from banks experiencing larger losses and thus under greater threat of going bankrupt. One interpretation of this evidence is that there was a "run" by corporations on weak banks under the fear that future credit supply may be choked off.

However, in a recent paper using loan-level data from the Fed's SNC program, Mian and Santos (2011) show that the increase in drawn lines of credit is not unique to the 2007 to 2009 crisis. The same pattern is seen in each of the previous two recessions of 1990 to 1991 and 2001 as well, and there was no banking crisis in 2001. Thus, an alternative demand-based explanation for the increase in draw-down ratio is that as the economy slows, firms draw down as much as they can before their credit worthiness deteriorates.

We can use the above-mentioned methodology to test if the corporate run on undrawn lines of credit was driven by credit supply shock. Using loan-level data on syndicate loans from the Fed, we estimate equation (1), with y_{ij} defined as change in draw down percentage of a syndicate loan from lead bank i to firm j. Variable δ_i captures the exposure of a lead bank to the crisis, which we proxy using the bank's ultimate charge-offs to assets. We also add the initial level of draw-down percentage on the right-hand side since the change in draw down is mechanically related to the initial draw-down percentage.

While simple OLS estimation of equation (1) over 2006 to 2007 and 2007 to 2008 shows that banks with larger ultimate losses experience larger increase in draw-down percentage, this result is entirely driven by less creditworthy firms more likely to borrow from banks with greater exposure to the crisis. The unbiased borrower fixed-effect estimate $\hat{\beta}_{FE}$ is no longer positive with reasonably small standard errors. Thus the correlation between bank losses and increase in borrower draw-down ratio is driven by the endogenous matching of firms with low credit worthiness to banks that end up experiencing large losses.

11.5   Concluding Discussion

Most concerns about systemic risk relating to the banking industry are based on the premise that bank credit supply may get out of whack with economic fundamentals. This chapter outlined a methodology that can be used to test specific hypotheses about the extent to which changes in credit are driven by supply-side factors. The methodology uses loan-level credit registry data that are increasingly available in many countries. However, surprisingly, the United States lags behind in the availability of detailed loan-level data. Ideally, one would like to have loan-level data that covers the entire banking sector, and follows not just loan quantities but also price terms such as interest rate, maturity, collateralization rate, and basic covenants.

While I discussed three examples relating to my own work, other scholars have also used the methodology highlighted here in conjunction with credit registry data to isolate credit supply effects. These include Cetorelli and Goldberg (forthcoming) on international transmission of credit supply shocks during 2007 to 2008, Lin and Paravisini (2010) on the credit supply effect of bank reputation in the United States, Paravisini (2008) on credit supply effects in Argentina, Jiménez et al. (2010, forthcoming) on credit supply effects of monetary policy in Spain, and Schnabl (forthcoming) on the international transmission of credit supply shocks in Peru.

I end with some caveats regarding the use of this methodology in practice. First, the use of credit registry data is feasible at a monthly or quarterly frequency only. Thus, analysis of the sort discussed in this chapter is more suitable for low-frequency analysis.

Second, the methodology is based on a cross-sectional comparison of changes in loans over time, and may be viewed as a specific version of the difference-in-differences approach. As such, the methodology is useful to the extent that there are legitimate reasons to believe that the impact of credit supply is not uniform across all banks.

Third, the methodology by design limits the analysis to borrowers with multiple banking relationships. There is thus a concern that single-relationship borrowers that may be most adversely impacted by credit supply shocks are left out. However, more than three quarters of bank lending often goes to borrowers with multiple relationships. Moreover, variation within multiple-relationship firms can also be used to test if credit supply shocks affect smaller firms differentially.

References

Cetorelli, Nicola, and Linda S. Goldberg. Forthcoming. "Global Banks and International Shock Transmission: Evidence from the Crisis." *IMF Economic Review*.

Ivashina, V., and D. Scharfstein. 2010. "Bank Lending during the Financial Crises of 2008." *Journal of Financial Economics* 97:319–38.

Jiménez, Gabriel, Atif Mian, José-Luis Peydró, and Jesús Saurina. 2011. "Local versus Aggregate Lending Channels: The Effects of Securitization on Corporate Credit Supply In Spain." Working Paper, Princeton University.

Jiménez, Gabriel, Steven Ongena, José-Luis Peydró, and Jesús Saurina. 2010. "Credit Supply: Identifying Balance-Sheet Channels with Loan Applications and Granted Loans." Discussion Paper 7655. Center for Economic Policy Research.

———. Forthcoming. "Hazardous Times for Monetary Policy: What do Twenty-Three Million Bank Loans Say about the Effects of Monetary Policy on Credit Risk?" *American Economic Review*.

Khwaja, Asim I., and Atif Mian. 2008. "Tracing the Impact of Bank Liquidity Shocks." *American Economic Review* 98 (4): 1413–42.

Lin, Huidan, and Daniel Paravisini. 2010. "What's Bank Reputation Worth? The Effect of Fraud on Financial Contracts and Investment." Working Paper, London School of Economics.

Mian, Atif, and Joao Santos, 2011. "Liquidity Risk, Maturity Management, and the Business Cycle." Working Paper, Princeton University.

Paravisini, Daniel. 2008. "Local Bank Financial Constraints and Firm Access to External Finance." *Journal of Finance* 63 (5): 2161–93.

Schnabl, Philipp. Forthcoming. "The International Transmission of Bank Liquidity Shocks: Evidence from an Emerging Market." *Journal of Finance*.

World Bank. 2011. "General Principles for Credit Reporting." Consultative Report, March. Washington, DC: The World Bank.

V Household Sector

12

Monitoring the Financial Condition and Expenditures of Households

Robert E. Hall

- Household expenditure accounts for about two-thirds of GDP; it accounted for a large fraction of the decline in GDP following the financial crisis.
- Households went on a spending binge in the middle of the 2000s, building up unusually high stocks of housing, cars, and other durable assets, along with a large volume of debt to finance the spending.
- The crisis resulted in a large volume of household deleveraging—households contracted consumption to pay off debt.
- The United States has excellent data on many categories of expenditure, asset holdings, and debt, summed across all households, but much less information about the variation of these quantities across the range of poor-to-prosperous households.
- Existing data sources could be improved, by collecting data more often and by collecting data from panels of households.
- Online and administrative sources not currently tapped could add a great deal to information about household finances and expenditure.

Households purchase about two-thirds of the output of the US economy. Cutbacks in household expenditure are a factor in every recession—the Great Recession starting at the end of 2007 was no exception. Because many households—arguably the majority—are dependent on financial insti-

Robert E. Hall is the Robert and Carole McNeil Joint Hoover Senior Fellow and Professor of Economics at Stanford University and a research associate and director of the Economic Fluctuations and Growth Program at the National Bureau of Economic Research.

For acknowledgments, sources of research support, and disclosure of the author's material financial relationships, if any, please see http://www.nber.org/chapters/c12550.ack.

tutions for credit, events in financial markets have immediate and powerful effects on household expenditure and thus on output and employment.

Figure 12.1 shows household purchases of new houses and consumer goods and services since 2001 along with business purchases of plant and equipment and government purchases. Household purchases began sagging at the end of 2007, reached their minimum in 2009, and have grown slowly since then. They are still well below their growth path from 2001 to 2007. Business purchases dropped sharply after the financial crisis of late 2008 and rebounded back to almost their earlier growth path before falling again in the slowdown of 2011. The level of household purchases dwarfs the other two components at all times. I should note that household purchases as shown here exceed consumption expenditure in the National Income and Product Accounts because they include purchases of new houses, which the NIPAs count as investment.

It is useful to divide household expenditure into three categories as shown in figure 12.2: (a) new houses, (b) cars and other consumer durables, and (c) nondurable goods and services. The third category is by far the largest,

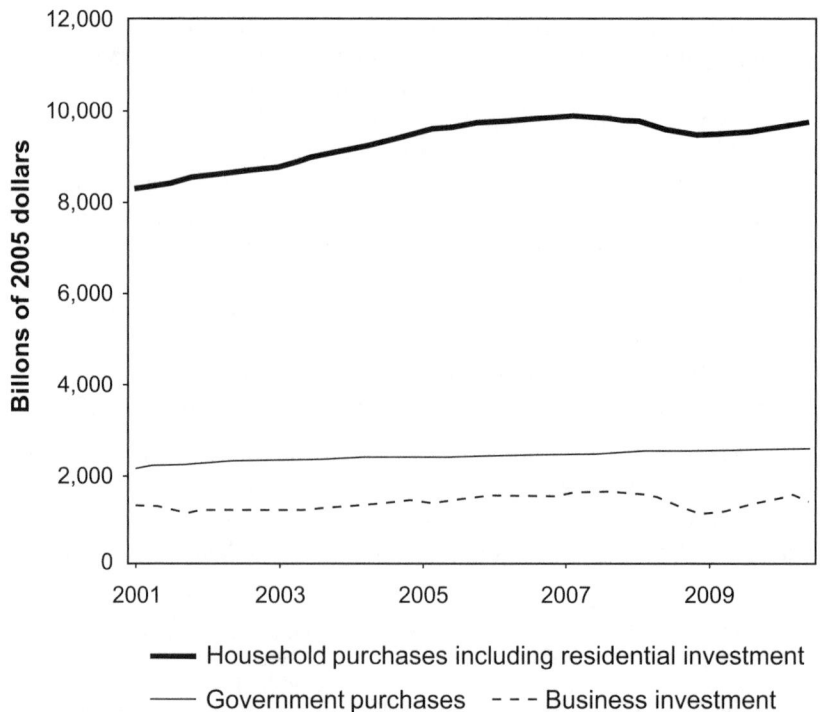

Fig. 12.1   Household purchases dominate the level and movements of output

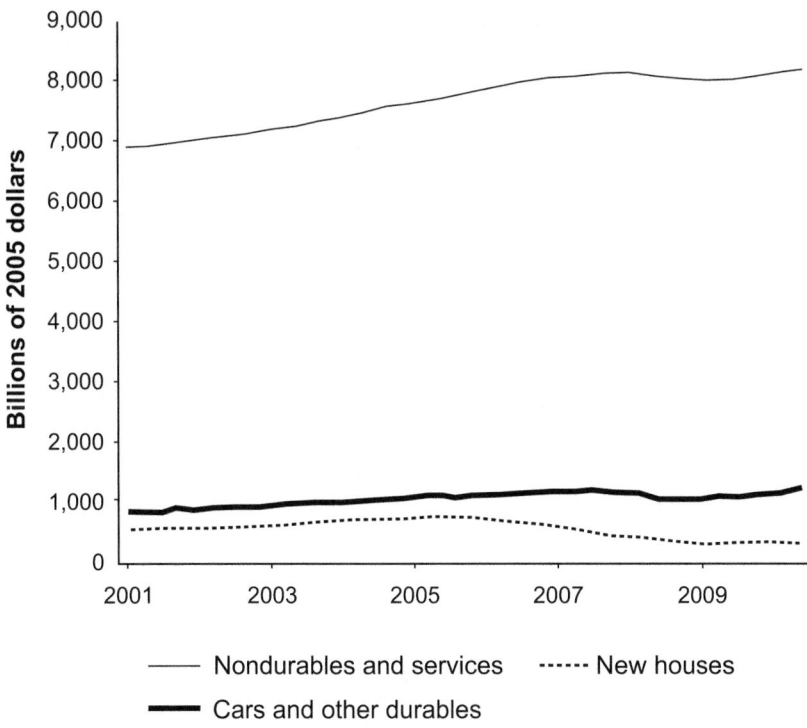

Fig. 12.2   Components of household purchases

but the first two are more volatile and more sensitive to financial events because most families borrow to buy houses and cars.

Macroeconomists are close to a consensus about the origins and mechanisms of the Great Recession. In the middle years of the decade, households were on a borrowing and buying binge. Figure 12.3 shows that household stocks of housing and durables reached an unusual level relative to the gross domestic product (GDP) in the second half of the decade. Although some economists have concluded that easy money and plentiful credit in general accounted for the binge, as figure 12.3 also shows, no similar binge occurred in business holdings of plant and equipment. Forces specific to households, including the expansion of subprime mortgages and the expectation of rising house prices, appear to be the main proximate causes.

Households took on large amounts of new debt to finance their binge purchases. Figure 12.4 shows that new borrowing considerably exceeded interest payments and repayment of principal until the middle of 2006. From 2002 to 2006, households played a Ponzi game. Then, in a sudden reversal, from 2007 to the present, households paid hundreds of billions of dollars back to lenders (net of debt forgiven on account of default).

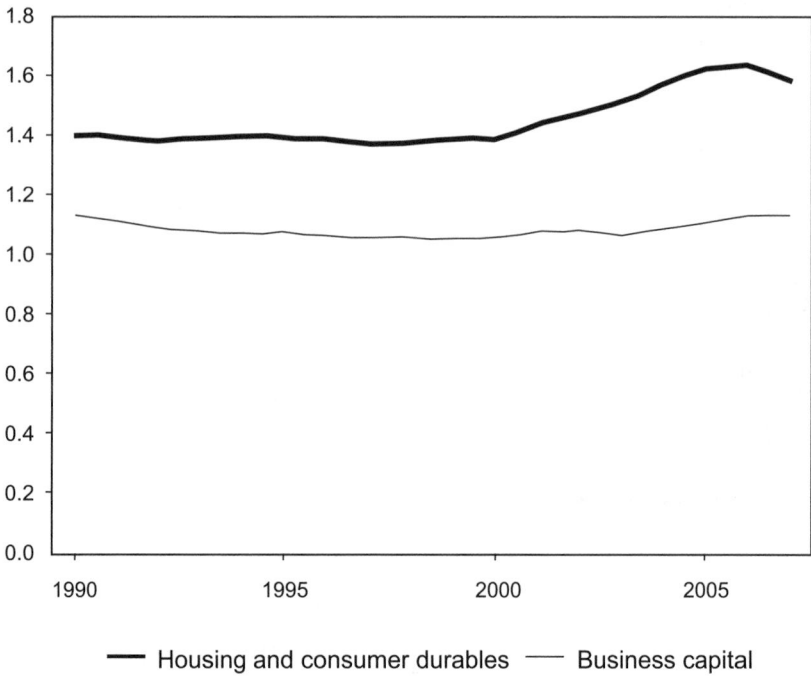

Housing and consumer durables ——— Business capital

Fig. 12.3   Ratios of capital and durables to GDP

Why did the reversal of cash flows occur? In the first place, a Ponzi game cannot go on forever, so at some point households would have shifted to making positive net cash payments to lenders. But the financial crisis appears to have contributed to the speed and magnitude of the reversal. As house prices reached their maximum values in 2006 and started downward, banks and other financial institutions began to suffer depletion of capital. One response was to cut back dramatically in lending to households and other borrowers. Figure 12.5 shows indexes of lending standards inferred from the Senior Loan Office Survey of the Federal Reserve Board.

Finally, households faced a large and continuing increase in financial stress. Figure 12.6 shows one measure, an index of Google queries for "withdrawal penalty." The upsurge in consumer concern about penalties for accessing retirement plans and other forms of wealth confirms that many households were unable to borrow on normal terms from financial institutions.

Data aggregated over all US households are readily available in great detail for expenditures and financial positions. The major sources are as follows:

- The National Income and Product Accounts of the Bureau of Economic Analysis, Department of Commerce, contain detailed monthly

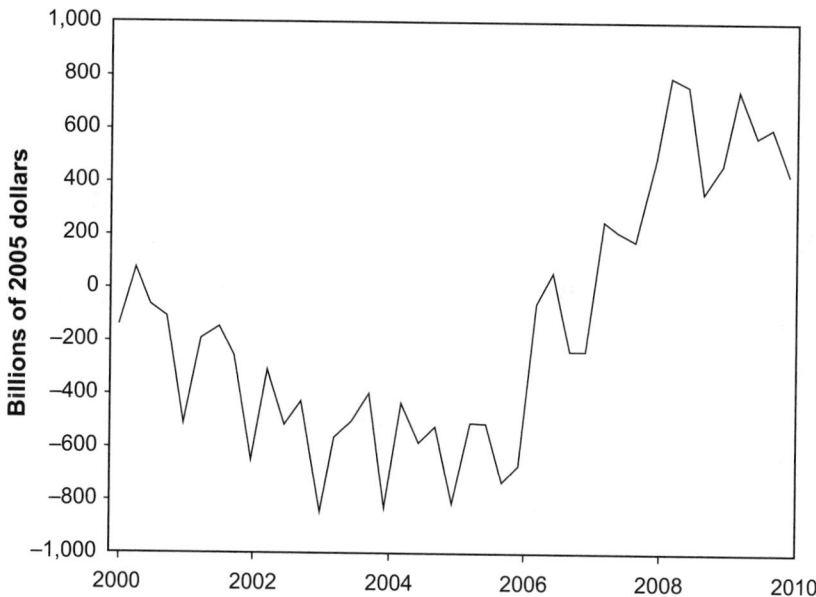

Fig. 12.4   Net cash flowing from households to lenders

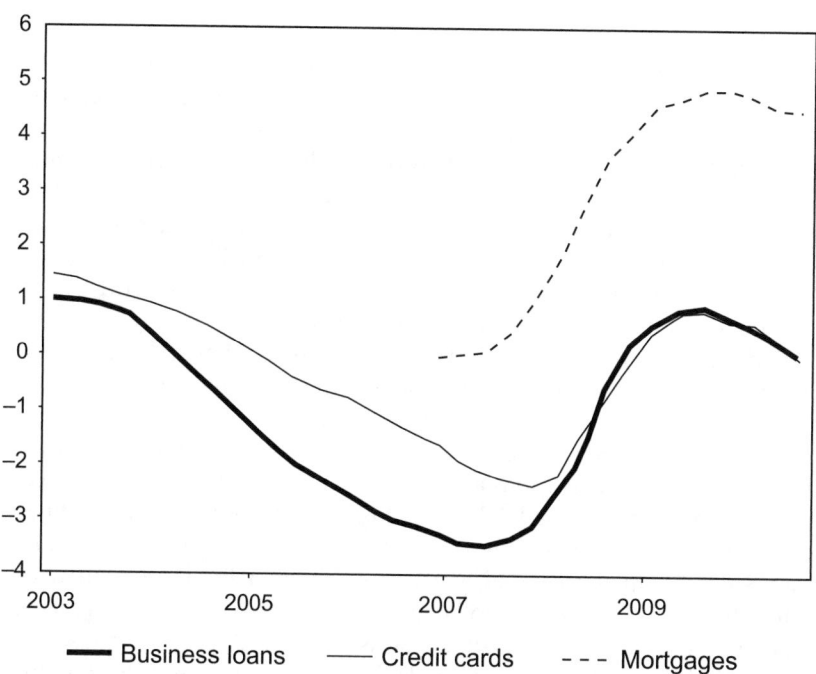

Fig. 12.5   Indexes of lending standards inferred from the FRB Senior Loan Officer Survey

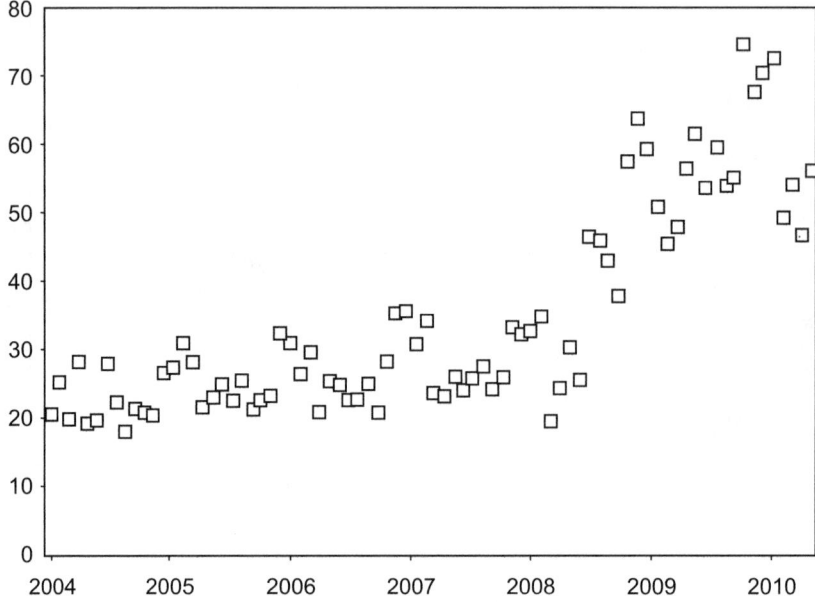

Fig. 12.6   Index of Google queries for "withdrawal penalty"

data on personal and disposable income and on expenditures in detailed categories, together with their prices. The satellite Fixed Asset Accounts report stocks of housing and consumer durables.

- The Flow of Funds Accounts of the Federal Reserve Board contain detailed balance sheets for US households.
- The Federal Reserve Board publishes data on interest rates and charge-off rates for a variety of types of consumer debt.
- The Bureau of Labor Statistics, Department of Labor, and the Department of the Census conduct the Current Population Survey, which provides monthly estimates of employment, unemployment, and related measures of household involvement in the labor market.

The aggregate data sources are inadequate for the task of monitoring household financial positions and expenditure levels, because they conceal vast heterogeneity among US households. In particular, holdings of financial wealth are extremely skewed. More than half of US families hold less than $10,000 in financial wealth apart from retirement funds, yet total wealth is hundreds of thousands of dollars per family. Table 12.1 shows aggregate financial assets and liabilities of US households, as dollars per household, in late 2011, from the Flow of Funds data. On average, American households hold substantial financial assets, well in excess of their borrowing. But the average conceals the fact that the majority of households hold no

Table 12.1   **Financial assets and liabilities of US households, thousands of dollars per household, third quarter, 2011**

	Thousands of dollars
Financial assets	418
Deposits and stocks	175
Other assets	244
Liabilities	121
Mortgages	87
Consumer credit	22

financial assets to speak of. Moreover, these are the households who owe *all* of the consumer debt and much of the mortgage debt. See Kaplan and Violante (2011) for a discussion of the role of illiquid high-debt house-holds, who include many with quite high incomes. The aggregate data fail to completely convey the reality among American families, most of whom are financially precarious. They deal with adverse shocks by cutting back consumption expenditures, especially cars and other durables, rather than by drawing down liquid savings. In times when consumer credit is plentiful, these families maintain consumption by running up credit card balances, but this habit makes their expenditure sensitive to credit tightening, as occurred during the financial crisis. For a theoretical model that gives a full treatment to the range of experiences among households depending on their liquid-asset positions, and to their response to credit tightening, see Guerrieri and Lorenzoni (2011).

Existing sources of data at the household level include the following:

- The Bureau of Labor Statistics's Consumer Expenditure Survey measures consumption at the family level but does not follow families over much time. Its aggregates over products disagree substantially with NIPA. The BLS is working on improving the survey. See Attanasio, Hurst, and Pistaferri (2012) for recent work on correcting the errors in the survey.
- The Panel Study of Income Dynamics measures consumption of a sample of families every two years. See Dynan (2012) for a study of the differences among consumer behavior during the crisis based on their immediate precrisis debt holdings, using PSID data.
- The Federal Reserve Board's Survey of Consumer Finances measures family assets and liabilities in great detail—every three years—but does not usually follow families over time. The Fed conducted a special resur-vey of the 2007 respondents in 2009 to track the effects of the financial crisis and Great Recession.

One improvement in the value of household data would involve conduct-ing the Survey of Consumer Finances annually and including families in it for two or more years. The 2009 resurvey demonstrated the practicality of gathering information a second time from the same respondents. The design of the resurvey carefully considered the burden on the respondents and avoided repeating many of the questions from the original survey.

A more ambitious and controversial approach would collect financial and flow data from families from administrative and financial institution records. This approach would blend data from the Internal Revenue Service and all financial institutions, linked by Social Security numbers. With reliable income and wealth data, expenditure could be measured as income less the increase in wealth. Jonathan Parker's chapter 13 in this volume explores the possibilities of comprehensive household data collected from administrative and other records.

Amir Sufi and Atif Mian have demonstrated the benefits of an intermediate level of data, from detailed geographic data. See, in particular, Mian and Sufi (2012). Sufi's chapter 14 in this volume pursues the idea of tracking dangerous expansions in household credit resulting from the easing of lending standards, using data at the zip code level.

References

Attanasio, Orazio, Erik Hurst, and Luigi Pistaferri. 2012. "The Evolution of Income, Consumption, and Leisure Inequality in the US, 1980–2010." NBER Working Paper no. 17982, Cambridge, MA.

Dynan, Karen. 2012. "Is a Household Debt Overhang Holding Back Consumption?" *Brookings Papers on Economic Activity* 44 (1): 299–362.

Guerrieri, Veronica, and Guido Lorenzoni. 2011. "Credit Crises, Precautionary Savings and the Liquidity Trap." NBER Working Paper no. 17583, Cambridge, MA.

Kaplan, Greg, and Giovanni L. Violante. 2011. "A Model of the Consumption Response to Fiscal Stimulus Payments." Unpublished Manuscript. Princeton University.

Mian, Atif, and Amir Sufi. 2012. "What Explains High Unemployment? The Aggregate Demand Channel." Chicago Booth Research Paper no. 13-43 (November). University of Chicago, Booth School of Business.

13

LEADS on Macroeconomic Risks to and from the Household Sector

Jonathan A. Parker

The household sector is both a propagator of shocks to the economy, as wealth is redistributed across households with differing propensities to consume, and an originator of risky claims held in systemically important places, as losses are shifted from households to creditors such as financial institutions. Information about these exposures, like information generally, is conveyed by prices and so is underproduced by markets. Thus increased public collection, analysis, and distribution of information on household exposures to macroeconomic risk factors can potentially lead to better macroeconomic performance, both through better informed private decision making and through better public policy.

This chapter describes a system for monitoring, measuring, and publicizing exposures to and from the household sector. This system, called the LEADS system, is designed to provide market participants, regulators, and households with additional information to understand the reallocation of resources within, from, and to the household sector in response to macroeconomic events. In short, the system is designed to stress test the balance

Jonathan A. Parker is the International Programs Professor of Management at the MIT Sloan School of Management and a research associate of the National Bureau of Economic Research.

For helpful comments, I thank Markus Brunnermeier, Andrea Eisfeldt, Arvind Krishnamurthy, and participants in the April 2011 NBER conference on systemic risk and macro modeling. This research was funded by the NBER Systemic Risk and Macro Modeling Project and the Kellogg School of Management at Northwestern University. In addition to being faculty at the Kellogg School, I served as an academic consultant and adviser for the Federal Reserve Bank of Chicago and served as a special adviser on financial stability for the US Department of the Treasury during 2009. For acknowledgments, sources of research support, and disclosure of the author's material financial relationships, if any, please see http://www.nber.org/chapters /c12551.ack.

sheets of the households and include the household sector in measurement of systemic risk.

The LEADS system has three components, of which the first is the main focus of this chapter. The first step is the collection of data on LEADS— liabilities, earnings, assets, demographics, and financial sophistication—at the household level. I argue that these categories are the key dimensions to measure, that measurement at the household level is critical for accurate measurement, and that much of this information is available in institutions already subject to government oversight and reporting requirements. The second step in LEADS is the measurement of the exposure of each asset, each liability, and each income stream to macroeconomic risk factors. This step is the subject of much of the field and practice of finance, and describing the vast and evolving set of techniques for this step is beyond this chapter. This component of the system requires historical data on returns (at a minimum) and modeling of future exposures.

The final step is the analysis and release of information. I propose analysis of the implications of changes in risk factors in four important dimensions: the distributional impacts on both liquid wealth and lifetime wealth; the changes in household demand; the effects of balance sheet adjustments on the prices and payouts of claims on the household sector held by other sectors; and the resulting impact on the revenues and liabilities of the government, through possible transfers and de jure and de facto guarantees to the household sector. Such projections necessarily involve household decisions. This information on exposures across groups of households could then be combined with information on financial sophistication. Where exposures to or from the household sector are large and sophistication low, macroeconomic risks may be mispriced or amplified by lack of sophistication and knowledge.[1] Finally, the results of the analyses could be made public— potentially pushed in some cases to "unsophisticated" households—and the underlying data made public in a suitably limited form that maintains privacy.

Together the LEADS system would uncover information relevant to addressing the following types of questions that are of interest to market participants and policymakers:

- How risky are loans to the household sector? Is a particular type of aggregate risk concentrated among households with few resources or little sophistication and so represents a potential source of losses for other claims on these households?

---

1. The focus of this chapter on sophistication in the household sector is not intended to single out or incriminate this sector. Systematic risks could be caused or hidden by lack of sophistication, limited knowledge and biases among legislators, regulators, and courts (as well as financial institutions, businesses, etc.). Lack of sophistication outside the household sector may have been a cause of the recent crisis, and may still cause systemic risk even with the LEADS information. This chapter simply focuses on measurement in the household sector.

- Is a particular type of macroeconomic or systematic risk held primarily by households with little financial sophistication and so potentially mispriced?
- How exposed is consumer demand to declines in different assets or asset classes? Is a particular type of aggregate risk concentrated in liquid wealth or on households whose demand is highly sensitive to losses?
- How likely are private losses to become public liabilities? Is a particular group of households, like pensioners, holding enough of a specific macroeconomic or systematic risk so that losses might lead to ex post public assistance?

With very narrow exceptions, these questions cannot be answered by analysis of existing data sets.

This chapter—and the NBER Initiative on Systemic Risk and Macro Modeling of which it is a part—are both motivated directly by the credit market disruptions and financial crisis of 2007 and early 2008, the contemporaneous declines in asset values, and the large macroeconomic consequences. At the time, most observers expected that the decline in demand for investment and consumption goods following these events would be both similar to that caused by the stock market decline in the year 2000 and concentrated on the construction sector (e.g., Bernanke 2008).[2] In fact, consumption demand fell significantly during the Great Recession—more than output—and has been slow to recover after (relative to most previous US recessions).

The financial crisis and recession of 2008 to 2009 illustrate the two main ways in which the household sector is important for measurement of systemic risks. First, household demand is critical for business cycles, and as such the monitoring of households' balance sheets and wealth is a natural part of the monitoring of macroeconomic risks. Second, systemically important institutions hold claims on the household sector, and so understanding the correlated risks of these institutions requires understanding the value of these claims in different macroeconomic scenarios. Section 13.1 contains a discussion of these issues.

Section 13.2 presents the structure of the LEADS data and describes how this structure allows one to measure aggregate risks to and from the household sector. Section 13.3 describes how the LEADS data can be collected and compiled. Current sources of information are disparate, do not cover the same households, lack sufficient detail on asset holdings, and do not measure household sophistication. The data set for the LEADS system can be constructed by merging administrative data on investments and debts

---

2. There were even reasons to believe the macroeconomic impact would be smaller than in 2000. Housing is consumption, and as house values decline, the (opportunity) cost of housing falls, providing insurance to households that own homes. Further, the structure of mortgages provides households with an option that increases in value when house prices decline, transferring wealth from high-wealth, high-saving households to low-wealth, high-consumption households.

with a panel survey of households that focuses on demographics, income, and financial sophistication.

Section 13.4 discusses analysis and dissemination. Analysis of the data can use existing tools employed in the study of financial risks and household finances. I sketch a three-step procedure to first measure individual-asset exposures, calculate liquid wealth and lifetime wealth exposures, and map these back to changes in both household demand and the value of claims on households. To allow better management of aggregate risks, the analysis, summary data, and an anonymous random sample of detailed data can be released to the public. Section 13.5 concludes, and an appendix discusses the role of the government in the provision of this type of information.

13.1   Why Monitor Household Exposures?

The exposures to and from the household sector are important for monitoring and measuring aggregate risks for three broad reasons.

First, movements in household expenditures amplify and propagate shocks to the economy. This was true in the recession of 2008 to 2009; during and following the recession, sluggish household expenditures have amplified and propagated slowdown. This has also been true more broadly. As Hall (1986 and forthcoming) shows, the volatility of GDP comes primarily from household spending. And long slumps from the Great Depression to the recent recession are arguably amplified by low consumer demand due in part to debt overhang (e.g., Melzer 2010).

Since households own firms and are the government, household demand is exposed to macroeconomic risks through changes in aggregate income and aggregate asset values (and gains or losses on net asset postions with foreign countries). Thus, a major part of risk in household demand can be measured from aggregate data on the share of wealth held in different asset classes and an evaluation of the riskiness of each asset class. But household-level data on individual asset holdings and their characteristics can provide a better understanding of the exposure of aggregate demand to asset values.

Any decline in any asset value has a disporportionate impact on household demand if it is accompanied by transfers among households of differing propensities to consume. This disproportionate effect can happen, for example, if shocks redistribute resources between middle-aged households, whose behavior is reasonably approximated by the life cycle model, and younger households, whose behavior is better characterized by the buffer stock model of consumption.[3] In the recent recession and in the Great

---

3. See Carroll (1997) and Gourinchas and Parker (2002). Kaplan and Violante (2011) provide a related model. Most current models of the macroeconomy are largely linear, even those with heterogeneous agents, so that the household-level data is not necessary in these *models* for predicting macroeconomic dynamics. This statement even applies to models with precautionary savings that match the large share of households with low wealth (Krusell and Smith 1998), although these models typically miss the volatility of asset markets.

Depression, for example, household demand seems to have been reduced by the concentration of losses among households with leverage.[4]

Thus, the household sector has historically been an important proximate source of output volatility and the household sector's response to wealth changes is determined by the distribution of wealth changes both across households and across two measures of wealth: short-term, liquid, financial resources and long-term, illiquid wealth, such as retirment accounts or future income.

The second reason to monitor household exposures is that both the government and systemically important institutions hold financial claims on the household sector. The ability of households to meet these claims and not default in different macroeconomic scenarios determines the exposure of these assets to systematic risks and thus the extent to which those holding the financial claims are exposed.

In the recession of 2008 to 2009, a significant reason for the depth and severity of the recession was large losses on loans to households that were held by systemically important financial institutions. These exposures may well have been smaller had the exposures to aggregate risk factors of the various dimensions of wealth of the households with mortgages been better understood by market participants or regulators.

The final reason to monitor household exposures is that, as with groups of banks, the government cannot commit ex ante not to make large transfers to groups of households following adverse outcomes.[5] And in general, monitoring is helpful in dealing with the moral hazard problems that accompany insurance. These types of assistance are public risks that expose aggregate growth to the risks born by these households through increased tax rates and decreased future spending and benefits.

Examples of governments assisting a subset of households that lose significant resources include those following natural disasters, and the bailout of the elderly following the Great Depression with the Social Security system (enacted in 1935 and 1939), which paid retirees benefits starting in 1940 to aid seniors whose wealth was wiped out by the Great Depression.[6] As long as the government ex post makes transfers to households that have suffered

---

4. See Fisher (1933), Eggertsson and Krugman (2012), Hall (2011). Parker and Vissing-Jorgensen (2009, 2010) find larger consumption declines for high-consumption or high-income households, implying an important role for declines in asset prices and expected future prospects of high-income households.

5. Farhi and Tirole (2012) clarify the point that it is not just that a single institution can be too big to fail, but also groups of institutions. The Troubled Asset Relief Program provided equity investments not just in large banks but in most small banks also.

6. And we may observe it if the Pension Benefit Guaranty Corporation (PGBC) fails or some US states go bankrupt. On the other hand, households facing foreclosure in the current recession were not bailed out. What little assistance that was provided—the Home Affordable Modification Program, which affected less than a million mortgages—focused on overcoming an ex post market inefficiency rather than being a transfer to households. Also, there was no government rescue for the employees of Enron or Arthur Anderson, nor for the victims of the Madoff fraud.

large losses, it is optimal for the government, like any private insurer, to monitor these households and react to these risks.[7]

These are the reasons that market participants and policymakers benefit from information on household asset holdings, but why does the government have a role in gathering, analyzing, and publicizing this information? There are two main reasons, addressed in more detail in the appendix. First, as a general principle, in markets the social value of information exceeds its private value, so information is underproduced by the market. Given too little information, mistakes are made relative to the economy with the socially optimal amount of information. And mistakes will tend to be based on the common information that exists, so that misestimation leads to coordinated mistakes that are by definition macroeconomic. Second, lack of financial sophistication (such as lack of financial knowledge, limited information processing abilities, and limited time allocated to financial decisions) can lead some households to misprice aggregate risks, both leading to misallocation by other sectors and exposing household demand and claims on households to "mispriced" aggregate risk factors.[8] While it is efficient to have the downside economic risk held by those most willing to hold it, it is generically inefficient to have it held by those least able to understand it or who most underestimate it.

These considerations imply that data collection and analysis focus on measuring the systematic exposure of two measures of household financial wealth—liquid financial resources over a few years and lifetime wealth—for not just the household sector but also for different households grouped according to consumption response to these two measures of resources, according to their importance for claims on the household sector, according to the likelihood of losses being born by the government, and according to measures of financial sophistication of the household decision makers.

13.2   LEADS Data

What information is required to measure exposures to and from the household sector? First, household-level data is necessary so that the common risks of different types of households can be studied across both different groups and risks of interest. That is, while the units of analysis will typically be groups of households, to characterize exposures among groups of households with differing propensities to consume, for example, one has to have information for many possible groupings defined by demographics

---

7. In terms of regulatory response, the government can simply disclose these exposures so that government accounting is more informative, or the government can hedge the exposures so that tax rates can be smoothed and market prices better reflect true risks, or finally, it can restrict or intervene to deter the exposures ex ante that lead to bailouts in some states ex post.

8. Mispricing relative to a benchmark in which people are not limited in knowledge or information-processing capacity.

and/or financial measures of interest such as liquid wealth or home owner-ship status. Individual-level data allow the study of the history of exposures and behavior of different groups or types of households through different aggregations of historical data. Further, to calculate the exposure of claims on household resources to an aggregate shock, one needs to model the default of each household, which again is most straightforward (and requires the least extraneous assumptions) using household-level data. For example, to predict how much default would accompany a 10 percent decrease in house values for a group of households, it would be useful to know not just that the average loan-to-value ratio of households in that group was 80 percent, but also the distribution of loan-to-value ratios and how correlated other household assets and incomes were with the considered aggregate risks. Finally, the study of household-level data is a useful input to risk calcula-tions, such as under what conditions households default or how different regulations might change household behavior. That is, household-level data allows one to use existing variation in laws, regulation, prices, and so forth across households to study and measure household behavior and thus infer better what losses to and from the sector would occur in response to what aggregate events.

In terms of the information on each household, the arguments in sec-tion 13.1 imply that the data contain enough detail on assets, income, and liabilities to accurately measure the extent to which a household's *liquid wealth* and *lifetime wealth* are correlated with macroeconomic risk factors. This requires knowledge about the nature of income, of assets held in each asset class, and of credit terms for debt, so that the impact of changes in each on liquid wealth and on total wealth can be calculated. For example, holdings in retirement accounts clearly expose lifetime wealth and not liquid wealth, while temporary shocks to income affect liquid wealth more than lifetime wealth. In sum, a system to monitor systemic risk in the household sector requires data on assets and liabilities both at the household level and in enough detail to assess their roles in liquid wealth and lifetime wealth.

What actual financial information about households is needed? As in the monitoring and regulation of the US banking system, one would like to observe sufficient detail about household balance sheets to accurately measure the exposure of each asset and liability to aggregate risk factors of interest. To this end, the data need to contain information not just on the holdings in any asset class, but on the actual details of the securities held. It is insufficient to measure the risk of a class of assets because one group of households may differ significantly from another in the actual securities held within that class, and so actually have quite a different exposure to a macroeconomic risk factor. As examples, among mortgages, the extent to which households default will differ dramatically with the terms of the mortgage. Stocks can have high exposure to aggregate risk or provide insur-ance against aggregate shocks. Hedge funds can be highly levered and lose money in response to credit shock, or provide liquidity in a credit shock and be highly profitable.

A similar argument applies to labor and benefit income. One needs to know enough details of the labor income of the household to measure the exposure of labor income to macroeconomic risk factors and to measure the household's ability to avoid default or bankruptcy. Some households have stable labor and benefit incomes and others are highly exposed to business cycles. The actual exposures, as for assets, can be estimated from existing data on historical labor incomes of similar households. And benefits and income amounts from each source are necessary to infer total exposure.

Finally, an important part of monitoring banks is the quality of management and its plans for future contingencies. The measurement of financial sophistication in the household sector is similarly important for measuring and monitoring risks and for providing clues as to which risks might be mispriced. In banking regulation, the quality of management informs the regulator about the likelihood that the financial institution can manage the exposures inherent in the bank's asset and liability positions. In the recent financial crisis, measurement of this dimension for Fannie Mae and AIG Financial Products would have shown poor management practices, been easy to correlate with massive exposures to real estate prices and price impact, and potentially been useful to other investors taking prices as informative about the riskiness of mortgage-backed securities. While poorly managed firms tend to suffer a Darwinian fate, this argument has little bite for households living well above subsistence. And regulation today reflects this: regulations restrict most households from making many investment choices, which are available only to qualified investors.[9]

While financial sophistication has many dimensions, the most pertinent to measure is the extent to which households are informed about aggregate risks and their exposures to them. If households are not informed, that is not proof that they are incorrectly exposed, but it suggests that greater information about exposures might change behavior for the better. The measures, discussed later, capture the extent to which households are informed about the financial decisions they are making, the extent to which they have the abilities to make reasonable financial decisions, and the extent to which

9. Would information on sophistication have been helpful before the financial crisis and 2008 to 2009 recession? Probably not (although Lusardi [2010] argues to some extent otherwise). This sort of information on households seems unlikely to have been useful in monitoring the systematic risks and in avoiding them, since closely related data was available. The information in credit ratings bureaus showed that subprime borrowers had very poor credit ratings, which probably correlates highly with lack of financial sophistication. But this does not mean that this type of information will not be useful next time. In the next potential crisis, it might be that households take on more risk than they intend absent LEADS-type information, or that markets or regulators would find information on the sophistication of the households driving financial flows to be a useful signal to help interpret price movements and measure macroeconomic risks.

Table 13.1   **An overview of LEADS for households**

Data at the household level on:

*L*iabilites	Measure terms of each borrowing instrument and calculate exposure—collateral information, commitment/term, interest-rate determination, penalties, etc. *Details almost completely lacking in current data sets.*
*A*ssets	Details on each investment, including restricted accounts like retirement. Examples: name of hedge fund, actual security, house address, etc. *Details almost completely lacking in current data sets.*
*E*arnings	Measure of current and past incomes at the household level as well as dynamics. *Current data sets strong (PSID, NLSY, CPS, ACS, IRS).*
*D*emographics	(Age, family structure, geographic location, occupation, industry, etc.) For grouping households into groups to study exposure, for public data. *Details available but not tied to data other than earnings and course measures of assets and liabilities.*
Financial *S*ophistication	Measures of households' expectations and subjective probabilities of different scenarios and responses to tests of understanding of investment choices and consumption smoothing in the markets in which they are operating. *Completely lacking in current data sets*

they exhibit characteristics correlated with good financial decision making. We would better understand macroeconomic risks if we were always able to observe when credit was increasing to households with low financial sophistication and when households with low financial sophistication were increasing their exposures to macroeconomic risks.

In sum, the needed data is information collected at the household level on the following categories, summarized in table 13.1: Liabilities, Assets, Earnings, Demographics, and financial Sophistication (LEADS). Table 13.1 also highlights what is missing from current data sets. The two main missing items are (a) the details on assets and liabilities at the household level, and (b) measures of financial sophistication.

The fact that the LEADS data would contain a host of information on household financial positions raises important issues of privacy. It will be necessary to insure the anonymity of households in any summary statistics released to the public or limited data sets released to researchers. I do not address these issues in this chapter, but merely note that these issues are of great import and surmountable. They are important, as the provision of accurate information in part relies on the confidence of the provider that the information will not be misused. That these issues are surmountable is shown by the regulation of the banking sector in which bank regulators have been able to preserve the privacy of confidential bank information.[10]

13.3   How to Collect the LEADS Data

How could a statistical agency gather the LEADS data? While the details of the system could rival the documentation of the measurement of risk in the traditional banking sector, in short there are several principles that are necessary to gather this information.

First, the collection of data must rely heavily on administrative data. Survey response rates are declining, and administrative data is increasingly detailed, already computerized, and has low rates of error. Even cooperating households with good intentions are likely not to know the details of their financial contracts or holdings. This happens in two ways. The household may simply not know the details of the asset or liability that are available to them, like a household not knowing the aggregate and idiosyncratic risks of the returns on a stock they own, or whether their mortgage gives the lender recourse or not, or the covenants and seniority of a bond they own. Or the household may not have access to this information, as would be the case for a household holding a mutual fund or hedge fund, or having its investment advisor allocating its assets.

This information, however, is available through financial institutions, all of which are already (or seemingly will be) covered under the large umbrellas of financial regulation and reporting. The organizations that sell the assets or hold claims on households either understand the details of the payments that must be made in different states of the world or have on file the terms of the mortgage contract, the National Securities Identification Number (or CUSIP) of the security, and so forth. One approach is for the appropriate regulator to gather reports on all financial holdings by or against a given household by all financial entities.[11] The gold standard for information on financial positions—assets and liabilities—is administrative data from the universe of financial institutions, merged by household for a subset of households. The universe of financial institutions would have to include everything from hedge funds to payday lending to limited partnerships.[12]

---

10. The IRS has also not allowed leaks of confidential tax return documents while allowing researchers to use the data for important social scientific research.

11. There are questions of feasibility and privacy issues that this chapter does not address. Presumably one could gather this administrative data with the consent of the surveyed household. Another option would be to require universal reporting by financial institutions for certain types of financial transactions. Household information is gathered by credit bureaus and households wishing to engage in certain financial transactions are also choosing to be monitored. Tax law requires reporting of all dividends.

12. It is unclear how to handle international holdings, although one could cover a large portion through intermediaries who sell (or lend) from abroad.

Even if this is not completely possible, it seems necessary to rely as much as possible on administrative data to avoid significant loss in detail on holdings.

Could statistical agencies use private companies that serve households and collect financial information, such as Mint.com? Data from these private money management companies suffers from a serious shortcoming: the sample of the population they cover are not representative of households in the United States. These data cover only households that choose to manage their finances and do so online. Households that use these types of services are not the average household, and in particular they probably display more than average financial sophistication—certainly in the dimension of planning—and so likely have different wealth and incomes and take different financial risks.

Second, household demographics are probably most accurately gathered by a household-level survey or possibly even simply gleaned from existing household surveys. Administrative data may provide better coverage, since any household survey will suffer the usual problems of surveys, including potentially low response rates. But much of the basic demographic and even income data already exists for many households in several extant data sets. Using the various surveys of households conducted by the Census Bureau, and combining data across existing data sets within the US government at the household level could yield an accurate picture of household demographics and income. With household permission, the government agency could merge this extant survey data with the financial information provided by the financial sector to create a close-to-ideal data set. A further improvement would be to merge with the income and tax return data in the Internal Revenue Service.[13] There are, of course, many hurdles to these coordinated efforts, including issues of consent, issues of biasing responses and data provision, and issues of interference with the primary missions of the original data sources.

Third, financial sophistication can be measured using a combination of data from financial institutions and survey methods. Financial institutions have information on household choices and responses to financial offers. These responses have been used by economists to measure financial sophistication in behavior from dominated choices (see Agarwal et al. 2009, 2010). Detailed holding can also be used to ask to what extent observed behavior conforms to an economic model's views of what optimal behavior ought to be (see, for example, Calvet, Campbell, and Sodini 2007, 2009). In either case, financial institutions have some existing information on the quality of financial management within a given household. However, this information is unlikely to prove sufficient, and the collection of this type of information may distort the incentives for financial institutions to create the information.

---

13. While historically these data have been very difficult to use for confidentiality reasons, the data at least could be used to construct group-level statistics available outside the IRS.

Complementarily, many dimensions of financial sophistication can be measured by suvey methods, as shown by existing surveys. A notable example is the Financial Industry Regulatory Authority (FINRA)'s National Financial Capability Study (2009). At this point, however, there is insufficient previous research on the usefulness of different dimensions of sophistication to know exactly which questions or information will be most useful. And to some extent flexibility must be maintained in data collection so that measures can evolve with the financial situation and the risks percieved as potentially most interesting.

Despite these caveats to measurement of financial sophistication, three types of data are potentially useful indicators of suboptimal responses of household spending or mispricing of claims on the household sector. The first type of information is measures of household contingency plans for macroeconomic events of interest.[14] This information would be directly useful for understanding default on credit instruments and indirectly for modeling whether expectations of actions are inconsistent across households (and potentially financial institutions). The information that everyone plans to run for the same exit in the event of a fire is useful information for households themselves.

The second class of useful information concerns whether households understand the financial products they are using. Lack of understanding would suggest suboptimal exposure to macroeconomic risk factors, and potential exploitation leading to increased aggregate exposures. Of course this is far from proof, as illustrated by the analogy of the pool player who plays well but does not understand classical mechanics.[15] But there is strong evidence that measures of this type of financial sophistication are correlated with financial choices.[16]

Note that the motivation to measure macroecomomic risk exposure is distinct from the motive to protect investors; that is, the goal of the newly legislated Consumer Financial Protection Agency. While the methods may overlap and the data may be of interest for both purposes, the measurement of aggregate risk exposures requires a focus on common misunderstandings that align with measured exposures.

Finally, the third dimension of sophistication to measure is general abilities and behaviors related to good financial decision making. For example, saving for retirement is much larger among households that report that they plan for vacations (Ameriks, Caplin, and Leahy 2003). While it is probably

---

14. Brunnermeier, Gorton, and Krishnamurthy (2012) provide a modeling strategy for financial institutions that makes use of these type of questions of financial institutions.

15. Note that an important aspect of the analogy is inconsistent with our modeling of agents as pool players. There is no uncertainty in pool. If an *economist's* agent played pool, in theory, the agent would always win by sinking all the balls in the right order on the first shot.

16. See, for example, Lusardi and Mitchell (2007).

not realistic to measure IQ for these purposes, IQ does correlate with financial decision making (Grinblatt, Keloharju, and Linnainmaa 2011).

Turning to the structure of the data, for accurate measures of systemic risk, it will generally be necessary that all data be in the same data set—that is, that one has all LEADS information for a set of households. Short of this, if groups of interest can be defined based on observables that are measured in two different data sets, then the group averages can be constructed for each group in each data set and combined. For example, if assets, liabilities, and income are well measured in one data set with demographics, and financial sophistication is well measured in another data set with demographics, then one can calculate statistics about financial sophistication for any demographic group. What one cannot do is observe if, within any demographic group, it is the less sophisticated households that are holding particular assets held by that group and not other assets. With some loss of accuracy, one can extrapolate from a small sample with complete information to a larger sample with information on different dimensions for different households.

Finally, to what extent is repeated cross-sectional data sufficient, or would the LEADS system be significantly stronger with panel data that follows the same households over time? The risks of assets and liabilities require that one track the performance of these assets, and not that one track the same households over time. To measure income dynamics and correlations with macroeconomic risks requires repeated measures of a household's income, but there are data sets from which measures could be constructed with long time series already. The Panel Study of Income Dynamics, the Current Population Survey, and the Social Security Earnings Records in the Health and Retirement Study all provide long histories of earnings on households that could be mapped to demographics and then applied to households in the new data set. I expect that the heterogeneity within a demographic group missed by this method would be of little systemic interest. That said, repeated cross-sectional data will reduce the power of many measures, particularly when studying household-specific changes to better understand behavior or when tracking the impact of changes over longer periods of time.

13.4   Outline of LEADS Data Analysis and Dissemination

The LEADS system is designed to allow the measurement of the exposure of the liquid wealth and lifetime wealth of different groups of households to different macroeconomic shocks and the construction of measures of the exposure of both aggregate consumption demand and claims on the household sector to these macroeconomic shocks. This section first outlines a framework for analysis of three steps: (a) measure the risk exposure of each asset, each liability, and each income stream to macroeconomic risk factors; (b) aggregate exposures to household-level liquid wealth and lifetime wealth and then aggregate exposures to groups of households; and (c) model the exposures of aggregate consumption demand, claims on the household sector and government liabilities. Second, dissemination of both analysis and anonymous raw data is critical. While regulators may find patterns of exposure informative, the private sector can also better respond to and price risks when it is better informed of their aggregate consequences, as would be the case if it had access to both the analyses and some of the data.

To begin, the measurement of the risk exposure of assets and liabilities can be based on textbook asset pricing and its application, which necessarily involves the difficulties of the real world. This part of the analysis of the LEADS system is not novel and is reasonably well understood by academics and practitioners. I simply propose standard modeling of asset and debt cash flows that makes up the bulk of quantitative finance and fundamental analysis.[17] Returns, cash flows, and prices, are described as a sum of exposures (betas) times realizations of aggregate risk factors and idiosyncratic or deterministic components. Modeling income risk is similarly reasonably well understood and applied in labor economics. Here "understood" does not mean straightforward. Perhaps the most important assumptions are those about the behavioral responses over the period studied in cases where these responses affect cash flows, which as noted subsequently, may depend on other holdings of a given household.

Given estimated exposures, the liquid wealth of a household can be written as a sum of stochastic cash flows into and out of liquid assets from income, assets, and liabilities, and of terminal prices of liquid assets and liabilities. And the lifetime wealth of a household can be written similarly, but for all assets (not just liquid assets). Thus, we would have measures of the exposure of these two concepts of wealth to variation in aggregate risk factors. Finally, aggregating across households, one calculates the implications of a change in any set of aggregate factors for the liquid wealth and lifetime wealth for any group of households.

The third step in analysis is to use a model of the consumption sensitivity of different households to these two types of wealth to measure the exposure to aggregate risk factors of the aggregate demand for consumption. As discussed shortly, this requires modeling household behavior. But having modeled household saving, consumption, default, and portfolio behavior, the LEADS system provides a measure of the exposure to default of any set of claims on the household sector.[18] Finally, one can examine under what

---

17. One danger going forward is that new financial products have limited histories and so are potentially the most subject to misestimation.

18. Similarly, given decision rules about portfolio choice, one can evaluate the change in asset demand from the household sector. With assumptions about the potential other buyers of the asset, one can check the aggregate risk factor exposures are reasonable or reasonably consistent with the household responses.

scenarios there are significant direct or possible effects on the government budget through explicit or implicit guarantees or legislative responses.

As noted, the modeling of household behavior is a critical step in the construction of both income and asset/debt outcomes as well as household consumption, saving and rebalancing in response to events. In short, we need to model how households respond to changes over any horizon considered. In terms of risks to the household sector, most relevant are exposures of household income, where cash flows depend on household labor supply responses, and exposures of household debt, where the household can choose to exercise an option to default or change portfolio or saving behavior. In terms of outcomes, the LEADS analysis needs to model household consumption behavior to understand how the demand of different households are more and less exposed to macroeconomic events. Further, to understand claims on households, one has to make assumptions that determine the situations in which households default. Fortunately, many of these behaviors have been or can be measured from past experiences and existing data, so that modeling assumptions can be disciplined by data. Further, one advantage of LEADS data is that, because it represents a significant increase in the quality of available information, it will increase the ability to learn about these behaviors from future events. Nevertheless, given the importance of these assumptions, any analysis will have to carefully evaluate robustness to alternative assumptions.

Household financial sophistication may be quite useful in modeling household behavior. Household decision rules may differ importantly with financial sophistication. The second use of financial sophistication is in grouping households for analysis, in combination with information on exposures. Where exposures—to or from the household sector—are large and sophistication low, this is suggestive that macroeconomic risks may be mispriced or amplified by lack of sophistication or information.

In sum, the proposed analysis produces information on the exposure of aggregate demand to various risks, information helpful for the private sector and the government. The analysis measures the size of risks emanating from the household sector, and allows them to be evaluated and tracked into other sectors of the economy. Finally, the analysis contains information on the potential costs to the government in terms of likely payouts through automatic means-tested programs and possible payouts through ex post bailouts to subgroups of the household sector.

Finally, the LEADS information could be made public, in three ways. First, the results of the analysis—the range of possible impacts on aggregate demand and defaults and asset prices for many aggregate scenarios under any assumptions—could be made public. This dissemination can lead to many benefits, as discussed in section 13.1 and the appendix. Further, if regulators were concerned about the possibility of "unsophisticated" households unintentionally holding too much risk, then particular results about riskiness could be pushed to the type of household that might most benefit from this information. Similarly, if regulators were concerned about the exposures of some market participants, they again could highlight the risks and allow participants to react to the information as they see fit.

Second, a data set of aggregated data could be made publically available for analysis and investigation by academics and investors. Ideally this data set would combine analysis and raw data. A large number of government agencies produce detailed tables based on data that they collect through surveys. A reasonable model for the LEADS summary data is the published tables based on the Survey of Consumer Finances (SCF). But the LEADS tables would be better if summary statistics were released by demographic groups of possible interest including financial sophistication, and if the focus were not on current value of holdings but on asset detail and riskiness. Further, it would be useful to observe not just mean holdings, but covariances of holdings across assets within a group and quantiles of holdings—both of which would allow a better understanding of the possibility that large shocks lead to large movements for some households in the group. Finally, to be most useful, the statistics should, to the extent possible, convey information about exposure to both liquid wealth and lifetime wealth.

Third, a household-level data set could be made accessible to researchers working to improve our understanding and modeling of macroeconomic risks and financial stability. In keeping with standard survey data protocols, this data set can omit enough detail to ensure confidentiality and anonymity of individual agents. The data set would be useful to bring new evidence on the behavioral assumptions inherent in the extant measures of systematic exposures.

13.5   Conclusion

Macroeconomic shocks can lead to large changes in demand from the household sector and can lead to large changes in cash flows from debt claims on the sector. The LEADS system outlined in this chapter is designed to measure sufficient detail on household liabilities, assets, earnings, demographics, and financial sophistication, to project these large changes.

This LEADS system would help households, firms, and policymakers determine what sources of aggregate risk are most pertinent for claims on the household sector and household demand, and when these exposures are likely to be large. More specifically, the system is designed to allow measurement of (a) the distributional impacts on both the distribution of liquid wealth and lifetime wealth, and the resultant changes in household demand; (b) the effects of balance sheet adjustments on the prices and payouts of claims on the household sector held by other sectors; and (c) the resulting impact on the revenues and liabilities of the government, through possible transfers and de jure and de facto guarantees to the household sector. While the scope of the LEADS system implies that this chapter can only provide an overview of the system, methodologies exist for most of the individual component tasks.

While it is beyond the scope of this chapter to lay out a complete framework for macroprudential data analysis and regulation of the household sector, the analogy between banks and households suggests that policymakers want to consider three tools. First, policymakers might consider capital requirements, such as existed in mortgage markets in practice in the period of the conforming mortgage. A related system is the Social Security system, which guarantees/imposes a basic standard of living for elderly households by requiring young households to pay while working for health insurance and basic retirement income when elderly. Second, policymakers might consider restrictions on what financial assets households can use. This regulation is in place as restrictions on what investors can invest in unless they are qualified investors. It seems suboptimal to make this determination based on wealth—errors are made both by excluding sophisticated investors from markets and by allowing wealthy unsophisticated investors to invest in any assets. A better regulation might license an investor on the basis of a test, like what is required to get a driver's license to drive. Finally, the regulator may want to inform the public and warn them about specific exposures, or even lean against the wind and try to change prices, limit access, or tax certain investments or strategies that they see as destabilizing. A good data measurement system is an essential guide to evaluate the benefits and, just as important, the costs of any potential regulation.

Appendix
Why the Government Has a Role in Monitoring Household Systemic Exposures

There are two benefits to measuring the exposure of the household sector to systemic risk.

First, as a general principle, in markets the social value of information exceeds its private value. Because information has some of the features of a public good, markets tend to lead to the production of too little information. This result comes from the power of markets to create efficient allocations given the available information. Prices aggregate and convey information to market participants, and optimizing agents can coordinate behavior to efficiently produce and allocate goods. However, this benefit implies that when an individual produces information, others benefit. Thus the social value of information exceeds its private value.

When there is too little information, mistakes are made relative to the economy with the socially optimal amount of information. Mistakes will tend to be based on the common information that exists, so that misestimation leads to coordinated mistakes that are by definition macroeconomic if not systemic. Misestimation propagates; misestimation of the positions of the household sector can lead to systemic risk elsewhere.

This externality implies that there is a role for a governmental or quasi-governmental agency to produce information. This is not a new role. The government does this for a large number of macroeconomic variables. The government also regulates the production and disclosure of information by firms. The goal of this chapter—and this NBER project—is to modernize data production and provision, updating it to account for the modern financial landscape and redirecting some of its focus from the measurement of means to the measurement of covariances—risks, and macroeconomic and systemic risks in particular.

There are many potential benefits of more information. Market participants would be able to allocate resources more efficiently across potential outcomes given better information on exposures to aggregate risks in places in the household sector. Better measurement of the risk exposure of consumer demand and claims on household resources would also allow the government and the market to better predict consumption demand, and so better understand risks given their observed prices.

The second reason that the government has a role in monitoring household exposures is that some households lack financial sophistication, due, for example, to a lack of financial knowledge, limited information-processing abilities, and limited time allocated to financial decisions. Thus, some households can make significant financial mistakes relative to the decisions they would make if they had the ability and took the time to collect and process fully all available information and knowledge. The provision of information about the holdings of agents with different levels of sophistication can make behavior closer to that of the full-information or full-sophistication economy, which can increase the information content of prices, and lead to better private decision making and better management of systematic exposures.

When the mistakes of market participants are common, they can lead to noise or bias in prices that other agents are using as sources of information for their choices, and may lead to larger systemic exposure of both household demand and claims on households.[19] In financial markets, financial institutions that all expect to be able to sell the same assets or all draw on credit but fail to recognize the extent to which other institutions have made the same plans create a systematic risk. For households, this misestimation can create a similar dynamic or exposure. In the recent crisis, households

19. A typical argument is that agents do not make similar mistakes over many time periods, not that many agents do not make similar mistakes at the same time.

that had planned on using home equity to stabilize consumption across bad shocks found that credit was available only at very high prices and that their collateral values had declined, further limiting the extent of borrowing.

Further, when a sophisticated/informed investor observes a price, they must try to infer the information in this price. This inference can involve estimating the shares of price movement caused by agents with different levels of motivation and sophistication trading in the market. And so the inference could be improved by information on these shares—whether observed prices are due to the actions of other sophisticated/informed investors or instead the actions of unsophisticated investors or "noise traders," whose choices are not based on as much information or are motivated by different concerns. For example, a large exposure among a group of households that are (in some sense) making unsophisticated choices can distort prices and pass systematic risk through the household sector into other parts of the economy through default on claims on the household sector.

Public provision of information about the sophistication of groups of agents who are holding different assets can partly reveal how informative market prices are, and again can lead to, better private sector decision making.[20]

Finally, while it is efficient to have the downside economic risk held by those most willing to hold it, it is generically inefficient to have it held by those least able to understand it or who most underestimate it. Lack of sophistication can be exploited and there is always the risk that this exploitation can cause systemic exposure.[21] A signal of the size of systemic risk is its price. And regulators interested in regulating systemic risks need to be able to observe clues as to whether the risk is correctly priced and correctly placed.

Thus, the LEADS data can be informative about whether downside economic risk is being shifted to the unsophisticated part of the household sector, or passed through the unsophisticated part of the household sector to other systemically important sectors. This argument implies that data collection should support these types of inference and should be designed to provide the information necessary for market participants and good regulatory responses. There may be situations where aggregate risk can be reduced by some consumer financial protection, and where regulation of financial

20. This information would allow lenders to these households to observe their sophistication, which can be useful as a signal of the quality of their financial decision making in other areas. Thus, an investor with insufficiently detailed information (or sophistication) to evaluate the exposure of the household balance sheet might still learn from the disclosed abilities of households that are holding certain assets.

21. While not a group of households, one can make the argument that AIG financial products, by mispricing credit default swaps on mortgage-backed securities, lead market participants to underestimate the exposure of these assets to aggregate risk and lead to its being held in systemically important places. Unsophisticated households could play a similar role in the next crisis.

choices may avoid "unintentional" systemic exposures.[22] Even without government intervention, information on sophistication is likely to be useful for targeting the provision of information about systemic exposures (or the provision of the implications of analysis of systemic exposures), with the goal of allowing household and firm choices that are more consistent with those that they would have made given complete information.

References

Agarwal, Sumit, S. Chomsisengphet, C. Liu, and Nicholas S. Souleles. 2010. "Do Consumers Choose the Right Credit Contracts?" Working Paper. http://www.chicagofed.org/digital_assets/publications/working_papers/2010/wp2010_05.pdf.

Agarwal, Sumit, John Driscoll, Xavier Gabaix, and David Laibson. 2009. "The Age of Reason: Financial Decisions over the Life Cycle and Implications for Regulation." *Brookings Papers on Economic Activity* Fall:51–117.

Ameriks, John, Andrew Caplin, and John Leahy. 2003. "Wealth Accumulation and the Propensity to Plan." *Quarterly Journal of Economics* 118:1007–47.

Bernanke, Ben. 2008. "Remarks on the Economic Outlook." Speech at the International Monetary Conference, Barcelona, Spain (via satellite), June 3.

Brunnermeier, Markus K., Gary Gorton, and Arvind Krishnamurthy. 2012. "Risk Topography." In *NBER Macroeconomics Annual 2011*, vol. 26, edited by D. Acemoglu and M. Woodford, 149–176. Chicago: University of Chicago Press.

Calvet, Laurent E., John Y. Campbell, and Paolo Sodini. 2007. "Down or Out: Assessing the Welfare Costs of Household Investment Mistakes." *Journal of Political Economy* 115 (5): 707–47.

———. 2009. "Measuring the Financial Sophistication of Households." *American Economic Review* 99 (2): 393–8.

Carroll, Christopher D. 1997. "Buffer Stock Saving and the Life Cycle/Permanent Income Hypothesis." *Quarterly Journal of Economics* 107 (1): 1–56.

Eggertsson, Gauti, and Paul Krugman. 2012. "Debt, Deleveraging, and the Liquidity Trap: A Fisher-Minsky-Koo approach." *Quarterly Journal of Economics* 127 (3): 1469–1513.

Farhi, Emmanuel, and Jean Tirole. 2012. "Collective Moral Hazard, Maturity Mismatch and Systemic Bailouts." *American Economic Review* 102 (1): 60–93.

Financial Industry Regulatory Authority. 2009. "National Financial Capability

---

22. The field of economics has a long history of taking individual choices as optimal and basing policy advice on arguments that rely not on individual mistakes but on market failures due to externalities, for example. Both of the previous arguments—that markets naturally produce too little information and so there is a government role in the provision of information—are in this spirit. However, the field tends to ignore the possibility that agents differ in sophistication and sophisticated agents can regulate the behavior of the unsophisticated and improve welfare. The general commitment to the sovereignty of the decision maker is the real divide between behavioral economics and the rest of the field. In cases where sophistication is about education and information, in theory, revealed-preference tests and utility constructs could lead to welfare measures that proscribe such regulations as welfare improving in the standard approach. Obviously, we are some distance from this point.

Study, 2009 Questionnaire." http://www.finrafoundation.org/web/groups/foundation/@foundation/documents/foundation/p120537.pdf.

Fisher, Irving. 1933. "The Debt-Deflation Theory of the Great Depressions." *Econometrica* 1 (4): 337–57.

Gourinchas, Pierre-Olivier, and Jonathan A. Parker. 2002. "Consumption Over the Life Cycle." *Econometrica* 70 (1): 47–89.

Grinblatt, Mark, Matti Keloharju, and Juhani Linnainmaa. 2011. "IQ and Stock Market Participation." *Journal of Finance* 66 (6): 2121–64.

Hall, Robert E. 1986. "The Role of Consumption in Economic Fluctuations." In *The American Business Cycle: Continuity and Change*, edited by Robert J. Gordon. Chicago: University of Chicago Press.

———. 2011. "The Long Slump." *American Economic Review* 101 (2): 431–69.

———. Forthcoming. "Household Consumption and Debt Data." In *Systemic Risk and Macro Modeling*, edited by Markus K. Brunnermeier and Arvind Krishnamurthy. Chicago: University of Chicago Press.

Kaplan, Greg, and Gianluca Violante. 2011. "A Model of the Consumption Response to Fiscal Stimulus Payments." University of Pennsylvania. Unpublished Manuscript.

Krusell, Per, and Anthony Smith. 1998. "Income and Wealth Heterogeneity in the Macroeconomy." *Journal of Political Economy* 106 (5): 867–96.

Lusardi, Annamaria. 2010. "Americans' Financial Capability." Testimony before the Financial Crisis Inquiry Commission, February. http://fcic-static.law.stanford.edu/cdn_media/fcic-testimony/2010-0226-Lusardi.pdf.

Lusardi, Annamaria, and Olivia Mitchell. 2007. "Baby Boomer Retirement Security: The Roles of Planning, Financial Literacy, and Housing Wealth." *Journal of Monetary Economics* 54:205–24.

Melzer, Brian T. 2010. "Mortgage Debt Overhang: Reduced Investment by Homeowners with Negative Equity." Unpublished Manuscript. Kellogg School of Management.

Parker, Jonathan A., and Annette Vissing-Jorgensen. 2009. "Who Bears Aggregate Fluctuations and How?" *American Economic Review* 99 (2): 399–405.

———. 2010. "The Increase in Income Cyclicality of High-Income Households and its Relation to the Rise in Top Income Shares." *Brookings Papers on Economic Activity* Fall:1–55.

Detecting "Bad" Leverage

Amir Sufi

14.1 Introduction

The key question I seek to answer in this chapter is the following:

How do regulators and policymakers know when a large increase in leverage will end badly?

A large body of evidence suggests that the sharp increase in household debt during the years prior to the Great Recession of 2007 to 2009 was perhaps the most important factor explaining the severity of the downturn.[1] Seeing this sharp increase in household debt during the housing boom was not difficult. Instead, the difficulty was determining whether regulators and policymakers should be concerned about the increase.

My analysis seeks to answer the following question: How does a regulator know when a large increase in household debt will end badly? I argue that the answer to this question lies in the ability to detect whether an increase in household leverage is due to an expansion in the *supply* of credit or whether it is due to improvements in the *productivity* of borrowers. The essence of the strategy I propose is to use microeconomic data on borrowers with a high elasticity of borrowing with respect to credit availability to isolate the supply

Amir Sufi is professor of finance at the Booth School of Business at the University of Chicago and a research associate of the National Bureau of Economic Research.

I thank Atif Mian, Robert Vishny, and participants in the NBER Systemic Risk Initiative in April 2011 in Chicago. This chapter was prepared for the NBER Systemic Risk Initiative. An online appendix with the data description and figures is available at http://www.nber.org /data-appendix/c12552/appendix8-15-11.pdf. For acknowledgments, sources of research support, and disclosure of the author's material financial relationships, if any, please see http:// www.nber.org/chapters/c12552.ack.

1. See, for example, Mian and Sufi (2010, 2011), Glick and Lansing (2010), and Hall (2011).

versus productivity effects. If a sharp increase in leverage is due primarily to an increase in the *supply* of credit, the regulator should be concerned. While I focus here on the household sector, the approach I describe could easily be applied to other sectors, such as nonfinancial corporations or banks.

Three preliminary facts will help motivate the methodology. First, when fueled by an expansion in the availability of credit, dramatic increases in leverage typically end badly. Kindleberger and Aliber (2005) conducts a careful historical analysis of financial crises and argues that they are often preceded by the "expansion of credit result[ing] from the development of substitutes for what previously had been traditional monies." My assertion is that serious dangers lurk when financial innovation leads to a sharp increase in debt levels that are unaccompanied by improvements in borrowers' permanent income or productivity.[2]

Second, there is a segment of the US population that displays a very high elasticity of borrowing with respect to credit availability. This has been shown in a variety of contexts including credit cards (Gross and Souleles 2002), home equity loans (Mian and Sufi 2011), and auto loans (Einav, Jenkins, and Levin 2011). The aggressiveness shown by borrowers is notable: in my joint work with Atif Mian, we show that borrowers in the lowest quartile of the credit rating distribution borrow up to $0.40 for every $1.00 of increase in home equity.

Third, asset prices are often a function of debt levels. There are both theoretical (e.g., Allen and Gale 2000; Geanakoplos 2010; Simsek 2011) and empirical studies (Mian and Sufi 2009; Favara and Imbs 2010) that support this view. As a result, debt-to-value ratios are often misleading in the midst of an expansion in debt. A critical mistake is to justify high levels of debt with an appeal to high asset values. If the expansion of debt is causing the increase in the value, the higher values will likely prove to be temporary.

These three facts are important to keep in mind as I outline the methodology.

14.2   The Methodology

The methodology I propose is as follows.[3] Conditional on seeing a sharp increase in leverage in some sector of the economy, use microeconomic data to implement the following three steps:

---

2. This is, of course, a controversial assertion. However, it is supported by evidence from a variety of sources, including Kindleberger and Aliber (2005), Eichengreen and Mitchener (2003), Mian and Sufi (2009), and Schularick and Taylor (2009). There is an indisputably strong predictive relation between sharp increases in debt and subsequent financial crises. I do not take a stand on the underlying model that is consistent with this relation. While I fully agree that more research on this issue is needed, I believe the evidence is strong enough to warrant careful monitoring of debt levels in the economy.

3. A simple model to motivate this test is in Mian and Sufi (2009).

1. Determine who the marginal borrowers are that have a very high elasticity of borrowing with respect to credit availability. Ideally, one wants to classify marginal borrowers before the large increase in debt. These borrowers will often appear "constrained" from receiving credit before the increase in leverage.

2. Ask the question: During the period of increasing debt levels, has the flow of credit to these marginal borrowers increased substantially relative to nonmarginal borrowers? Or in other words, are previously constrained borrowers responsible for a large fraction of the total increase in debt levels? In most circumstances where debt levels have increased sharply, the answer to this question will be yes.

3. If the answer to the previous question is yes, ask the question: Is the relative increase in the flow of credit to marginal borrowers driven by productivity improvements/increases in permanent income? Use current income growth as a proxy. This is the key step in the methodology and requires the most careful analysis.

If the answer to question 2 is yes and the answer to question 3 is no, then the evidence is supportive of credit supply as the driving force behind increases in debt levels. My assertion is that the regulator should show some concern if this is the case.

I do not take a stand on the precise steps that the regulator should take at that point in time. It will depend on the circumstances and the overall economic environment. But it is critical for the regulator to understand when sharp increases in debt levels are likely driven by an expansion in the willingness to lend by creditors, and not by improvements in productivity or permanent income.

14.3 An Example: The 2002 to 2007 Increase in US Household Debt

Figure 1 in the online appendix shows the sharp rise in household debt in the United States beginning in about 2000. While there was a general increase in household debt since the 1950s, the increase in debt from 2000 to 2007, measured either as a total or scaled by income, was stunning in historical perspective. Witnessing this sharp rise in household debt in real time, the regulator would now be in a position to implement the above-mentioned methodology.

The first step is to isolate marginal borrowers. I examine two measures used in the previous literature (Gross and Souleles 2002; Mian and Sufi 2009): the credit card utilization rate and the fraction of borrowers with a credit score under 660. I measure these variables at the zip code level as of 1998. In figure 2 in the online appendix, I show the correlation of these two variables with denial rates on mortgage applications as of 1998. Both of these measures were strongly correlated with the denial rate, which is consistent with the view that these measures capture "constrained" or "marginal" households.

For step 2, I measure the flow of credit to these marginal borrowers using new mortgage originations for house purchase. I split the sample of zip codes based on the fraction of individuals with a credit score below 660 as of 1992. In figure 3 in the online appendix, I show the growth in mortgage originations for house purchase from 1992 through 2009. As figure 3 shows, there was a dramatic relative growth in originations for zip codes with a large fraction of marginal borrowers, as measured by credit score. This corresponded closely to the period in which aggregate household debt levels increased sharply. The answer to the question in step 2 is yes: the sharp increase in overall household debt corresponded to a dramatic relative increase in the flow of credit to marginal borrowers.

For step 3, I measure relative income growth for marginal versus non-marginal borrowers. Figure 4 in the appendix shows income growth for high- versus low-credit quality zip codes. From 2002 to 2007—the period in which the relative growth in mortgage credit to low-credit quality zip codes was strongest—there was no evidence that low-credit quality zip codes experienced substantial gains in income. If anything, the opposite is true: marginal borrowers in the United States from 2002 to 2007 were experiencing a tremendous growth in mortgage credit while experiencing lower income growth relative to nonmarginal borrowers.

If the above-mentioned methodology had been implemented during the 2000 to 2007 explosion in US household debt, it would have been clear that the sharp increase was driven primarily by an expansion in the credit supply. This could have been seen as early as 2004 and very strongly in 2005.

14.4   Additional Notes on Methodology

The methodology explicitly ignores asset prices. It compares the flow of credit to marginal households with their income growth, but does not take into account the increase in the value of the asset being financed (in the case of 2000 to 2007, house prices). The justification for ignoring asset prices is that they are often a function of debt availability. In the context of the 2000 to 2007 credit expansion, figure 5 in the appendix shows that house prices increased by more in zip codes with a larger fraction of low-credit quality borrowers. This relative growth in house prices occurred despite the fact that income growth in these areas was relatively negative. Indeed, perhaps the biggest mistake made by regulators in the household debt run-up was to justify debt levels with high house prices, when high debt levels were likely pushing up house prices.

The methodology also explicitly ignores interest payments on debt. Expansions in credit correspond with declines in interest rates, and so a comparison of income to interest rates ("debt service ratio") can hide the danger of higher debt levels. This was especially true from 2002 to 2007 when lower interest payments were driven in part by teaser rates on adjustable-rate mortgages that depended on continued house price growth. Further, it is likely that the level of debt will be the biggest problem in a financial crisis (given debt overhang or risk-shifting tendencies), not the flow of interest payments to creditors.

This methodology is about aggregate patterns. A mistaken view is that this exercise only isolates patterns among marginal borrowers. Instead, the methodology uses marginal borrowers to make an assertion about what is driving aggregate economic patterns. If the flow of credit to marginal borrowers expands dramatically despite lower relative income growth, it is likely that the increase in debt levels even for nonmarginal borrowers is driven by credit supply. In appendix figure 6, I present a scatter plot of US states that supports this view. On the horizontal axis, I calculate for each state the zip code level correlation between low-credit quality share and mortgage origination growth from 2002 to 2006. States with a high score on this measure are states where the credit supply effect is strongest. On the vertical axis, I plot the total household debt growth over the same time period. As the figure shows, there is a very strong positive relation between overall debt growth in a state and the relative flow of mortgage credit to marginal borrowers.

Microeconomic data is critical. The aggregate debt-to-income ratio is a useful measure. But the nature of the income process at the aggregate level can lead regulators to discount a sharp increase in the debt-to-income ratio. For example, many regulators argued that productivity improvements led to a rise in long-run permanent income that justified higher debt levels relative to current income. The microeconomic data show explicitly that debt levels are rising in areas where income is not rising. The microeconomic data force regulators to understand the reasons why marginal borrowers are building up debt without any evidence of an increase in permanent income.

This methodology applies to other sectors of the economy. I focus here on the household sector, but this methodology can be implemented in other sectors easily. For example, Greenwood and Hanson (2010) implement a very similar test in the context of nonfinancial businesses. They show that a relative increase in credit to highly levered risky companies is followed by lower expected returns on bonds. In fact, they argue that expected returns on bonds are negative after sharp increases in credit to marginal borrowers on the corporate side.

Good shifts in credit supply? More evidence is needed to buttress the assertion that all shifts in credit supply end badly. Are there episodes in the past in which a shift in credit supply unaccompanied by productivity improvements did not end badly?

But what about the economics? I am very sympathetic to the complaint that we need to understand more about the underlying economics of credit expansion to marginal borrowers before implementing the methodology. For example, under a simple model of liquidity constraints, the consumer welfare improvements of credit expansion to marginal borrowers are large. But I believe it is equally important to give serious considerations to models in which debt amplifies negative shocks (e.g., Bernanke and Gertler 1989; Shleifer and Vishny 1992; Kiyotaki and Moore 1997; Krishnamurthy 2003; Allen and Gale 2004) and models that argue that debt levels can be inefficiently high (e.g., Lorenzoni 2008). Given the ambiguity on the ultimate welfare costs of intervention, I have purposely not recommended any specific intervention upon determining the importance of credit supply shifts in the economy.

14.5   Data

In terms of data, one advantage of the methodology is that it can be implemented immediately. In fact, most of the data for this exercise is available at the zip code level. Regulators can potentially construct a zip code data set to implement this approach going forward without requiring any additional surveys or data collection.

In order to construct the ideal data set, I will first list the existing data sources available at the zip code level. I will then highlight where more data is needed.

- Home Mortgage Disclosure Act. This provides excellent data on the flow of new mortgages. This is available at the individual application level, and can easily be aggregated to the census tract or zip code level. The frequency is yearly.
- Consumer Credit Bureau data. This provides excellent data on the debt side of the household balance sheet. These data could be broken down to the individual level, but are also widely available at the zip code level. The frequency is monthly.
- House price data. Data on house prices at the zip code level are available from Fiserv Case Shiller Weiss, CoreLogic, and Zillow. The frequency is monthly.
- IRS income data. The IRS Statistics of Income provides income data aggregated to the zip code level. The frequency is yearly.
- Auto sales data. Auto purchases at the zip code level are available from R. L. Polk. The frequency is monthly.
- Census. The decennial census provides a wealth of information at the zip code level. The primary drawback is that the information is only provided every ten years. But this snapshot is extremely valuable for understanding the microeconomic patterns behind macroeconomic trends.

In terms of improvements in data, I would emphasize the following:

- Data on consumption is very limited. The auto sales data is the only measure of consumption that I know of that is at the zip code level. One obvious source of such data would be credit card companies and the clearing houses. They should have data at the zip code level. Monitoring consumption levels is crucial for understanding how leverage is affecting the economy.
- Data on wealth is also very limited. The most commonly used source is the Survey of Consumer Finances. The drawback is that geographic identifiers are not widely available, and the sample is quite small. One possible source is IXI Corporation, which may have microdata available on the wealth distribution.
- The IRS data has a huge lag. If the IRS made their zip code–level data available more quickly, that would facilitate measurement. As of August 2011, the latest zip code–level IRS data available is for 2007.
- While zip code–level data is very useful for understanding what is happening in the economy, individual-level data is needed in some circumstances. One of the most important individual-level characteristics that is needed is whether someone owns a home or not. Being able to split home owners and renters and examine their patterns separately would be extremely useful.

References

Allen, Franklin, and Douglas Gale. 2000. "Bubbles and Crisis." *Economic Journal* 110:236–55.

———. 2004. "Financial Intermediaries and Markets." *Econometrica* 72:1023–61.

Bernanke, Ben, and Mark Gertler. 1989. "Agency Costs, Net Worth, and Business Fluctuations." *American Economic Review* 79 (1): 14–31.

Eichengreen, Barry, and Kris Mitchener. 2003. "The Great Depression as a Credit Boom Gone Wrong." Bank for International Settlements Working Paper no. 137. http://www.bis.org/publ/work137.htm.

Einav, Liran, Mark Jenkins, and Jonathan Levin. 2011. "Contract Pricing in Consumer Credit Markets." Working Paper, Stanford University.

Favara, Giovanni, and Jean Imbs. 2010. "Credit Supply and the Price of Housing." Working Paper, International Monetary Fund.

Geanakoplos, John. 2010. "The Leverage Cycle." In *NBER Macroeconomics Annual 2009*, edited by Daron Acemoglu, Kenneth Rogoff, and Michael Woodford, 1–65. Chicago: University of Chicago Press.

Glick, Reuven, and Kevin Lansing. 2010. "Global Household Leverage, House Prices, and Consumption." *FRBSF Economic Letter*, Jan 11. San Francisco: Federal Reserve Bank of San Francisco.

Greenwood, Robin, and Samuel Hanson. 2010. "Issuer Quality and Corporate Bond Returns." Working Paper, Harvard Business School, Harvard University.

Gross, David, and Nicholas S. Souleles. 2002. "Do Liquidity Constraints And Interest Rates Matter For Consumer Behavior? Evidence from Credit Card Data." *Quarterly Journal of Economics* 117 (1): 149–85.

Hall, Robert. 2011. "The Long Slump." *American Economic Review* 101 (2): 431–69.

Kindleberger, Charles P., and Robert Aliber. 2005. *Manias, Panics, and Crashes: A History of Financial Crises.* Hoboken, NJ: John Wiley & Sons.

Kiyotaki, Nobuhiro, and John Moore.1997. "Credit Cycles." *Journal of Political Economy* 105 (2): 211–48.

Krishnamurthy, Arvind. 2003. "Collateral Constraints and the Amplification Mechanism." *Journal of Economic Theory* 119:104–27.

Lorenzoni, Guido. 2008. "Inefficient Credit Booms." *Review of Economic Studies* 27:809–33.

Mian, Atif, and Amir Sufi. 2009. "The Consequences of Mortgage Credit Expansion: Evidence from the US Mortgage Default Crisis." *Quarterly Journal of Economics* 124:1449–96.

———. 2010. "Household Leverage and the Recession of 2007 to 2009." *IMF Economic Review* 58:74–117.

———. 2011. "House Prices, Home Equity-Based Borrowing, and the US Household Leverage Crisis." *American Economic Review*, August.

Schularick, Moritz, and Alan Taylor. 2009. "Credit Booms Gone Bust: Monetary Policy, Leverage Cycles, and Financial Crises, 1870–2008." NBER Working Paper no. 15512, Cambridge, MA.

Shleifer, Andrei, and Rob Vishny. 1992. "Liquidation Values and Debt Capacity: A Market Equilibrium Approach." *Journal of Finance* 47:1343–66.

Simsek, Alp. 2011. "Belief Disagreements and Collateral Constraints." Working Paper, Massachusetts Institute of Technology.

VI

Corporate Sector

A Macroeconomist's Wish List of Financial Data

V. V. Chari

15.1 Introduction

Developing an understanding of how financial market disturbances affect the broader economy is crucial for designing appropriate regulatory policy on financial markets. In this chapter I argue that both policymaking and research could be advanced with new data.

- What data do we need? We need financial statements of nonpublic firms. Recent research on general equilibrium models with financial frictions offers a great deal of promise in understanding links between financial markets and the rest of the economy. In particular, many recent models focus on how frictions in financial markets impede firms' investment decisions. Further development of this class of models requires data on the financial statements of nonfinancial firms. Such data is available for publicly traded firms but is not available for privately held firms in the United States.
- Where is this data available? Such data is available from the tax returns that corporations file, as well as the statements firms make available to financial intermediaries when they seek to borrow funds, but detailed

V. V. Chari is the Paul W. Frenzel Land Grant Professor of Liberal Arts and professor of economics at the University of Minnesota and an adviser at the Federal Reserve Bank of Minneapolis.

I thank the National Science Foundation for financial support, Alessandro Dovis and Ariel Zetlin-Jones for technical assistance and useful comments, and the participants at the NBER systemic risk conference, especially Markus Brunnermeier, Arvind Krishnamurthy, and Luigi Zingales for useful comments. The views expressed herein are those of the author and not necessarily those of the Federal Reserve Bank of Minneapolis or the Federal Reserve System. For acknowledgments, sources of research support, and disclosure of the author's material financial relationships, if any, please see http://www.nber.org/chapters/c12555.ack.

data on individual firms is not publicly available. If confidentiality concerns imply that data on individual nonpublic firms cannot be available, selected statistics can help.
- How would this data help? Making this kind of data more publicly available would help academics develop better models and would also help make policy.

The need for this kind of data starts with the recognition that financial crises are a recurrent feature of capitalist economies. Such crises manifest themselves in a variety of ways, including sharp declines in the value of assets traded in financial markets and the threatened or actual failure of financial intermediaries. Some crises are associated with banking panics and often a widening of interest rate spreads between relatively safe assets and relatively risky assets. Typically, financial crises are associated with sharp declines in economic activity. Such declines typically reach well beyond the financial sector and affect firms and households in a variety of industries. (See Reinhart and Rogoff [2009], for a recent study of financial crises in a variety of countries over a number of years, and the associated fluctuations in economic activity.) An understanding of the sources of financial crises and the mechanisms whereby disruptions in financial markets affect economic activity more generally is essential in developing policies and designing institutional arrangements whereby such crises can be avoided and the effects on economic activity mitigated.

Developing this understanding necessarily requires developing models in which financial market disturbances affect broader economic activity. One can imagine a variety of ways in which financial market disturbances affect real economic activity. Here, I focus on models in which financial market disturbances affect economic activity through the *investment channel*. Specifically, I will focus on models in which shocks affect the ability of firms to finance investment. Fluctuations in the volume of investment in such models affect output and employment. Focusing on such models excludes models in which financial market disturbances affect working capital, for example, though some of the issues that I raise also apply to such models.

An academic literature over the last decade or so has made a promising start at developing models in which financial frictions affect the aggregate economy primarily through their effect on investment decisions (see, for example, Bernanke, Gertler, Gilchrist [1999] and Kiyotaki and Moore [1997]). These models assume that firms are confronted with a variety of frictions arising from financial markets that limit the extent to which they can use external funds to make profitable investments. From a conceptual point of view, it is useful to divide these models into two broad classes. One class of such models uses what I will call the *representative firm* construct. The other class consists of models in which heterogeneity across firms plays an essential role in the way aggregate investment is affected by financial market disturbances and I will refer to this class as using a *heterogeneous firm* construct. With a representative firm, to a first approximation, all production of nonfinancial goods and services can be usefully thought of as occurring within a typical or representative firm. In particular, reallocation of funds from one set of firms to another set plays no essential role in the way financial frictions affect economic activity. Leading examples of the representative firm construct are Bernanke, Gertler, and Gilchrist (1999), Jermann and Quadrini (2012), and Eisfeldt and Rampini (2009). It is worth emphasizing that in Bernanke, Gertler, and Gilchrist's formulation, all firms are not alike but the economy behaves as if a nonfinancial activity occurs within a representative firm. Leading examples of models that use the heterogeneous firm construct are Kiyotaki and Moore (1997), Eisfeldt and Rampini (2006), and Shourideh and Zetlin-Jones (2012).

I argue that the data strongly suggest that the representative firm construct is not a useful way to proceed if one is interested in developing models in which financial frictions affect economic activity through the investment channel. I go on to argue that the heterogeneous firm construct is more promising. Realizing that promise requires, however, obtaining and using disaggregated data on fund flows between firms and financial intermediaries.

The main problem with the representative firm construct is that in the aggregate, nonfinancial firms generate significantly more cash from their operations than is needed to finance their investments. These excess funds are, of course, returned to shareholders in the form of dividends, stock buybacks, and the like. Using data from the Flow of Funds for the United States, I show that in essentially every quarter over the postwar period, firms in the aggregate generated more cash from their operations than they used for investment. That is, in essentially every quarter over the postwar period, in the aggregate, funds flow from nonfinancial firms to households after investment expenditures have been made. In models with financial frictions, external funds are more expensive than internal funds. This difference in costs creates strong incentives for firms to delay paying dividends rather than using external funds for investment. This delay delivers higher returns to shareholders, and to use those proceeds for investment. The observation that, in the aggregate, firms pay dividends rather than delaying them creates a challenge for representative firm models.

Heterogeneous firm models, however, hold promise. These models emphasize the role of financial markets in reallocating funds from relatively cash-rich firms without plentiful projects in which to make investments to cash-poor, project-rich firms. From the perspective of these models, disturbances in financial markets can adversely affect economic activity by reducing resource reallocation from firms with relatively poor investment opportunities to firms with good investment opportunities. Determining how financial market disturbances affect the broader economy requires a measure of the amount of resource reallocation across firms that is conducted through financial markets. A key statistic to measure this resource reallocation is what I call an *external funding measure*. This statistic measures the amount of investment that is financed by financial markets. Shourideh and Zetlin-Jones (2012) use this measure to discipline their general equilibrium model of financial frictions operating through the investment channel. In this sense this measure has already proven useful in academic work. This measure is also likely to be useful for policymakers. It provides them a real-time statistic that will be useful in determining the way financial market disturbances are affecting the broader economy.

Realizing the promise of heterogeneous firm models ideally requires that we have access to the financial statements of firms. Such data is typically available for firms whose shares are traded in public stock markets (from sources such as COMPUSTAT). Such data is available for European countries for the last decade or so for a broader set of firms, including privately held firms. Shourideh and Zetlin-Jones (2012) show that the amount to which privately held firms use external funding for investment is much greater than for publicly held firms. This finding is promising for heterogeneous firm models but also makes clear the urgent need to have such data for the United States.

These findings lead to a specific set of proposals. The ideal outcome would be to obtain financial statements, including balance sheets, income statements, and flow of funds statements for all nonfinancial corporations in the United States. Such data is available for publicly held firms, but as I have argued, appears to be most important for privately held firms. The Internal Revenue Service already has this data since all corporations, including privately held ones, are required to report extensive information on their finances along with their tax returns. In principle, the IRS could make available a suitably chosen random sample of this data.

If the IRS is unwilling to make this data public, the Federal Reserve or other organizations could conduct surveys to obtain this information. In essence, the survey would collect financial statements. In particular, the flow of funds statement is the most useful. One source of such data comes from financial intermediaries like banks. Such intermediaries invariably require financial statements from borrowers. It should be possible to obtain financial statements of borrowers while respecting privacy concerns. One example of such an exercise is Bachmann and Bayer (2011), who obtained German data on individual firms' financial flows for a limited number of years.

The most limited proposal is that the IRS could be asked to compute and report the external funding measure proposed here by size class in terms of assets, size class in terms of revenues, and by industry. The underlying data is already available and the computations are straightforward. Given the nature of the statistic, confidentiality is not an issue.

The value of this kind of data is that it will allow academics to develop better, more reliable quantitative models of the role of financial markets.

Such models are essential if we are to ask and answer what the economic consequences would be of policy interventions. For example, one proposal intended to reduce the likelihood of crises is to require banks to hold more capital. If this proposal simply raises borrowing costs for financially constrained firms, it will simply interfere with resource reallocation and will make the economy less efficient.

This kind of data can also be valuable to policymakers. Measuring changes in resource reallocation will allow policymakers to obtain signals about the likely consequences of financial market disturbances on the broader economy.

15.2   A Critique of Financial Friction Models with a Representative Firm

Over the last twenty years or so, macroeconomists have developed an array of models in which financial frictions play an essential role. Prominent examples include Bernanke and Gertler (1989), Bernanke, Gertler, Gilchrist (1999), Christiano, Motto, and Rostagno (2009), Jermann and Quadrini (2012), and Gertler and Karadi (2011). The basic idea in these models is that the ability of firms to access capital markets, particularly for investment expenditures, is limited. In Bernanke and Gertler (1989) and Bernanke, Gertler, Gilchrist (1999), for example, investment expenditures (at least at the margin) must be financed by external borrowing. The cost of this external borrowing is higher than the return that firms can receive because of agency problems. In Jermann and Quadrini's formulation, external funds are needed for firms to make profitable investments, and firms face collateral-like constraints on the amount of external funds they can raise. These constraints are thought to arise from the possibility that managers might decamp with some of these funds.

Here I critique this class of models. It should go without saying that the representative firm construct is an exceptionally useful formulation in a wide variety of models. My critique applies only to the role of financial frictions in such models. The main purpose of this critique is to demonstrate the need for disaggregated flow of funds data. Existing aggregate data sources are simply inadequate to analyze how financial market disturbances affect the broader economy.

To develop this critique I present a simple model with financial frictions. Consider the following version of a neoclassical stochastic growth model with financing frictions. I model the financing frictions in the spirit of Kiyotaki and Moore as constraints on the extent to which investment can be financed by borrowing. The time horizon is infinite, the underlying (finite) space of shocks in each period is denoted by s_t and the history of shocks is denoted by s^t with probability $\mu_t(s^t)$ A single consumption-capital good is produced using a neoclassical production function $z_t F(k_t, l_t)$ where z_t is a technology shock, k_t denotes capital, and l_t denotes labor input. The representative household's utility function is given by $\sum_{t=1}^{\infty}\beta^t U(c_t,l_t)$ where c_t denotes consumption, U is a standard utility function, and $0 < \beta < 1$ is the discount factor. The resource constraints are given by

$$c_t + x_t \le z_t F(k_t, l_t).$$

and

(1)
$$k_{t+1} = x_t + (1-\delta)k_t,$$

where x_t denotes gross investment and δ is the depreciation rate.

The market structure is as follows. Households and firms have access to one period risk-free bonds, which if purchased in period t pay an interest rate r_{t+1} together with the principal in period $t + 1$ Firms make investment decisions, employ labor, and distribute dividends denoted by d_t. The representative household chooses consumption, labor, and bond holdings to solve the following problem:

(2)
$$\max \sum_{t=0}^{\infty} \sum_{s^t} \beta^t \mu_t(s^t) U(c_t(s^t), l_t(s^t))$$

subject to

$$c_t(s^t) + b_{t+1}(s^t) \le w_t(s^t)l_t(s^t) + d_t(s^t) + (1 + r_t(s^{t-1}))b_t(s^{t-1})$$

and a no-Ponzi condition $b_{t+1} \ge -\underline{B}$ where $\underline{B}$ is a large number, taking the stochastic process for dividends as given. Let $m_t(s^t) = \beta^t \mu_t(s^t) U_c(c_t(s^t), l_t(s^t))$ denote the marginal utility of consumption at s^t or alternatively the price of consumption in terms of a numeraire good.

Firms make investment and employment decisions to solve the following problem:

(3)
$$\max \sum_{t=0}^{\infty} \sum_{s^t} m_t(s^t) d_t(s^t)$$

subject to

(4)
$$d_t(s^t) + x_t(s^t) \le z_t(s^t) F(k_t(s^{t-1}), l_t(s^t)) - w_t(s^t)l_t(s^t) + b_{t+1}(s^t)$$
$$- (1 + r_t(s^{t-1}))b_t(s^{t-1}),$$

equation (1), a nonnegativity constraint on dividends,

(5)
$$d_t(s^t) \ge 0,$$

and an enforcement constraint

(6)
$$k_{t+1}(s^t) - b_{t+1}(s^t) \ge \lambda_t(s^t),$$

where $\lambda_t(s^t)$ is a stochastic process that governs the tightness of the enforcement constraint. The idea is that firms are limited in the extent to which they can finance investment by borrowing and that the extent of this limit varies stochastically over time.

I argue that if the enforcement constraint is binding in any period t, the nonnegativity constraint must also be binding in that period. The argument is by arbitrage. Note that consumer optimality implies that

$$m_t(s^t) = \sum_{s^{t+1}} m_{t+1}(s^{t+1})(1 + r_{t+1}(s^t)).$$

The arbitrage argument is by contradiction. Suppose that the enforcement constraint is binding at some s^t and that $d_t(s^t) > 0$. Reducing $d_t(s^t)$ and $b_{t+1}(s^t)$ by a small amount leaves the value of the firm's objective unchanged but relaxes the enforcement constraint and allows for an improvement of the objective. We then have the following proposition:

PROPOSITION 1. *Suppose that the enforcement constraint in equation (6) is binding at some t and s^t. Then $d_t(s^t) = 0$.*

Thus, if a firm pays dividends at some date, then in the model, the enforcement constraint must not be binding in that period. As I will show, in the data for the United States, the aggregate of all firms (and therefore the representative firm in the model) pays dividends almost all the time. From the perspective of the model, the implication is that the enforcement constraint could not have been binding. Fluctuations in the financial frictions parameter, $\lambda_t(s^t)$ could not have had any effect.

Consider now alternative ways of modeling financial constraints. These alternative ways are simply different ways of writing the enforcement constraint and they allow for debt to have tax advantages over equity. I argue that financial frictions cannot matter as long as dividends are positive. To make this argument, I will say that financial frictions matter if they distort investment decisions relative to an economy without such constraints. Formally, I say *financial frictions matter at t* for investment if

(7) $$\frac{\sum_{s^{t+1}} m_{t+1}(s^{t+1})[z_{t+1}(s^{t+1})F_k(k_{t+1}(s^t), l_{t+1}(s^{t+1})) + (1-\delta)]}{m_t(s^t)} > 1.$$

The left side of equation (7) is the expected return to capital weighted by the household's marginal rate of substitution and the right side is simply the cost of investing. In an economy without frictions, the two sides of equation (7) are equal to each other. Consider now the problem of maximizing firm profits given by equation (3) subject to equations (4), (1), and (5), and a general formulation of the enforcement constraint of the form

(8) $$H(k_t(s^{t-1}), k_{t+1}(s^t), l_t(s^t), b_{t+1}(s^t), b_t(s^{t-1}); s^t) \geq 0,$$

where the function H is allowed to depend on inherited capital, debt, future capital, and labor. Assume that H is increasing in $k_{t+1}(s^t)$. It is clear that in any solution to this problem, if $d_t(s^t) > 0$, equation (7) cannot hold. The reason implies that it is feasible to reduce $d_t(s^t)$ by a small amount, increase investment in the current period by that amount, and raise dividends in the next period by the associated return to capital. We then have the following proposition:

PROPOSITION 2. *Assume that H is increasing in* $k_{t+1}(s^t)$. *Suppose* $d_t(s^t) > 0$. *Then financial frictions do not matter at t and state* s^t.

Note that if I also allowed for constant proportional taxes on dividends, proposition 2 still holds.

Figure 15.1 plots dividends for all nonfarm, nonfinancial corporate businesses relative to corporate gross domestic product (GDP) for the United States from 1952:01 to 2011:04. I have taken the data for dividends from table F.102, line 3, and obtained corporate GDP from National Income and Product Accounts (NIPA) table 1.14, line 17. Clearly, dividends are positive for every quarter and typically substantially so compared to gross investment. On average, dividends are 4 percent of corporate GDP. Gross investment (line 11 in table F.102) is 15 percent of corporate GDP on average. In light of propositions 1 and 2, these figures pose a significant challenge for financial friction models that use the representative firm construct.

More generally, it is useful to think of financial markets as consisting of pipes connecting nonfinancial firms to financial intermediaries and households, and to think of financial market disturbances as clogging the flow of funds in these pipes. Many models of financial frictions implicitly think of funds as flowing from households to nonfinancial firms. The problem is that

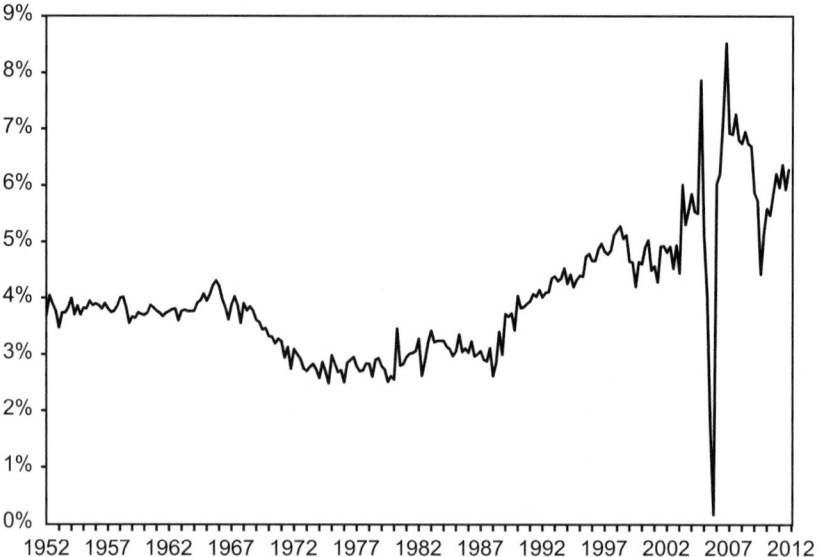

Fig. 15.1   Net dividends, US nonfinancial corporations
Note: See text for description of data.

in the data, in the aggregate, funds flow from nonfinancial firms to households so that it is hard to see how financial market disturbances interfere with the ability of firms to obtain financing.

To demonstrate the sense in which funds flow from nonfinancial firms to households, it is useful to define a variable that I will call *Available Funds*. In the context of the previous models , I define available funds as

(9) $$AF_t = y_t - w_t l_t - r_t b_t - T_t,$$

where $y = z_t F(k_t, l_t)$ denotes output, or value added, and T_t denotes taxes. The idea is that interest payments on debt and taxes are legal obligations. Note that I do not include maturing debt. In practice, most debt by nonfinancial firms is long-term debt and only a relatively small amount matures each quarter.

Conceptually, think of firms as obtaining revenues from operations. These revenues net of payments to other firms for materials is simply value added. Subtracting out payments to employees, interest payments on past debts and taxes gives a measure of funds that are available either for gross investment or for financial activities. Such financial activities consist of paying dividends, issuing new debt, retiring old debt, and accumulating financial assets such as claims on households and on financial intermediaries.

Substituting equation (9) into equation (4), we obtain the following accounting identity

(10) $$d_t - (b_{t+1} - b_t) = AF_t - x_t.$$

In equation (10), it is useful to note that if $(b_{t+1} - b_t)$ is negative, firms are effectively accumulating net financial assets.

Suppose now that firms follow a policy under which available funds exceed investment at all dates and states. Since it is feasible for firms to pay no dividends, it is feasible for firms to follow a financial policy under which eventually the net financial asset position of firms becomes positive and financing constraints never bind. Eventually, financial frictions cannot matter. Thus a comparison of the behavior of available funds and investment in the data can shed light on the importance of financing constraints.

15.2.1   Available Funds and Gross Investment in the Data

I use Flow of Funds data for the United States to construct a comparison between available funds and gross investment. Mechanically, in the Flow of Funds, available funds are computed by adding internal funds (table F.102, line 9) and dividends (table F.102, line 3). Internal funds, in turn, mainly consists of adding retained earnings to depreciation. For gross investment, I use line 11 in table F.102. These data are for all corporations in the United States, including those whose equity is publicly traded and those for which equity is not traded in public markets.

In figure 15.2, I plot available funds and gross investment scaled by gross

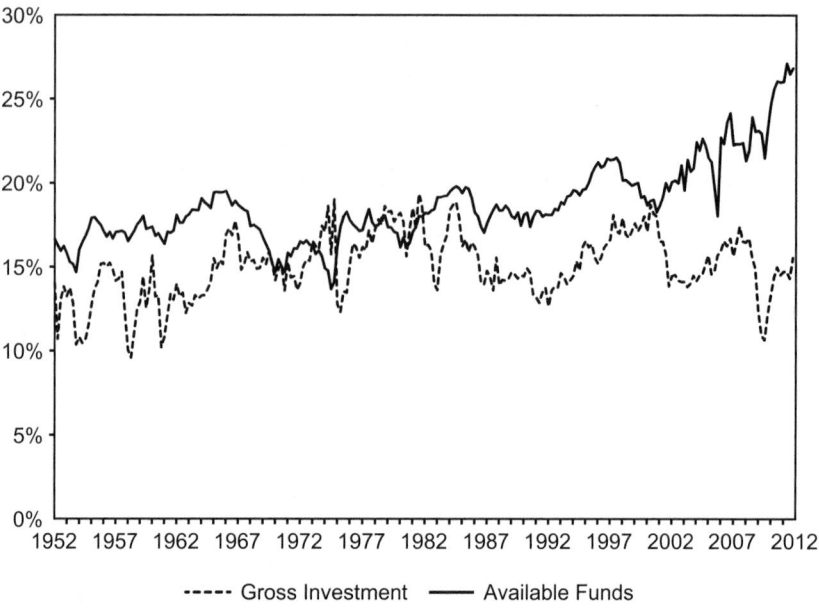

Fig. 15.2   Available funds and gross investment, US nonfinancial corporations
Note: See text for description of data.

domestic product for all nonfinancial corporations for the United States for each quarter from 1952:01 to 2011:04. The figure shows that the mean value of available funds relative to nonfinancial corporate GDP is 19 percent, and the mean value of gross investment is 15 percent. On average over the entire period, funds flow from the nonfinancial sector to other sectors. This finding is not surprising since these flows constitute net payments to shareholders of nonfinancial firms and we should expect that the shareholders will be compensated for their investment in these firms. More striking, the figure also shows that available funds exceed gross investment for 217 of the 240 quarters in the data. That is, in over 90 percent of the quarters, available funds exceeds gross investment, and by an economically large amount. Note also that since 1982 available funds has consistently exceeded gross investment, and, in general, by a substantial amount.

I also use the Statistics of Income from the Internal Revenue Service. This data contains summary statistics from tax returns of all corporations and is provided by size class. This data consists of a series of cross-sections. It is the source of much of the information in the Flow of Funds. Using this data, I construct measures of available funds and gross investment for the size classes in the Statistics of Income. This data shows that within each size class, available funds exceed gross investment. In this sense the data does not show any evidence that smaller firms, taken as a whole, are more reliant on external finance than larger firms. Figure 15.3 shows available funds and investment normalized by sales for large firms (the largest firms by asset size that account for 70 percent of sales and small firms (the remainder of firms). (The appendix describes the details of the construction.) The figure shows that when firms are aggregated within size classes, available funds consistently exceed gross investment.

Figure 15.4 displays similar statistics for the firms in the COMPUSTAT database where I have scaled available funds and investment by sales. In Compustat, to calculate available funds, I use OANCF when available and its equivalent FOPT for those firms that do not report OANCF at that date. For gross investment, I use CAPX + AQC − SPPE. (Shourideh and Zetlin-Jones [2012] show that the statistics computed from this figure are not driven by outliers.) This figure shows that for public firms, as an aggregate, available funds typically exceed gross investment.

These figures represent a challenge to the literature that uses the representative firm in models in which financial frictions operate through the investment channel. In this literature, financial frictions do end up mattering so next I explore the key ingredients that allow financial frictions to matter.

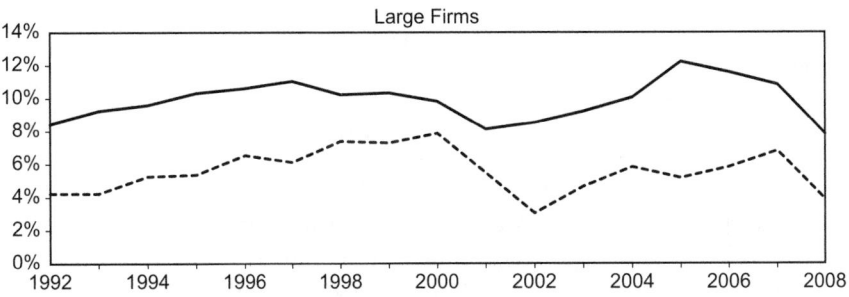

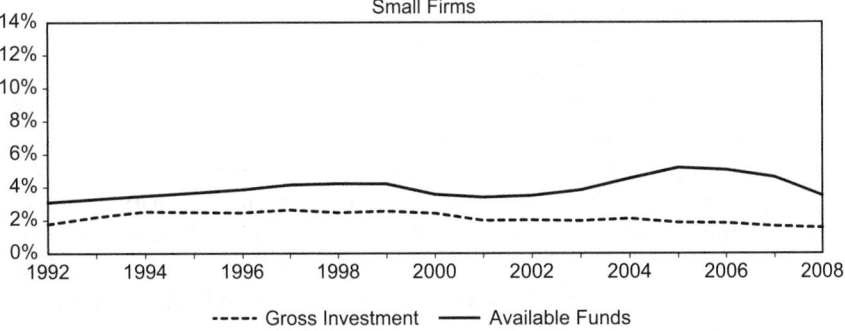

----- Gross Investment   —— Available Funds

Fig. 15.3   Available funds and gross investment by asset class
Note: See text for description of data.

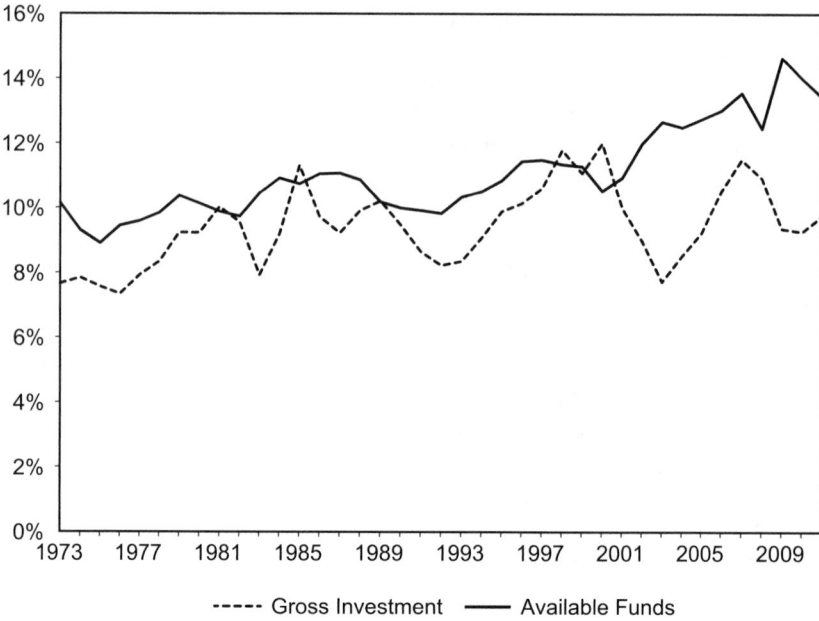

Fig. 15.4   Available funds and gross investment, COMPUSTAT nonfinancial corporations

Note: See text for description of data.

15.2.2   Adjustment Costs and Other Fixes

Jermann and Quadrini (2012), in an important paper, develop a model very similar to that previously outlined and argue that financial frictions and collateral shocks play an important role in accounting for the business cycle. The key assumption they make is that it is costly for firms to adjust dividends relative to the steady state level. This assumption implies that financial frictions could matter. The main concern with this fix is that it is not clear how we could measure these adjustment costs using data at the firm level. As a research agenda, it seems preferable to avoid adding ad hoc adjustment costs. Gertler and Karadi (2011), as well as a number of other papers, make similar assumptions about adjustment costs. Such adjustment costs are not easily rationalized as coming from other sources. For example, a large literature in finance (see, for example, Bhattacharya [1979] or Myers and Majluf [1984]) has argued that if managers are better informed than shareholders, dividends could serve as a signal of future cash flows. This literature could be regarded as a rationalization for the reluctance of managers to reduce dividends and their willingness to reduce capital expenditures instead in bad times. One problem with applying the lessons of that literature is that that literature is really about idiosyncratic shocks and not about aggregate circumstances. It is difficult to argue that managers have better information about macroeconomic aggregates than shareholders. Financial frictions matter when firms choose to use costly external finance while paying dividends at the same time. In response to an observable macroeconomic shock, any model of optimal contracting between shareholders and managers would allow managers to cut dividends rather than cutting back on profitable investments.

Bernanke, Gertler, and Gilchrist (1999) develop a contracting model in which agency problems induce firms to rely on debt to finance investment. In their model, all dividends are distributed when the entrepreneurs who manage the firm die. One problem with their formulation is that it implies an extremely counterfactual property of dividends at the level of individual firms. They are zero until the firm dies, at which point they spike. Similar concerns apply to Christiano, Motto, and Rostagno (2009).

It is worth emphasizing that this literature has been extremely valuable. It is quantitative and it deals with general equilibrium effects and tries to grapple with the effect of financial frictions on output, employment, investment, and so on. In that sense, it represents a considerable advance over illustrative two or three period models that are common in the literature on financial intermediation.

The concerns I have raised about the representative firm construct in models of financial frictions operating through the investment channel do not imply, of course, that all models of financial frictions are doomed. Models focusing on reallocation of investment funds offer a promising alternative.

15.3   Macroeconomic Models with Reallocation and Disaggregated Data

Models that focus on the role of financial frictions in inhibiting the reallocation of funds across firms seem promising. In Kiyotaki and Moore (1997), Eisfeldt and Rampini (2006), Buera (2009), or Shourideh and Zetlin-Jones (2012), the key role of financial markets is that they allow funds to be reallocated from cash-rich, project-poor firms to cash-poor, project-rich firms. Disturbances in financial markets can then be thought of as affecting the reallocation of funds and therefore the efficiency with which the economy operates.

In this context, I propose a statistic that I will call the *external funding measure*. This measure is computed using the concepts of available finds and gross investment defined earlier. Specifically, suppose we have data on available funds and gross investment for a sample of firms. Let x_{it} and AF_{it} denote gross investment and available funds for firm i in period t. Then the external funding measure in period t is given by

$$EF_t = \frac{\sum_i (x_{it} - AF_{it} * x_{it} > AF_{it})}{\sum_i x_{it}},$$

and the average over the sample period is given by

$$EF = \frac{1}{T}\sum_{t=1}^{t=T} EF_t.$$

This statistic is a measure of the extent to which firms rely on external funds to finance investment. To obtain it, I add up all investment in excess of available funds and scale it by aggregate investment. This statistic is a natural measure of the reliance of firms in making investments on financial markets. This natural measure is useful for two reasons. Measuring the extent to which it fluctuates over time and determining its correlation with other measures of stress in financial markets provides real-time information on the extent to which real variables like investment are affected by financial market disturbances. Second, obtaining data on the business cycle properties of this statistic can discipline the building of quantitative general equilibrium models. Shourideh and Zetlin-Jones (2012) show that this measure plays a central role in calibrating their quantitative general equilibrium model.

Like all statistics of the data, this one should be treated with caution. For example, in a world where financial markets do not function at all, no firm is able to obtain external financing and the value of the statistic is zero. This observation suggests that the value of this statistic is to provide clues, rather than definitive answers, in real time and to discipline the construction of quantitative models.

Computing the external finance measure requires disaggregated data at the level of individual firms. For the United States, data on the balance sheets and income statements are not publicly available for all firms. Such data is available for firms whose shares are traded in public markets. Compustat offers a convenient source for these statements. Using data from Compustat, it is possible to calculate available funds and gross investment (as described earlier) for publicly traded firms. Figure 15.5 shows the time series for the external funding measure. The sample average is 23 percent. Note also that this measure varies considerably over time and seems to be procyclical. While this finding is promising, Shourideh and Zetlin-Jones (2012) show that when a model is calibrated to data from Compustat, the effects of financial frictions are fairly modest.

Shourideh and Zetlin-Jones (2012) obtain data from a data set called Amadeus. This data set contains financial information for a much larger set of firms for a number of European countries. This data contains financial information for both publicly traded companies and for privately held ones. Using this data, they show that for the United Kingdom, the sample average of the external finance measure for the period from 2000 to 2009 is 90 percent. The observation that privately held firms are so much more reliant on external finance is promising for models that emphasize the role of financial markets in reallocating investment funds from cash-rich, project-poor firms to cash-poor, project-rich ones.

A key lesson from the Shourideh and Zetlin-Jones exercise is that publicly

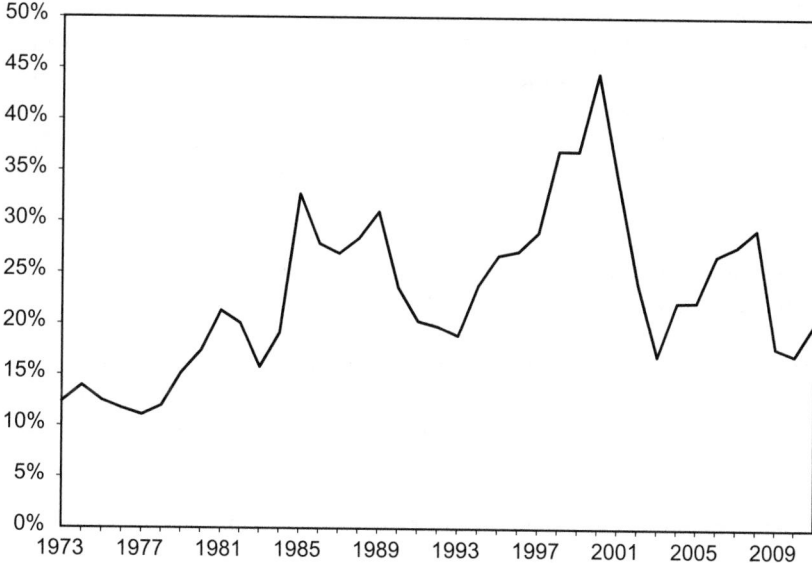

Fig. 15.5   External funding measure, COMPUSTAT nonfinancial corporations
Note: See text for description of data.

held and privately held firms are very different in terms of their reliance on financial markets for financing investments. This lesson suggests that policymakers and academics would benefit greatly from access to financial statements of privately held firms in the United States.

4.15.4   A Proposal for Disaggregated Data

I have argued that representative firm models are not useful for studying the role of financial frictions operating through the investment channel and that heterogeneous firm models are much more promising in this regard. In order to discipline the development of heterogeneous firm models, however, we need disaggregated data on financial statements of individual firms. Such data is available for publicly held firms. In terms of privately held firms, financial statements are available for the last decade or so for a number of European countries and the Amadeus data set offers a convenient way of accessing the data. For the United States, it would be exceptionally useful if financial statements were available for privately held firms. Here, I outline three options starting with the ideal outcome and proceeding toward acceptable outcomes for obtaining similar data for the United States.

The Internal Revenue Service already has this data since corporations are required to report extensive information on their finances along with their tax returns. The ideal outcome would be for the IRS to make available the underlying balance sheet information for privately held firms. Obviously, academics and policymakers do not necessarily need data for the entire population. A suitably chosen random sample should suffice. It is worth emphasizing that this random sample should be in the form of a panel rather than a repeated cross-section. One reason is that many firms may choose to access financial markets in times when their individual fortunes are relatively good in order to have funds available when investment needs are particularly high.

If the IRS is unwilling to make this data public, the Federal Reserve or other organizations could conduct surveys to obtain this information. In essence, the survey would collect financial statements. One possible source of such financial statements is banks. Borrowers are invariably required to provide financial statements to banks. As with all corporations, such statements consist of a balance sheet, an income statement, and a flow of funds statement. Of these, the flow of funds statement is the most useful.

If such surveys cannot be conducted, for example, because of concerns of low response rates, the IRS could be asked to compute and report the external funding measure proposed earlier by size class in terms of assets, size class in terms of revenues, and by industry. The underlying data is already available and the computations are straightforward. Given the nature of the statistic, confidentiality is not an issue.

Appendix

Appendix for the Statistics of Income Analysis

This appendix describes the computation underlying figure 15.4. All data are taken from Annual Statistics of Income, Corporation Income Tax Returns, Table 2: Balance Sheet, Income Statement, and Selected other items, by size of total assets (Returns of Active Corporations), 1992 to 2008.

Data Definitions

- Available funds = total receipts less total deductions plus deductions for depreciation (including depreciation, amortization, and depletion).
- Fixed assets = depreciable assets less accumulated depreciation plus depletable assets less accumulated depletion plus intangible assets less accumulated amortization plus land.
- Sales = total receipts.
- Depreciation = change in accumulated depreciation plus accumulated depletion plus accumulated amortization.
- Investment = fixed assets plus other assets plus depreciation.

Note that deductions for depreciation is *not* equal to accumulated depreciation.

Computing Statistics for Small and Large Firms

The statistics of income reports data for all firms within a given bin for nominal assets. Let the upper bound of the bins on nominal assets be denoted

$$(x_0, x_1, x_2, x_3, x_4, x_5, x_6, x_7) = (.5, 1, 5, 10, 25, 50, 100, 250),$$

representing $500,000, $1 million, $5 million, $10 million, $25 million, $50 million, $100 million, and $250 million.

Step 1: Aggregate to consistent bins.

Nominal bins changes in 2001. We aggregate the highest values after 2001 (values between $250 million and ∞) and we aggregate up to $500,000 before 2001.

Let $Y_t^{raw}(x_i)$ denote the raw series level in year t for all firms with assets between x_{i-1} and x_i.

Let $\bar{Y}_t$ denote the raw series level in year t for all firms.

Step 2: Convert to (level of) real data.

Let $y_t(x_i)$ denote the raw data after it has been made real using the implicit GNP deflator (my current base year is 2005).

Step 3: Compute empirical cumulative distribution.

Let

$$S(x_i, t) = \sum_{j=0}^{i} y_t(x_j).$$

Note that $S(x_7, t) \neq \bar{Y}_t$, since I have not included a "highest" bin value.

Step 4: Construct a continuous function $S(x,t)$.

We use the spline.m function provided by matlab applied to the log of $S(x_i, t)$ and the log of x_i. (Specifically, let $\bar{x}$ be the vector of $\log(x_i)$ and $\bar{S}$ the vector of $\log(S(x_i, t))$. Then for any value, x,

$$S(x, t) = \exp(spline(\bar{x}, \bar{S}, \log(x))).$$

Step 5: Defining cutoffs.

We use sales to define the small and large asset cutoffs. Suppose we assume that small firms make up 30% of sales in any year. Then, in each year, t, let $c(t)$ be the value such that

$$S^{sales}(c(t), t) = .3\bar{Y}_t^{sales}.$$

Available funds for small firms is then given by

$$AF_t^S = S^{in.funds}(c(t), t) + S^{dep}(c(t), t),$$

and for large firms

$$AF_t^L = \overline{Y}_t^{in.\,funds} - S^{in.\,funds}(c(t),t) + \overline{Y}_t^{dep} - S^{dep}(c(t),t).$$

To compute capital expenditures, we need the change in fixed assets. For this, we need to correct for growth in total assets and inflation to ensure firms stay approximately within the same bin. In particular, in any year t, let

$$z_{t,t-1} = c(t)(1 - g_{t-1,t} + \pi_{t-1,t}).$$

Then, capital expenditures for small firms is given by

$$Cap X_t^S = S^{fixa}(c(t),t) + S^{dep}(c(t),t) - S^{fixa}(z_{t,t-1},t-1),$$

and for large firms

$$Cap X_t^L = \overline{Y}_t^{fixa} + \overline{Y}_t^{dep} - \overline{Y}_t^{fixa} - Cap X_t^S.$$

References

Bachmann, R., and C. Bayer. 2011. "Uncertainty Business Cycles—Really?" NBER Working Paper no. 16862, Cambridge, MA.

Bernanke, B., and M. Gertler. 1989. "Agency Costs, Net Worth, and Business Fluctuations." *American Economic Review* 79:14–31.

Bernanke, B., M. Gertler, and S. Gilchrist. 1999. "The Financial Accelerator in a Quantitative Business Cycle Framework." In *Handbook of Macroeconomics*, edited by John B. Taylor and Michael Woodford, 1341–1393. Amsterdam: Elsevier Science, North-Holland.

Bhattacharya, S. 1979. "Imperfect Information, Dividend Policy, and the 'Bird in the Hand' Fallacy." *Bell Journal of Economics and Management Science* 10:259–70.

Buera, F. 2009. "A Dynamic Model of Entrepreneurship with Borrowing Constraints." *Annals of Finance* 5 (3–4): 443–64.

Christiano, L., R. Motto, and M. Rostagno. 2009. "Financial Factors in Economic Fluctuations." Working Paper, Northwestern University.

Eisfeldt, A. L., and A. Rampini. 2006. "Capital Reallocation and Liquidity." *Journal of Monetary Economics* 53:369–99.

———. 2009. "Financing Shortfalls and the Value of Aggregate Liquidity." Working Paper, Duke University.

Gertler, M., and P. Karadi. 2011. "A Model of Unconventional Monetary Policy." *Journal of Monetary Economics* 58 (1): 17–34.

Jermann, U., and V. Quadrini. 2012. "Macroeconomic Effects of Financial Shocks." *American Economic Review* 102 (1): 238–71.

Kiyotaki, N., and J. Moore. 1997. "Credit Cycles." *Journal of Political Economy* 105:211–48.

Myers S. C., and N. Majluf. 1984. "Corporate Financing Decisions When Firms Have Information That Investors Do Not Have." *Journal of Financial Economics* 13:187–220.

Reinhart, C., and K. Rogoff. 2009. *This Time is Different: Eight Centuries of Financial Folly*. Princeton, NJ: Princeton University Press.

Shourideh, A., and A. Zetlin-Jones. 2012. "External Financing and the Role of Financial Frictions over the Business Cycle: Measurement and Theory." Working Paper, University of Minnesota.

VII

International Sector

Systemic Risks in Global Banking
What Available Data Can Tell Us and What More Data Are Needed?

Eugenio Cerutti, Stijn Claessens, and Patrick McGuire

16.1 Introduction

The global financial crisis has shown how interconnected the financial world has become and how a shock that originates in one country or asset class can quickly have sizable impacts on the stability of institutions and markets around the world. As in the closed-economy case, the nature of the balance sheet linkages between financial institutions and markets affects the size of spillovers and their direction of propagation. At the global level, however, financial linkages and channels of propagation are more complex. Global systemic risk analysis is severely hampered by the lack of consistent data that capture the international dimensions of finance. Many of the data needed for identifying and tracking international linkages, even at a rudimentary level, are not (yet) available, and the institutional infrastructure for global systemic risk management is inadequate or simply nonexistent.

Eugenio Cerutti is a senior economist in the Research Department of the International Monetary Fund. Stijn Claessens is assistant director in the Research Department of the International Monetary Fund. Patrick McGuire is a senior economist in the Financial Institutions Section at the Bank for International Settlements.

The views expressed in this chapter belong solely to the authors. Nothing contained in this chapter can be reported as representing IMF policy or the views of the IMF, its executive board, or its member governments; the Bank for International Settlements or its board or management; or any other entity mentioned herein. We would like to thank Claudio Borio, Markus Brunnermeier, Giovanni Dell'Ariccia, Robert Heath, Arvind Krishnamurthy, and Kostas Tsatsaronis for their helpful comments and suggestions. A more extended version of this chapter was previously issued as IMF Working Paper 11/222 and BIS Working Paper 376. For acknowledgments, sources of research support, and disclosure of the authors' material financial relationships, if any, please see http://www.nber.org/chapters/c12557.ack.

This chapter highlights some of the unique challenges to global systemic risk measurement with an eye toward identifying those high-priority areas where enhancements to data are most needed. It shows the following:

- While currently available data can be used more effectively, supervisors and other agencies need more and better data to construct even rudimentary measures of risks in the international financial system.
- Similarly, market participants need better information on aggregate positions and linkages to appropriately monitor and price risks.
- Ongoing initiatives that will help in closing data gaps include the G20 Data Gaps Initiative, which recommends the collection of consistent bank-level data for joint analyses and enhancements to existing sets of aggregate statistics, and the enhancement to the BIS international banking statistics.

The starting point of systemic risk analysis for a single country is typically the banking system.[1] This is due to banks' significant role in financial intermediation and maturity transformation, and their highly leveraged operations. The approach often taken at central banks and supervisory agencies is to identify systemic risks using disaggregated data, including information on the composition of banks' assets and liabilities, maturity and currency mismatches, and other balance sheet and income metrics. These analyses attempt to capture systemic risks stemming from common exposures, interbank linkages, funding concentrations, and other factors that may have a bearing on income, liquidity, and capital adequacy conditions.[2] This approach does not, however, directly extend to the multicountry level. At least three additional challenges arise:

1. Lack of institutional mechanisms that ensure coordination of national approaches. International financial linkages, by definition, involve more than one legal jurisdiction. For various reasons (legal framework, accountability to parliaments and taxpayers, etc.), policymakers tend to focus on national objectives. At times, they may not even be aware of the international implications of their domestic actions or, conversely, of the effect of others' actions on their own economies. This raises a problem intrinsic to any system with multiple stakeholders: authorities in each jurisdiction pursue their

---

1. Attention to systemic risk assessment and contagion has dramatically increased with the global financial crisis, although a precise definition of systemic risk is still lacking. See Borio and Drehmann (2009) and Kaufman and Scott (2003) for a discussion of the definition, and de Bandt, Hartmann, and Peydro (2009) for a recent literature survey.

2. Examples of such quantitative approaches are Boss et al. (2006) and Alessandri et al. (2009) for Austria and the UK, respectively. Much of the work done under the Financial Stability Assessment Program (FSAP)—a joint IMF/World Bank effort introduced in 1999—has documented and analyzed such risks in individual countries. Global systemic risks are being analyzed in the joint IMF-FSB Early Warnings Exercise (IMF 2012), and by the Committee on the Global Financial System (CGFS 2010a, 2010b, 2010c).

own objectives, which do not necessarily maximize global welfare. In such a world, global financial stability may receive too little attention. A related problem is that many of the institutional mechanisms available at the national level to achieve (more) optimal outcomes before, during, and after a financial crisis are lacking at the global level. Although initiatives to enhance multilateral surveillance are underway, most regulatory oversight is still nationally oriented.[3] Supervision of large, internationally active financial institutions is dispersed among agencies in many countries, with imperfect sharing of information and limited tools to coordinate remedial actions. Moreover, a global framework for the resolution of these institutions is lacking,[4] and there is no formal lender of last resort to address liquidity problems in foreign currencies.[5]

2. *Greater complexity in the international context.* Differences in firms' organizational structures and legal status, which play limited roles in a strictly national context, complicate systemic risk measurement and (crisis) management internationally. Large global banks are composed of literally thousands of entities located in many countries. They can lend cross border directly from headquarters, and/or be active in host countries through subsidiaries or branches that also take local deposits. Analyzing vulnerabilities related to banks' operational structure purely using *group-level* consolidated data can be problematic. Such data implicitly assume that resources available at one office location can be freed up and immediately used elsewhere, a very strong assumption.[6] Similarly, group-level (consolidated balance sheet) data obscures hierarchical ownership structure, thus making it difficult to accurately compare a bank's global exposures to a particular asset class to the capital in the banking group.[7] And from a borrower country's perspective, assessing the fragility of credit received *from* foreign banks (either cross

3. The crisis also showed that international institutions' surveillance was often not effective in bringing about policy adjustment in key countries and did not highlight enough global risks (IMF 2011).

4. See IMF (2010) and Claessens, Herring, and Schoenmaker (2010).

5. A domestic central bank can supply liquidity in its domestic currency. But liquidity provision in foreign currencies is limited by the available foreign exchange reserves or borrowing capacity of the central bank.

6. Market frictions, illiquid asset markets, or government interventions can limit an institution's ability to unwind intragroup funding and/or transfer funds across locations, especially during times of financial turmoil. Cerutti et al. (2010) and Cerutti and Schmieder (2014) document that some host regulators ring-fenced foreign affiliates in their territory during the recent crisis. They quantified that banking groups' inability to reallocate funds from subsidiaries with excess capital to those in need of capital would imply substantially larger capital buffers at the parent and/or subsidiary level. Similarly, the crisis showed that netting a bank's balance sheet positions across offices, through consolidating statements, can mask funding risks (Fender and McGuire 2010).

7. For example, while a group is fully exposed to all losses at its local branches and through direct cross-border exposures, its losses from subsidiaries are capped by the parent's equity plus any nonequity intragroup claims. (For more details on the differences between branches and subsidiaries, see Cerutti, Dell'Ariccia, and Martinez Peria [2007].)

border or local) requires information on the types of funding that supports these banks' credit.

3. Scarcity of data that capture the international dimensions of systemic risk. Supervisors in each jurisdiction have access to granular data for banks operating in their jurisdiction. However, the supervision of the activities of internationally active institutions relies on data collection practices that tend to differ across jurisdictions. Moreover, confidentiality concerns generally restrict the sharing of data, even within the supervisory community. Publicly disclosed bank-level data (e.g., from commercial vendors) generally lack (consistent) information about banks' international activities (e.g., cross-currency and cross-border positions). The BIS international banking statistics, which track internationally active banks' foreign positions, are a key source of information for many analytical questions. But these statistics are aggregated across banks and have limited breakdowns of assets and liabilities, and as is are thus not appropriate for many analytical questions.

The following section provides four examples of data-related challenges that arise in the international context, as examples to demonstrate that many aspects of global systemic risk simply can not be captured using existing data. The final section discusses the most significant data limitations and provides a brief overview of international initiatives to deal with them. First, the ongoing G20 initiative to close data gaps (see IMF-FSB (2009) and box 16.2) has put forth twenty recommendations that call for improvements to bank-level and aggregate statistics, a framework for the collection and sharing of these data across jurisdictions, and rules governing access and use of the data. The recommendations specifically highlight the need for more *bank-level* data, including information on firm-level *bilateral* linkages, banks' organizational structures, and broad breakdowns of banks' total assets and liabilities (e.g., by instrument, counterparty-country, counterparty-sector, currency, and residual maturity). Second, enhancements to the *aggregate* BIS international banking statistics, which cover a much wider universe of banks, are also moving forward. These enhancements will shed more light on how banks organize their operations across jurisdictions. Together, these enhancements will go some way in providing a public good—financial data—that is fundamental to the ability to provide global perspectives on potential risks and financial stability concerns and conduct (multilateral) surveillance.

16.2   Measuring Systemic Risks: Examples and Challenges

While progress has been made in measuring global systemic risks, further improvements are possible, especially in the analysis of banks' contribution to systemic risk. This section highlights four data challenges that arise internationally: (a) accurately measuring banks' foreign asset exposures;

(b) measuring a borrower country's reliance on credit from foreign banks; (c) tracking banks' cross-currency funding and maturity transformation activities; and (d) capturing the endogenous interaction of asset and funding positions in scenario analysis.

A key input here is the BIS international banking statistics (IBS), which tracks developments in banks' foreign positions and cross-country financial linkages (see box 16.1). These data are not bank level, but rather are aggregated at the level of national banking systems; that is, the set of internationally active banks headquartered in a particular country (e.g., UK banks). The data cover banks' worldwide *consolidated* exposures to borrowers in particular countries and sectors, and can provide banks' asset and liability positions in specific currencies.

16.2.1 Measurement of Banks' Foreign Credit Exposures

How big are banks' exposures to a particular country or a sector within a country? Which banks are most exposed? How do exposures compare to the parent bank group's consolidated capital? Answering these questions is difficult with available data. Commercially available bank-level data do not contain enough detail on foreign exposures (i.e., the borrowers' country location and/or sector). Aggregated bank data, such as the BIS international banking statistics, do track banks' exposures to countries and sectors, but lack granularity.

To illustrate, consider assessing the potential losses a banking system i faces through its asset exposures to a particular sector in a particular country j. Banking system i's foreign credit exposure to country j is composed of three parts: (a) direct cross-border exposures to borrowers in country j booked by all offices of banking system i located outside of country j, (b) effective exposures via the local positions booked by bank i's subsidiaries and branches located in country j, and (c) all off-balance sheet exposures (derivatives, credit guarantees, and credit commitments) related to borrowers in country j. For the second of these components, note that a bank's exposure to its *subsidiaries* in country j is, from a strictly legal perspective, limited to the capital of the subsidiary plus any other nonequity funds provided by the parent bank. In contrast, the bank absorbs *all* losses on branch exposures most often.[8]

---

8. Of course, reputational concerns play a key role as well. While parent banks have supported foreign subsidiaries beyond their legal obligation, this is not always the case. Hryckiewicz and Kowelewski (2011) document 149 episodes when subsidiaries were abandoned between 1997 and 2009. Regarding branches, some countries (e.g., United States) have explicit provisions establishing that parent banks are not required to repay the obligations of a foreign branch if the branch faces repayment problems due to extreme circumstances (such as war or civil conflict) or due to certain actions by the host government (e.g., exchange controls, expropriations, etc.). This aspect was not considered in the analysis. (See Cerutti [2013] for more detail on the exposure calculations and the differences between branches and subsidiaries.)

Box 16.1   The BIS International Banking Statistics

The BIS international banking statistics (IBS) track internationally active banks' foreign positions through two main data sets: the BIS Consolidated Banking Statistics (CBS) and the BIS Locational Banking Statistics (LBS). Collectively, they are a key source of country-level aggregate information for analyzing financial stability. This box describes the characteristics of the IBS data that make them unique.

BIS Consolidated Banking Statistics

The CBS track banks' worldwide consolidated gross claims and other exposures to individual countries and sectors.[1] They thus provide internationally comparable base measures of national banking systems' exposures to *country risk* (e.g., *cross-border* asset exposure).[2] Reporting banks' foreign claims are composed of several pieces (see figure below). Cross-border claims (A) are claims on nonresidents booked by either a bank's head office or a foreign affiliate (branch or subsidiary) in a third country. Local claims are those booked by a foreign affiliate on borrowers residing in the host country of the affiliate. Local claims can be denominated in foreign currencies (B) or in the local currency of the host country (C).

Banks report foreign claims (A + B + C) on borrowers in individual countries on both an immediate borrower (IB) basis and an ultimate risk (UR) basis. In the CBS (IB), banks' claims are allocated directly to the country where the borrower resides. In addition, banks' foreign claims are reported as *international claims* (A + B) and *local claims in local currency* (C). In contrast, in the CBS (UR), banks allocate their claims to the country where the ultimate obligor resides, defined as the country where the guarantor of a claim resides or the head office of a legally dependent branch is located. Here, banks' foreign claims are reported as *cross-border claims* (A) and *local claims in all currencies* (B + C). Also in the CBS (UR), banks separately report off-balance sheet items such as derivative contracts and contingent exposures (undisbursed credit commitments and guarantees).[3]

---

1. See McGuire and Wooldridge (2005) for further discussion on the uses and structure of the BIS-CBS.

2. Banks net out intergroup positions and consolidate positions across offices worldwide, an advantage over residence-based data, such as the BIS locational banking statistics (LBS) and the IMF's Coordinated Portfolio Investment Survey (CPIS).

3. Derivatives exposures include the positive market value of outstanding contracts covering foreign exchange, interest rate, equity, commodity, and credit risks. Contracts with negative market value are classified as liabilities, and are not reported and/or netted out. Guarantees and credit commitments are reported at face value; that is, at maximum possible exposures.

Box 16.1   (*continued*)

BIS Locational Banking Statistics

Unlike the CBS, the LBS are *residence-based* data (i.e., they follow balance-of-payments accounting), and track the cross-border positions and the local positions in foreign currencies of banks *located* in a particular country. Banks' positions are broken down by currency, by sector (bank and nonbank), by country of residence of the counterparty, and by nationality of reporting banks. Both domestically owned and foreign-owned banking offices in the reporting countries record their positions on a gross (unconsolidated) basis, including positions vis-à-vis own affiliates in other countries.

The LBS are one of the few sources of information about the currency composition of banks' balance sheets, and so aids in tracking system-level funding risks. Because reporting jurisdictions also provide information on the nationality (i.e., the country of headquarters) of the reporting banks in their jurisdiction, the statistics can also be aggregated (across reporting locations) along the lines of consolidated national banking systems, as in the CBS described earlier. These data provide a broad picture of the currency breakdown of banks' consolidated foreign assets and liabilities. When combined with the CBS data, they help to track, at the bank nationality level, cross-currency funding and investment patterns (figure 16.3), which proved fragile during the crisis.

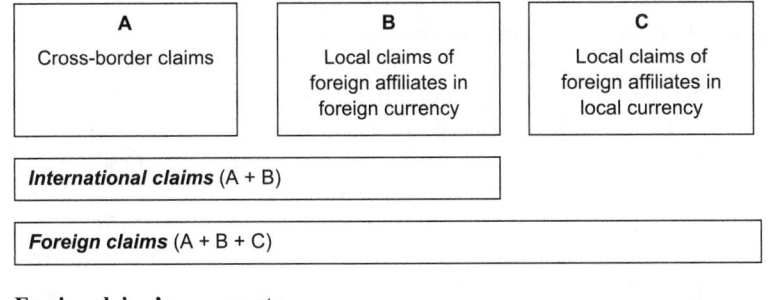

Foreign claims' components

The BIS consolidated banking statistics (CBS) on an ultimate risk basis are of some help in this analysis, but they have their limitations. They track banking system *i*'s *foreign claims* on borrowers in country *j*, which include its worldwide consolidated direct cross-border claims on country *j* plus the positions booked by its affiliates (subsidiaries *and* branches) in country *j* vis-à-vis residents of country *j*. That is, they capture consolidated *gross* exposures to particular countries/sectors, regardless of the branch/subsidiary structure of the reporting banks, and thus provide *upper-bound* measures of a banking system's exposure to country *j*. Supplementing these statistics with bank-level data yields *lower-bound* measures that take into account the legal *limited* exposure of parent banks to their subsidiaries.[9]

Figure 16.1 presents a comparison of foreign claims (upper bound) and the adjusted asset exposure (lower bound) measures, where values are expressed as a percentage of gross domestic product (GDP) and the bubble sizes are proportional to total domestic banking assets. As of September 2010, the adjusted lower-bound measure is, on average, about 10 percent below the upper-bound gross foreign claims measure. The two measures differ little for Swiss banks, but more for Canadian, Greek, and Spanish banks. And when off-balance sheet exposures are included in the calculations (figure 16.1, right-hand panel), the adjusted lower-bound measures fall below the gross measures, especially for Belgian, Swiss, and US banks.

This analysis of foreign credit exposures highlights how differences in banks' organizational structures and legal status need to be taken into account in an international context, and that available data only allow calculations at the level of whole banking systems rather than at the level of individual banks.

16.2.2 Measurement of Borrowers' Reliance on Foreign Bank Credit

Similar problems arise in measuring risks from the perspective of a borrower country. For example, many borrower countries experienced disruptions in international credit flows during the recent financial crisis. This is because the creditor banking systems themselves had balance sheet problems elsewhere that forced them to reduce exposures globally. As a result, they did not roll over all cross-border credit, and diverted funds raised locally by their subsidiaries in particular countries.

The BIS consolidated banking statistics are one of the few sources of information on the extent to which borrowers in a country rely on credit from a *particular* consolidated banking system (e.g., UK banks, Swiss banks, etc). However, because these data were not designed with the borrower's perspective in mind, they may overestimate reliance on a particular national banking system in cases where at least part of the banking system's funding comes from sources in the borrower country. Again, combining these data with bank-level data helps to illustrate the scale of the problem. Specifically, bank-level data provides an indication of the financing that subsidiaries and

---

9. Information on the branch/subsidiary structure is not included in the BIS-CBS statistics. For this analysis, as detailed in the appendix, proxies are derived using bank-level data by subtracting total customer deposits in the subsidiary from total assets of the subsidiary, and then aggregating to the level of banking systems.

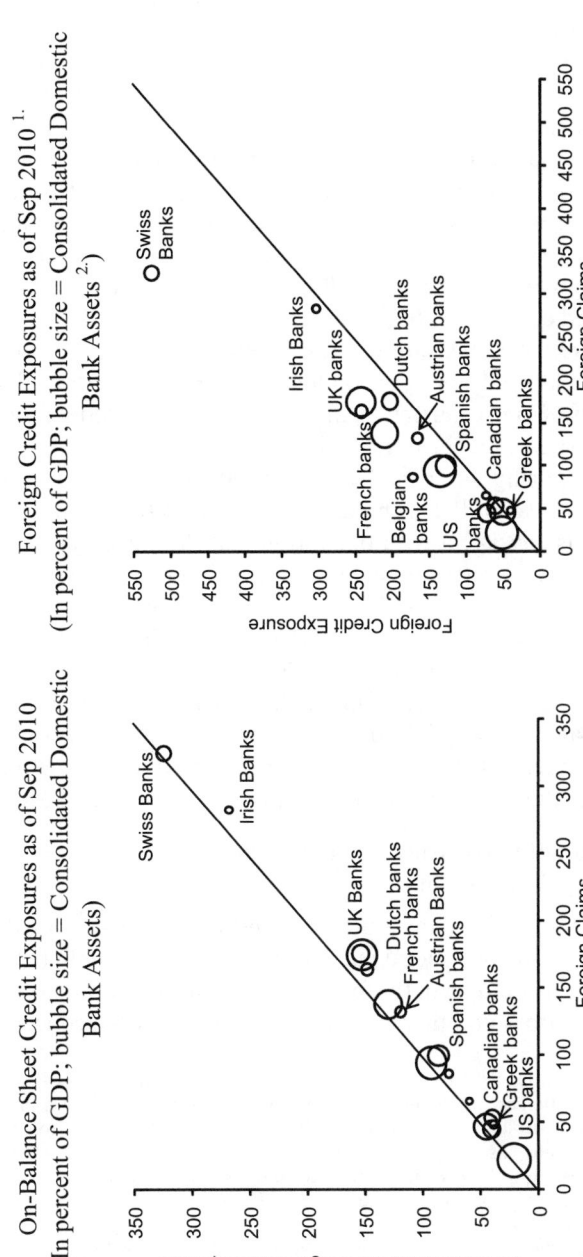

Fig. 16.1 Foreign credit exposure measure

Sources: BIS consolidated banking statistics, WEO, IMF, and authors' estimations.

[1]. The foreign credit exposure is equal to the sum of on-balance sheet foreign credit exposure and off-balance sheet liabilities (credit commitments, credit guarantees, and derivatives).

[2]. Consolidated Domestic Bank Assets refers to the aggregate consolidated assets (domestic and external) of domestically owned banks (i.e., those banks incorporated in the respective country).

branches obtain from local customer deposits, which can then be subtracted from the banking system's gross foreign claims on the country.[10]

The differences between the gross BIS foreign claims and the adjusted rollover risk figures (figure 16.2, left-hand panel) tend to be large for emerging market borrowers. This is because (a) large foreign affiliates located in many of these countries account for a significant share of gross foreign claims (i.e., the share of direct cross-border lending in total foreign claims is generally low), and (b) these affiliates are funded primarily by local deposits. For example, the adjusted measure for Latin America is, on average, only 40 percent of banks' foreign claims. Similarly, the exposures for emerging Asia and Europe are on average roughly half of foreign claims. By contrast, the ratio for advanced countries is 65 percent.

The ratio of the adjusted measure to gross foreign claims captures the borrower country's relative dependence on local resources. Countries that depended more heavily on resources from parent banks located outside going into the crisis (i.e., a higher ratio) saw a greater contraction in their total foreign funding during the crisis (December 2007 to September 2010; figure 16.2, right-hand panel).[11] This holds even if outliers (black squares) are eliminated. This is consistent with the notion that the global shock to wholesale funding markets, rather than deterioration in borrower-country fundamentals, played a major role in the contraction of foreign claims.

The analysis of borrower countries' dependence on credit from foreign banks requires data that preserve banks' multinational structure rather than consolidates it away. It also requires granular data on banks' internal capital markets and wholesale sources of funds (e.g., interbank repo market borrowing, and other nondeposit funding, etc.), information which is generally not available at either the individual bank or banking system level.

16.2.3   Measurement of Cross-Currency Funding and Maturity Transformation

In the run-up to the crisis, many European and other non-US banks invested heavily in US dollar–denominated assets, and increasingly relied on short-term US dollar funding in the form of direct interbank borrowing and the swapping of euros and other currencies for dollars. When concerns

10. As detailed in the appendix, the adjusted rollover risk measure sums direct cross-border claims and affiliates' claims that are not financed by local consumer deposits, the latter proxied by the bank-level deposit-to-loan ratio of foreign subsidiaries and affiliates. This rollover risk measure could, in principle, also be calculated by combining the BIS locational banking statistics by nationality and consolidated statistics (immediate borrower basis). However, a complete picture is possible only for those countries that are reporters of BIS data, which excludes many emerging markets.

11. The change in foreign claims is calculated after correcting the data for breaks in series, an expansion in the population of reporting banks, and for movements in exchange rates. The BIS reports forty-one series breaks during the 2007 to 2009 period in the BIS consolidated banking statistics, many of which are large (e.g., the Italian 2007Q1 USD 622 billion and the US 2009Q1 USD 1,334 billion break-in-series due to the coverage expansion).

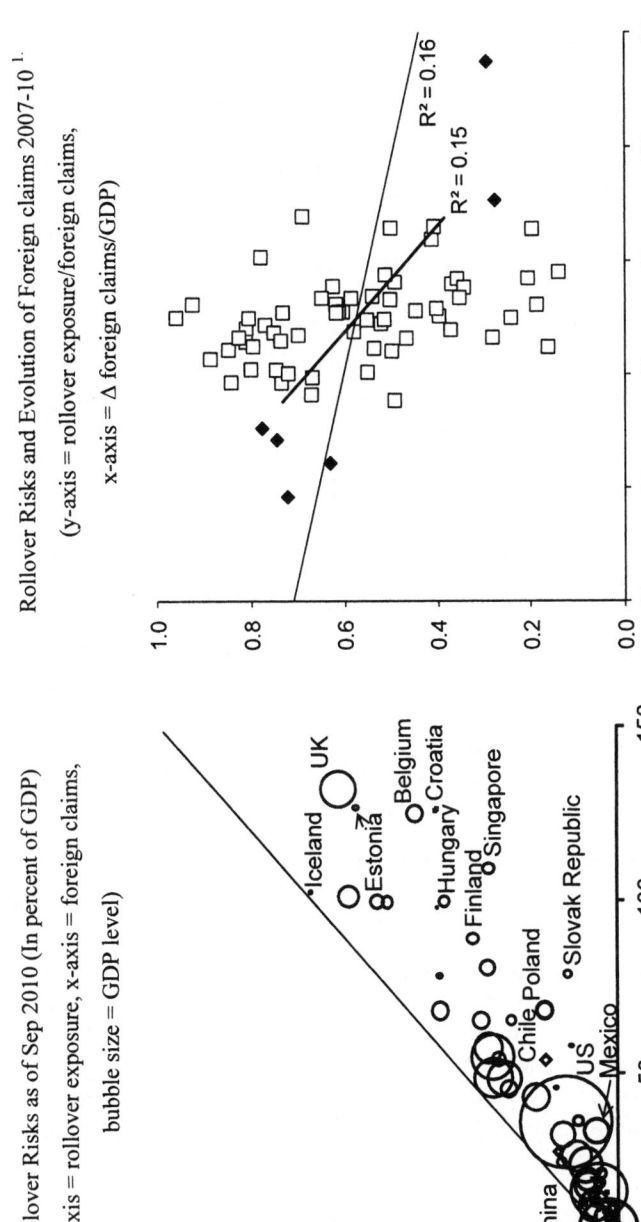

Fig. 16.2 Reliance on foreign bank credit

Sources: BIS consolidated banking statistics, WEO, IMF, and authors' estimations.

[1]The evolution of foreign claims between the period December 2007–September 2010, as percentage of 2010 GDP, is corrected for structural breaks in BIS series (e.g., increase in reporting banks and misreporting) and exchange rate fluctuations.

over exposures to toxic assets mounted, these banks found it difficult to roll over their dollar funding positions, driving up the overall costs of dollar funds. Throughout much of the crisis, but particularly following the collapse of Lehman Brothers in September 2008, the global demand for short-term dollar funding could only be met through the establishment of central bank swap lines.[12] In the wake of these experiences, central banks and other regulatory authorities have a greater interest in monitoring the international use of their currency. This requires comprehensive information about aggregate international balance sheet positions by currencies, including gross and net currency derivatives, for institutions operating both in and outside the currency issuing country.

While imprecise, BIS data help to illustrate the size of the problem since they provide some indirect information on non-US banks' dollar funding needs in the run-up to the crisis. Figure 16.3 shows the net US dollar asset and liability positions of major European and Japanese banks since 2000. The figure suggests a growing risk of funding problems prior to the crisis, as longer-term investments in nonbanks became increasingly dependent on short-term foreign currency funding. By these estimates, large European banks depended on some $1 trillion in short-term funding on the eve of the crisis, much of it obtained via FX swaps.

With these data, however, only broad tendencies can be identified since there are no actual data on residual maturities or the use of FX swap markets. Instead, information on the counterparty type (bank, nonbank, central bank) is used to proxy for the (unavailable) residual maturities, and interbank (thick line in right-hand panel) and net foreign exchange swap positions (bars in right-hand panel) are assumed to have a shorter average maturity than positions vis-à-vis nonbanks (dotted line in right-hand panel).

16.2.4 Modeling Systemic Risks for International Banks

Systemic events typically involve a combination of self-reinforcing asset and funding shocks, which then spill over to banks in other countries. While the origins of shocks are often difficult to identify (and model) a priori, assessing the size and direction of the subsequent spillovers can be easier. One approach is that of the International Monetary Fund (IMF) cross-border bank contagion scenario module used for surveillance, spillover analyses, and early warning exercises.[13] The scenario starts from asset credit exposures, differentiating between potential losses on cross-border claims, affiliates' claims, and off-balance sheet exposures. It then captures the propagation of shocks across borders through bank losses, funding shocks, and deleveraging. Again, however, it suffers from the weaknesses of existing data.

---

12. Estimates (McGuire and von Peter 2009) suggest that the wholesale US dollar funding needs of many European banks during the crisis greatly exceeded the dollar lending capacity of their home central banks.

13. See Tressel (2010) for the methodological framework and IMF (2012) for some recent modifications.

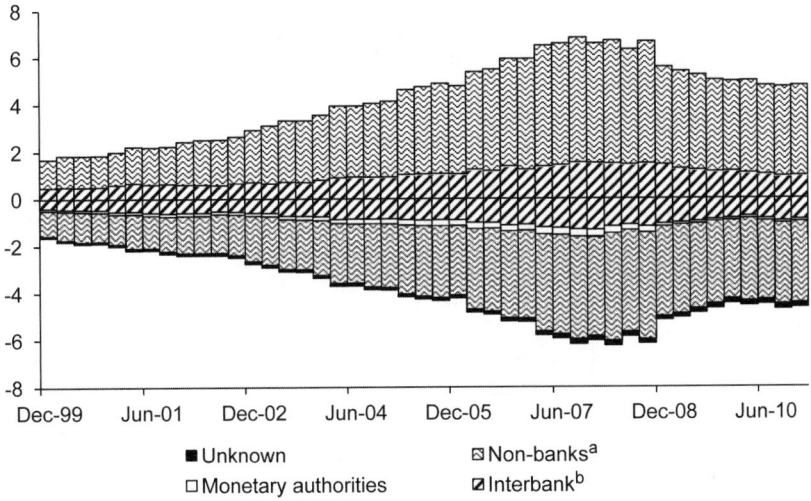

Gross, by counterparty sector

■ Unknown   ⊠ Non-banks[a]
□ Monetary authorities   ⊠ Interbank[b]

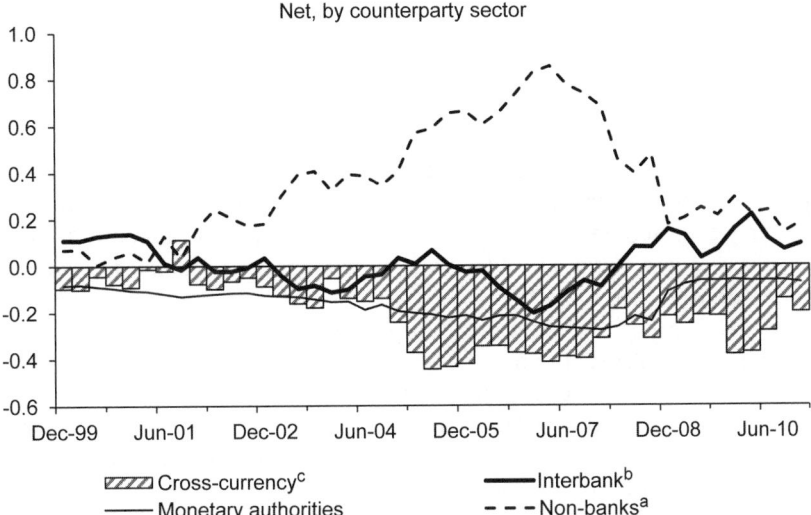

Net, by counterparty sector

▨ Cross-currency[c]   —— Interbank[b]
—— Monetary authorities   - - - Non-banks[a]

Fig. 16.3   On-balance sheet USD positions at long-USD European banks (in USD trillions)

Sources: BIS locational banking statistics by nationality, BIS consolidated banking statistics (immediate borrower basis), and authors' calculations.

Notes: Estimates are constructed by aggregating the worldwide on-balance sheet cross-border and local positions reported by internationally active banks headquartered in Germany, the Netherlands, Switzerland, and the United Kingdom.

[a]International positions vis-à-vis nonbanks plus local positions vis-à-vis US residents (all sectors) booked by banks' offices in the United States. No sectoral breakdown is available for these positions.

[b]Estimated net interbank lending to other (unaffiliated) banks.

[c]Implied cross-currency funding (i.e., FX swaps), which equates US dollar assets and liabilities.

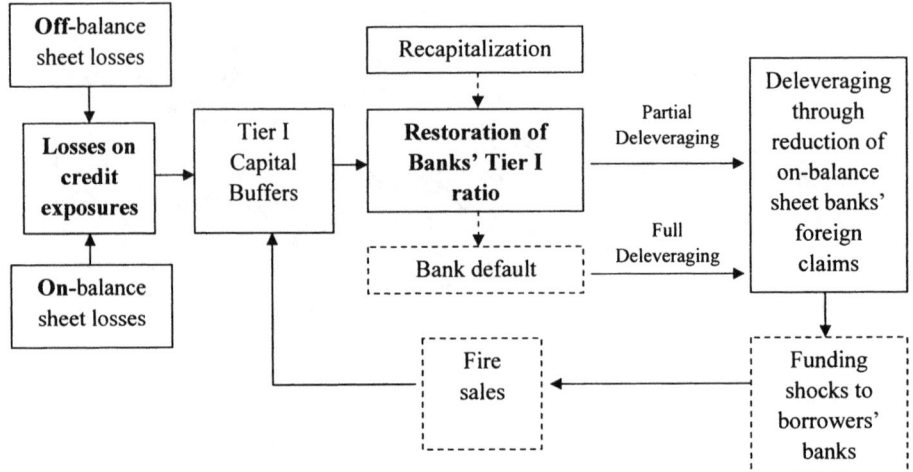

Fig. 16.4   **Shock propagation across borders through bank losses and deleveraging**

The scenario analysis allows for shocks to affect assets and funding through several rounds (figure 16.4). The first round considers losses on assets that deplete bank capital partially or fully. It relies on assumptions about the percentage loss on particular types of assets (e.g., claims on the public sector, banking sector, and nonbank private sector of an individual country or group of countries). Losses can also occur through off-balance sheet exposures. In the second round, if losses are large, banks are assumed to restore their capital adequacy to at least a certain threshold (here, the Basel III Tier I capital asset ratio) through deleveraging (i.e., sale of assets and refusal to roll over existing loans). In the third round, banks are assumed to reduce their lending to other banks (funding shocks), potentially triggering fire sales, further deleveraging, and additional losses at other banks. Final convergence is achieved when no further deleveraging occurs. The possibility of (public) recapitalization allows one to simulate how policy could mitigate the deleveraging process and reduce systemic risks.

Contagion across borders and through common lender effects can now be analyzed. Consider a common shock, due to a crisis in a particular sector/s in one or more countries, that involves losses of X_i percent on the foreign assets of banks from country i (illustrated in figure 16.5). If capital buffers are not large enough, and/or without bank recapitalization, deleveraging will need to occur to restore capital (e.g., to a Tier I capital ratio of 6 percent).[14]

14. Figure 16.5 implicitly assumes that deleveraging occurs proportionally across domestic and foreign assets. In practice, when deleveraging, banks often liquidate more risky assets first. This can be captured by assuming that banks disproportionately liquidate claims on more vulnerable countries or sell all types of foreign assets first.

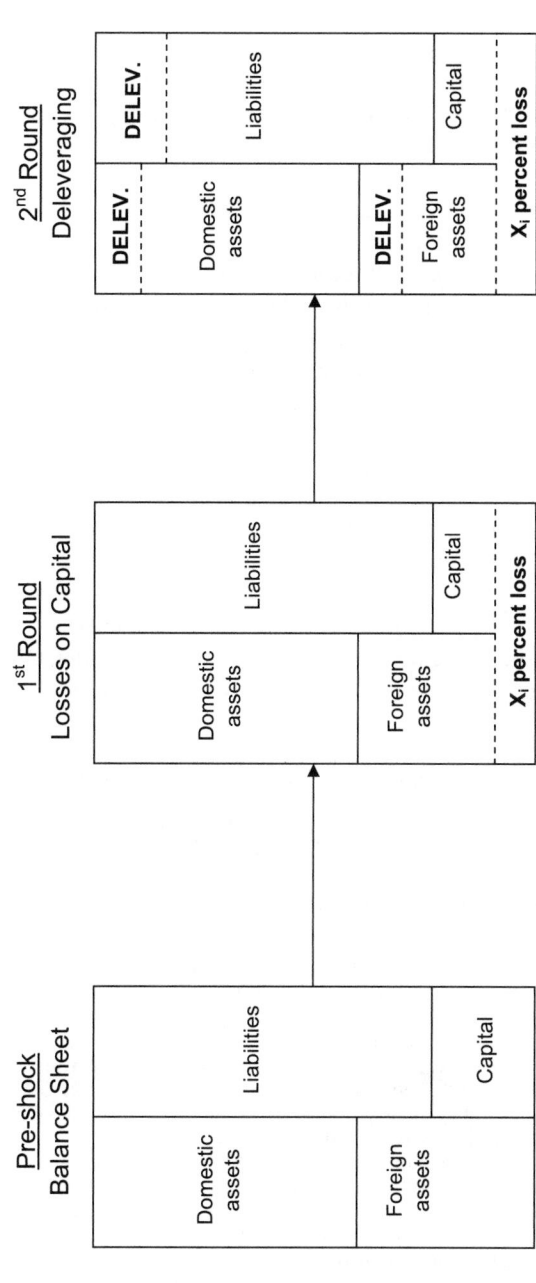

Fig. 16.5 Effect of foreign credit losses on the balance sheet of country *i* banks

The process of deleveraging then means a global reduction in loans of all banks affected, either directly or indirectly, impacting financing and economic activity in various countries. For banks in borrower country j, the funding shock (Y_j) equals the deleveraging across all its creditor countries (figure 16.6). If the funding shocks trigger fire sales, banks could experience further losses, triggering additional deleveraging if capital buffers are not large enough and/or in the absence of bank recapitalization. The system converges to a steady state when no further deleveraging takes place (i.e., banks meet their capital adequacy requirements).

While the model is quite rich, the lack of detailed and consistent input data limits its use. Ideally, comprehensive scenario analyses of this sort would be conducted using *bank-level* data, which also track *bilateral* linkages in the interbank market. Currently, BIS consolidated banking data are used to model the losses due to direct exposures of banking systems to the public sector, banking sector and/or nonbank private sector, and indirect exposures via off-balance sheet contingent positions, to borrowers in an individual country or group of countries.[15] Bank-level data (aggregated) provide the estimates of these banking systems' positions vis-à-vis borrowers in the home country and of their Tier I capital needed in the analysis, neither of which is available in the BIS data.[16] While the BIS data track many of the international dimensions of interest, the costly implicit assumption, of course, is that an entire banking system can be treated as a single bank.[17] Thus, problems that arise within a group of banks of a particular nationality cannot be uncovered, limiting the effectiveness of the analysis in policy discussions.

15. In the IMF model, scenarios are calculated for those countries for which consolidated BIS banking statistics on an ultimate risk basis are currently available (Austria, Belgium, Canada, France, Germany, Greece, Ireland, Italy, Japan, Netherlands, Portugal, Spain, Sweden, Switzerland, United Kingdom, and United States). The deleveraging impact is, however, estimated for almost all 180 countries, except for the potential additional impact triggered by funding shocks, which are only calculated for the domestic consolidated banking sector of BIS-reporting countries.

16. Comprehensive international data on banks' consolidated balance sheets that follow the BIS-CBS aggregation structure but include banks' domestic positions (i.e., positions vis-à-vis residents of the home country) are not yet available. Only the ECB-Banking Supervision Committee, which reports a national balance sheet for the aggregated domestically owned consolidated banks in each EU state, provides national aggregates similar to the BIS-CBS for some concepts, such as Tier I capital and capital ratios, and total bank assets. In other cases, it is necessary to sum individual domestically owned consolidated banks' balance sheets, or alternatively, depending on the number of foreign subsidiaries, subtract from national aggregates foreign-owned subsidiaries' balance sheets.

17. There are some additional data limitations: (a) the counterparty-sector breakdown is available only for total foreign claims, but not separately for the components of foreign claims (i.e., cross-border claims and local claims); (b) maturity breakdowns are available only for international claims (immediate borrower basis), which include both cross-border claims (in all currencies) and locally extended claims in foreign currencies; and (c) the interaction between funding and deleveraging risks is restricted to those countries that report BIS data on an ultimate risk basis (for several important markets; e.g., in China, Brazil, and Korea such data are not available).

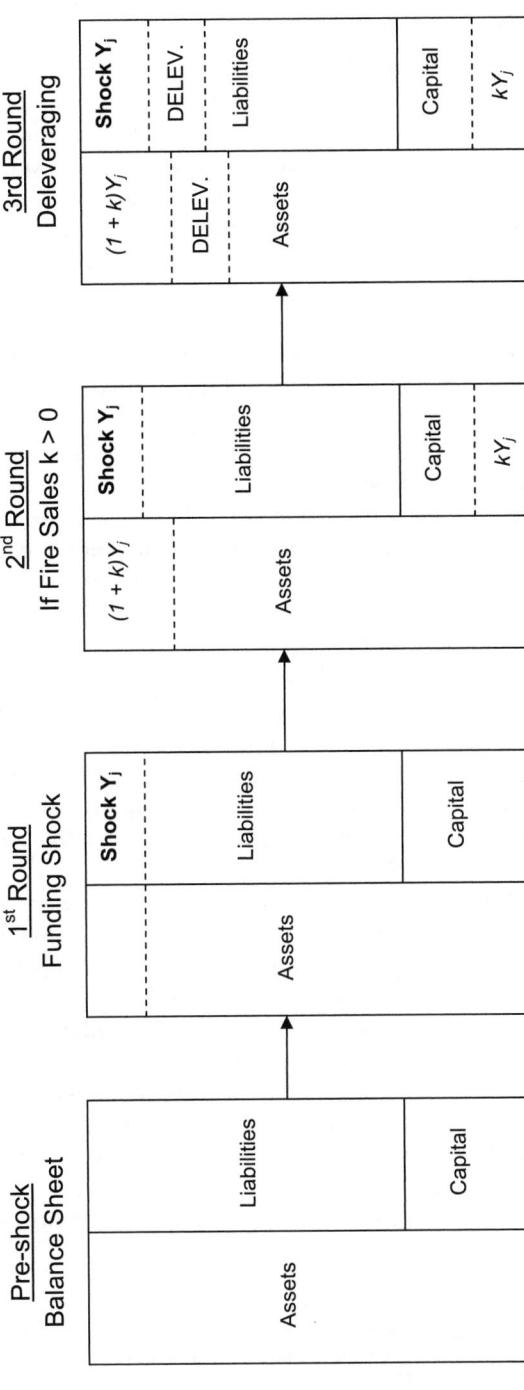

Fig. 16.6 Effect of a funding shock on balance sheet of borrower country _j_ banks

16.3   What More Data Are Needed?

Institutional and regulatory differences across countries can greatly affect the scale of shocks and the direction of their propagation across borders. These differences also make it difficult to construct analytical indicators that track the buildup of vulnerabilities at the system level. And the lack of internationally comparable data for the largest global institutions complicates things further. Drawing on the lessons of the recent crisis, this section reviews gaps in currently available data, outlines the G20 data initiative to close these gaps, and makes suggestions on areas that should be given high priority.

Analyzing systemic risks in international banking (e.g., common exposures across institutions, cross-currency funding patterns and maturity transformation, and the volatility of cross-border capital flows) requires the *joint* analyses of data covering *many* financial institutions. Common exposures to a particular asset class or funding source are easily masked in aggregate data. To detect these types of vulnerabilities requires data at the *individual bank level*, which is collected in a consistent and comparable format across banks, so that subsequent aggregation is possible.

Bank-level data obtained by national supervisors contain some of the needed information. But the experience during the crisis showed that, in many jurisdictions, supervisors lacked critical pieces of information; specifically, data on how international banks are connected to each other. During periods of market turmoil, real-time information on how the failure (or not) of a particular institution might impact other institutions is crucial for policy decisions, but was lacking in the days leading up to the collapse of Lehman Brothers. Thus, for crisis management purposes, there is a need for more information on bank-level *bilateral* linkages.

The bank-level data that are collected by supervisors are not widely shared, generally not even across supervisory jurisdictions, and only broad aggregates (if anything) are publicly disclosed.[18] No single supervisor, therefore, has a detailed overview of the global system. And without such a view, system-level vulnerabilities can go undetected. It was difficult (even late in the crisis), for example, to gauge the size of European banks' global exposures to US dollar collateralized debt obligations (CDOs), and there was virtually no system-level information on the scale of these banks' reliance on short-term dollar funding (e.g., money market funds), which dried up suddenly amidst the turmoil. Detecting these types of stresses early on requires detailed breakdowns of banks' assets and liabilities (i.e., by currency, instru-

---

18. Access to supervisory data is limited outside the home country. In some cases memorandums of understanding allow specific data to be exchanged between two countries. Also, in some cases, data are made available to teams conducting the joint IMF-World Bank Financial Sector Assessment Program (FSAP).

ment, residual maturity and, if possible, counterparty-type and country), and their joint analysis across many banks.

Bank-level data available outside the supervisory community are generally not detailed enough. Commercial databases compile information from banks' annual reports, but have considerable data lags and gaps. Information on the counterparty-sector and country are generally missing, and coverage of branches is particularly poor. In many countries, standard balance sheet data (e.g., capital asset ratios) are not even publicly disclosed (or are disclosed without much detail). Banks generally also do not report information on the currency of their positions or their exposures to particular counterparty types. Moreover, many banks disclose only their globally consolidated financial statements, which aggregate their positions across all their subsidiaries and branches (at home or abroad), and thus the information on the geographic structure of banks' operations is not preserved. As a result, much of the information about the funding and asset structures of banks' operations (branches and subsidiaries) is lost, limiting the usefulness of these data for global risk analysis.

As our earlier examples illustrate, global systemic risk analysis with currently available data rests on a myriad of tenable assumptions and yields very imprecise results. In this context, the IMF and the Financial Stability Board (FSB) have jointly issued a report to the G20 finance ministers and central bank governors with twenty recommendations on reducing financial data gaps (see box 16.2). Recommendations eight and nine in this report require the creation of a common reporting template for globally systemically important financial institutions (G-SIFIs). An international working group has already produced a set of draft data templates designed to capture detailed information about banks' asset and funding positions, and on the linkages between banks and other individual institutions. The group also outlined a framework for the collection and storage of highly confidential bank-level data, and a framework governing the access to and use of the data (see IMF-FSB 2011).

If these initiatives go forward, the resulting data would, for the first time, permit joint analyses of the global positions of many banks from different jurisdictions, thus substantially improving the ability to detect vulnerabilities in common exposures or concentrated funding positions and to assess the vulnerabilities in the global system. Moreover, when crises do occur, supervisors and macroprudential authorities would have some information to assess the potential for spillovers from the failure of a particular institution to other institutions, national markets and sectors, and evaluate the impact of various regulatory responses (e.g., whether ring-fencing restrictions in one or a group of countries would trigger spillovers to other countries and banking groups). The envisioned data would also facilitate more realistic modeling of how asset and funding exposures endogenously interact during periods of stress.

Box 16.2   G-20 Data Gaps Initiative

The Financial Crisis and Information Gaps, the joint IMF-FSB report to the G20, has made twenty recommendations on reducing financial data gaps. The recommendations that are most related to the topics covered in this chapter are

- development of measures of system-wide, macroprudential risk, such as aggregate leverage and maturity mismatches (4);
- development of a common data template for systemically important global financial institutions for the purpose of better understanding the exposures of these institutions to different financial sectors and national markets (8 and 9);
- enhancement of BIS consolidated banking statistics, including the separate identification of nonbank financial institutions in the sectoral breakdown, and the tracking of funding patterns of international financial systems (11); and
- development of a standardized template covering the international exposure of large nonbank financial institutions (14).

Efforts to fulfill these recommendations are underway. An international working group has created a draft template for the collection of bank-level data which, if adopted, would provide information on banks' exposures and funding positions with breakdowns by counterparty country and sector, instrument, currency, and remaining maturity. In addition, the collection of information on banks' intragroup positions and the number of branches and subsidiaries is also under consideration.

The other recommendations focus on improvements in country aggregate financial soundness indicators and implementation of standard measures that can provide information on tail risks, concentrations, variation in distributions, and the volatility of indicators over time (2 and 3), improved understanding of risk transfers from credit default swaps (5), improved securities data through better disclosure requirements for complex structured products and new common templates (6 and 7), increased frequency and participation in the coordinated portfolio investment survey (10 and 11) and international investment position survey (12), monitoring and measuring nonfinancial corporations' cross-border exposures (13), promotion of compilation of sectoral accounts (15), compiling distributional information (such as ranges and quartile information) alongside aggregate figures (16), standardized presentation of government finance statistics (7 and 18), improved public sector debt data (18), completion of a real estate prices handbook (19), and enhancement of principal global indicators (20).

In parallel with these efforts, enhancements to the aggregate BIS international banking statistics, which cover a much wider universe of banks, are underway.[19] In broad terms, these enhancements aim to: (a) provide more information on the currency of banks' positions; (b) provide more information on banks' counterparties, specifically on their location and sector; and (c) extend coverage to banks' entire balance sheets, not just their foreign positions (see BIS 2011). In addition, coverage will be broadened so as to capture all banks' financial assets and liabilities. That is, banks will start to also report their local currency positions vis-à-vis residents of the host country. This will make it easier to assess system-level funding risks across a much wider range of currencies. It will also allow the scale of banks' international activities to be compared with their total balance sheets.

Importantly, the enhanced BIS banking data will reveal more information about banks' operational structures.[20] That is, it is currently not possible to simultaneously know a bank's location, its nationality, and the location of its counterparties (e.g., aggregate liabilities to Middle Eastern oil exporters booked in the UK offices of Swiss-headquartered banks). Information on the country location of banks' counterparties started to be available from 2013 separately for banks of a particular nationality in each reporting jurisdiction. Once completed, going forward, this would facilitate more detailed analysis of how shocks in a banking system might affect borrowers elsewhere (see Fender and McGuire 2010).

In addition to official authorities, market participants also need better information if they are to appropriately monitor and price systemic risks. Public dissemination of raw data when possible—and consistent aggregates of the data by market, sector, and country when absolutely not—has the potential to help market participants discipline themselves. The release of bank-level sovereign exposure data in the framework of the European stress tests has shown that public dissemination of bank-level data is feasible even during periods of financial distress.

Even with improved aggregate banking statistics and better bank-level data, other dimensions of systemic risk will likely remain inadequately covered. While better coverage of banks is a top priority, nonbanks, including pension funds, insurance companies, and large multinational corporations, can also be systemically important. This suggests going forward including not only such nonbank institutions in the counterparty sector breakdown of banks' exposures, but also bringing large nonbank firms under the data-gathering umbrella.

---

19. See BIS (2011), Cecchetti, Fender, and McGuire (2010), and Fender and McGuire (2010) for a discussion of how well-designed aggregate statistics can enhance the monitoring of systemic risks, and for more detailed discussion on the structure of banks' international operations as revealed in the BIS banking statistics.

20. The FSB-IMF initiative described earlier focuses on bank-level worldwide *consolidated* data, and thus will not contain information on the positions of the individual banks' entities.

Appendix

Methodology Underlying the Foreign Credit Exposure and Rollover Risk Analysis[21]

Improving the Measurement of Foreign Credit Exposures

Bank-level balance sheet data are not often used in cross-country studies due to the difficulty of mapping major international banks' group structure across countries and compiling their balance sheet data. Organizing the bank data involves mapping both the parent banks and their network of subsidiaries, which is an extensive task.

More formally, a creditor country's *foreign credit exposure* would be equal to:

$$A_{ij} + B_{ij} + C_{ij} + D_{ij},$$

where A_{ij} = *Crossborder claims$_{ij}$* captures the direct cross-border exposure from creditor banks in country i on debtor country j;

$B_{ij} = total\_assets_{ij}^{subs} - deposits_{ij}^{subs} + total\_assets_{ij}^{branch}$ captures the exposure to subsidiaries and branches, taking into account the legal differences between them;

$C_{ij} = local\ claims_{ij} - \sum_{subs\ \&\ branch} total\_assets_{ij}$ represents the nonidentified exposure by bank-level data with respect to BIS-reported affiliates claims (i.e., individual bank-level data on branches in particular are often not reported in many countries); and

$D_{ij} = derivatives_{ij} + guarantees_{ij} + credit\_commitments_{ij}$ capture off-balance sheet exposure from country *i* banks on country *j* based on BIS data.

The *foreign credit exposure* (FCE_i) measures, those exposures as a percentage of GDP or total banking sector assets in country *i*, are as follows:

$$FCE_i = \sum_{j=1}^{N} \frac{A_{ij} + B_{ij} + C_{ij} + D_{ij}}{Z_i},$$

where Z_i is a scaling factor (GDP or total banking sector assets in country *i*).

Improving the Measurement of Foreign Rollover Risks

The foreign rollover risk analysis focuses on a borrower country's rollover risk to crises in its creditor foreign banking systems. For each borrower country, it summarizes the potential rollover risks of direct cross-border

---

21. See Cerutti (2013) for more details about the foreign credit exposure and rollover risk analyses, including information about necessary corrections for breaks in series and exchange rate movements.

lending from banks in creditor countries, as well as the lending by foreign affiliates funded by their creditor countries' parent banks.

Therefore, a borrower country j's *foreign rollover risk* (*Rollover Risk*) can be captured by:

$$Rollover Risk_j = Crossborder\ claims_{ij} + Local\ claims_{ij}$$
$$* (1 - Min(deposit\ loan\_ratio_{ij}, 1))$$

where *Crossborder claims*$_{ij}$ captures the volume of direct cross-border claims from country i on country j; *Local claims*$_{ij}$ the volume of affiliates (subsidiaries and branches) claims of parent banks from country i on country j; and $1 - Min(deposit\_loanratio_{ij}, 1)$ is a proxy of the proportion of loans not financed by local consumer deposits. The higher the deposit to loan ratio, the lower is the share of local claims financed by parent bank resources and/or wholesale financing, which is implicitly assumed to be correlated with the parent bank problems. The amount of lending by affiliates funded by their parent banks cannot be directly measured since the available bank-level balance sheet data from Bankscope is not detailed enough to identify all parent banks' nonequity claims. Therefore, the *foreign rollover risk* measure could also overestimate the effective rollover risks.[22]

Modeling Together International Banks' Assets and Liabilities

The scenario analysis of the contagion of a crisis across borders and through common lender effects is based on considering a stylized bank balance sheet given by:

$$Assets = Capital + Other\_Liabilities$$

where *Assets* = *Foreign_Assets* + *Domestic_Assets*. To quantify the effect of a shock on assets, we assume that, when facing a loss of LLR percent on, for example, its foreign assets, a bank combines asset sales *DEL* and recapitalization *RECAP* to maintain a sound capital (e.g., Tier I) to asset ratio of *CAR*. For a given loss on its asset portfolio and leaving aside risk-weight considerations, the set of possible combinations of deleveraging (asset sales) and recapitalization is given by:

$$Capital - LLR \cdot Foreign\_Assets + RECAP =$$
$$CAR \cdot (Assets - LLR \cdot Foreign\_Assets - DEL).$$

22. In the cases where affiliates' bank-level data are not available, the borrower country national deposit-to-loan ratio is used in order to have larger country coverage. Using affiliates' total assets minus deposits, as in the case of the foreign default exposure to subsidiaries, as the proxy of the amount of lending by affiliates funded by their parent banks produce similar results but lower country coverage.

Hence, in the absence of a recapitalization of the banking sector, the extent of deleveraging by the financial institutions of a creditor country is given by:[23]

$$DEL = Assets - LLR \cdot Foreign\_Assets$$
$$-\frac{1}{CAR} \cdot (Tier\,I\,Capital - LLR \cdot Foreign\_Assets).$$

The process of deleveraging results in a global reduction of cross-border claims by all international banks affected by the shock, either directly or indirectly. For each recipient country, the extent of capital outflows is the aggregation of the deleveraging process by all creditor countries.

Additional rounds of deleveraging may take place if shocks are large enough to cause international bank insolvencies, and if fire sales of assets occur, triggering further losses. The system converges to an equilibrium when no further deleveraging takes place.

(1.) *Insolvency of upstream countries' banks*: Following a given shock in a market j, the banking system of country i becomes insolvent (e.g., losses exceed capital) and defaults on a proportion of its liabilities to the banks of other countries. This may occur if the initial shock is large enough.

(2.) *Funding shock*: Following a given shock, the banks of country i reduce their lending to the banks of country j, which therefore face a *funding shock* Y_{ij}. If assets are sold at book value, no further deleveraging occurs; if, however, assets are sold at fire sale, the loss ($\kappa \cdot Y_{ij}$) is absorbed by the bank capital, which may result in further deleveraging DEL'_j according to:

$$Capital - \kappa \cdot Y = CAR \cdot (Assets - (1+\kappa) \cdot Y - DEL'_j).$$

The scenario analysis simulations assume that deleveraging occurs whenever the capital-to-asset ratio falls below a given threshold, implying that deleveraging is possible even if banks' equity is not entirely wiped out by the shock. The deleveraging is assumed to be proportional, such that the deleveraging of country i in country j is given by:

$$DEL_{ij} = X_i \cdot (A_{ij} + B_{ij} + C_{ij})$$

where X_i is the loan-loss ratio and $A_{ij} + B_{ij} + C_{ij}$ is the amount of cross-border and affiliates-related foreign credit exposures of country i's banks on country j.

---

23. Financial institutions are assumed to be able to sell their assets at book value. Fire sales at below book value may amplify deleveraging.

References

Alessandri, P., P. Gai, S. Kapadia, N. Mora, and C. Puhr. 2009. "A Framework for Quantifying Systemic Stability." *International Journal of Central Banking* 5 (3): 47–81.

Bank for International Settlements (BIS). 2011. "Chapter VI: Closing Data Gaps to Enhance Systemic Risk Measurement." *BIS 81st Annual Report*, June. Basel, Switzerland: Bank for International Settlements.

Borio, C., and M. Drehmann. 2009. "Towards an Operational Framework for Financial Stability: 'Fuzzy' Measurement and Its Consequences." BIS Working Paper 284, Bank for International Settlements, Basel, Switzerland.

Boss, M., G. Krenn, C. Puhr, and M. Summer. 2006. "Systemic Risk Monitor: A Model for Systemic Risk Analysis and Stress Testing of Banking Systems." Oesterreichische Nationalbank, *Financial Stability Report* 11 (June): 83–95.

Cecchetti, S., I. Fender, and P. McGuire. 2010. "Toward a Global Risk Map." BIS Working Paper no. 309, Bank for International Settlements, Basel, Switzerland.

Cerutti, E. 2013. "Foreign Credit Exposures and Rollover Risks: Measurement, Evolution, and Determinants." IMF Working Paper 13/9, International Monetary Fund, Washington, DC.

Cerutti, E., G. Dell'Ariccia, and S. Martinez Peria. 2007. "How Banks Go Abroad: Branches or Subsidiaries?" *Journal of Banking & Finance* 31 (6): 1669–92.

Cerutti, E., A. Ilyina, Y. Makarova, and C. Schmieder. 2010. "Bankers without Borders? Implications of Ring-Fencing for European Cross-Border Banks." IMF Working Paper 10/247, International Monetary Fund, Washington, DC.

Cerutti, E., and C. Schmieder. 2014. "Ring-Fencing and Consolidated Banks' Stress Tests." *Journal of Financial Stability* 11 (April): 1–12.

Claessens, S., R. J. Herring, and D. Schoenmaker. 2010. "A Safer World Financial System: Improving the Resolution of Systemic Institutions." Center for Economic Policy Research-International Center for Monetary and Banking Studies (CEPR-ICMB), July.

Committee on the Global Financial System (CGFS). 2010a. "The Functioning and Resilience of Cross-Border Funding Markets." Committee on the Global Financial System Publications no. 37, March. http://www.bis.org/publ/cgfs37.htm.

———. 2010b. "Funding Patterns and Liquidity Management of Internationally Active Banks." Committee on the Global Financial System Publications no. 39, July. http://www.bis.org/publ/cgfs39.htm.

———. 2010c. "Long-Term Issues in International Banking." Committee on the Global Financial System Publications no. 41, July. http://www.bis.org/publ/cgfs41.htm.

de Bandt, O., P. Hartmann, and J. Peydro. 2009. "Systemic Risk in Banking: An Update." In *Oxford Handbook of Banking*, edited by Berger, Molyneux, and Wilson. Oxford: Oxford University Press.

Fender, I., and P. McGuire. 2010. "Bank Structure, Funding Risk and the Transmission of Shocks Across Countries: Concepts and Measurement." *BIS Quarterly Review* September:63–79.

Hryckiewicz, A., and O. Kowelewski. 2011. "Why Do Foreign Banks Withdraw from Other Countries?" *International Finance* 14 (1): 67–102.

International Monetary Fund (IMF). 2010. "Resolution of Cross-Border Banks—A Proposed Framework for Enhanced Coordination." June 11. Washington, DC: International Monetary Fund.

———. 2011. "Camdessus Group Report." Washington, DC: International Monetary Fund. www.imsreform.org/surveillance.html.

———. 2012. "The IMF-FSB Early Warning Exercise: Design and Methodological Toolkit." IMF Occasional Paper 274. Washington, DC: International Monetary Fund.

International Monetary Fund-Financial Stability Board (IMF-FSB). 2009. "The Financial Crisis and Information Gaps: Report to the G20 Finance Ministers and Central Bank Governors." October. www.imf.org/external/np/g20/pdf/102909.pdf.

———. 2011. "The Financial Crisis and Information Gaps: Progress Report to the G-20 Finance Ministers and Central Bank Governors." http://www.imf.org/external/np/g20/pdf/063011.pdf.

Kaufman, G., and K. Scott. 2003. "What Is Systemic Risk, and Do Bank Regulators Retard or Contribute to It?" *Independent Review* Winter:371–91.

McGuire, P., and G. von Peter. 2009. "The US Dollar Shortage in Global Banking and the International Policy Response." BIS Working Paper no. 291, Bank for International Settlements, Basel, Switzerland, October.

McGuire, P., and P. Wooldridge. 2005. "The BIS Consolidated Banking Statistics: Structure, Uses, and Recent Enhancements." *BIS Quarterly Review* September:73–86.

Tressel, T. 2010. "Financial Contagion through Bank Deleveraging: Stylized Facts and Simulations Applied to the Financial Crisis." IMF Working Paper no. 10/236, International Monetary Fund, Washington, DC, October.

Contributors

Viral V. Acharya
Stern School of Business
New York University
44 West 4th Street
New York, NY 10012

Tobias Adrian
Capital Markets Research
Federal Reserve Bank of New York
33 Liberty Street
New York, NY 10045

William F. Bassett
Division of Monetary Affairs
Board of Governors of the Federal
   Reserve System
20th Street and Constitution
   Avenue, NW
Washington, DC 20551

Brian Begalle
Federal Reserve Bank of New York
33 Liberty Street
New York, NY 10045

Juliane Begenau
Department of Economics
Stanford University
Stanford, CA 94305

Markus Brunnermeier
Department of Economics
Bendheim Center for Finance
Princeton University
Princeton, NJ 08540

Eugenio Cerutti
International Monetary Fund
700 19th Street, NW
Washington, DC 20431

V. V. Chari
Department of Economics
University of Minnesota
271 19th Avenue South
Minneapolis, MN 55455

Stijn Claessens
International Monetary Fund
700 19th Street, NW
Washington, DC 20431

Adam Copeland
Money and Payments Studies Function
Federal Reserve Bank of New York
33 Liberty Street
New York, NY 10045

Darrell Duffie
Graduate School of Business
Stanford University
Stanford, CA 94305

John Geanakoplos
Department of Economics
Yale University
Box 208281
New Haven, CT 06520-8281

Simon Gilchrist
Department of Economics
Boston University
270 Bay State Road
Boston, MA 02215

Gary Gorton
Yale School of Management
135 Prospect Street
P.O. Box 208200
New Haven, CT 06520-8200

Robert E. Hall
Hoover Institution
Stanford University
Stanford, CA 94305-6010

Lars Peter Hansen
Department of Economics
University of Chicago
1126 East 59th Street
Chicago, IL 60637

Arvind Krishnamurthy
Kellogg School of Management
Northwestern University
2001 Sheridan Road
Evanston, IL 60208

Augustin Landier
Toulouse School of Economics
31 Allée de Brienne
31000 Toulouse
France

Antoine Martin
Money and Payments Studies Function
Federal Reserve Bank of New York
33 Liberty Street
New York, NY 10045

Robert L. McDonald
Kellogg School of Management
Northwestern University
2001 Sheridan Road
Evanston, IL 60208

Patrick McGuire
Bank for International Settlements
Centralbahnplatz 2
Basel 4002
Switzerland

Atif Mian
Bendheim Center For Finance
Princeton University
26 Prospect Avenue
Princeton, NJ 08540

Jonathan A. Parker
Sloan School of Management
Massachusetts Institute of Technology
77 Massachusetts Ave., Bldg. E62-642
Cambridge, MA 02139-4307

Lasse Heje Pedersen
Stern School of Business
New York University
44 West 4th Street
New York, NY 10012

Monika Piazzesi
Department of Economics
Stanford University
579 Serra Mall
Stanford, CA 94305-6072

Martin Schneider
Department of Economics
Stanford University
579 Serra Mall
Stanford, CA 94305-6072

Amir Sufi
Booth School of Business
University of Chicago
5807 South Woodlawn Avenue
Chicago, IL 60637

David Thesmar
HEC School of Management
1 rue de la Libération
78351 Jouy en Josas cedex
France

Gretchen C. Weinbach
Division of Monetary Affairs
Board of Governors of the Federal
  Reserve System
20th Street and Constitution
  Avenue, NW
Washington, DC 20551

Egon Zakrajšek
Division of Monetary Affairs
Board of Governors of the Federal
  Reserve System
20th Street and Constitution
  Avenue, NW
Washington, DC 20551

Author Index

Subject Index